THE TRIBES OF AMERICA

D0973157

Also by Paul Cowan

The Making of an Un-American
State Secrets (with Nick Egleson and Nat Hentoff)
An Orphan in History
A *Torah Is Written* (with photographs by Rachel Cowan)
Mixed Blessings (with Rachel Cowan)
Only Yesterday

THE TRIBES
OF AMERICA

Journalistic Discoveries of Our People
and Their Cultures

Paul Cowan

Introduction by Rick Perlstein

THE NEW PRESS

NEW YORK
LONDON

© 1971, 1972, 1973, 1974, 1975, 1978, 1979 by Paul Cowan
Introduction © 2004, 2008 by Rick Perlstein
All rights reserved.
No part of this book may be reproduced, in any form, without written permission
from the publisher.

Requests for permission to reproduce selections from this book should be mailed
to: Permissions Department, The New Press, 38 Greene Street, New York, NY
10013.

Published in the United States by The New Press, New York, 2008
First published by Doubleday, New York, 1979
Distributed by W. W. Norton & Company, Inc., New York

Two lines from "The City of New Orleans" by Steve Goodman are quoted on
page 46. Copyright © 1970, 1972 Buddah Music and Turnpike Tom Music.
All rights administered by United Artists Music Co., Inc.

Most of the material in this book originally appeared, in slightly different form,
in The Village Voice.

Rick Perlstein's introduction was originally published as "Second Read:
Rick Perlstein on Paul Cowan's The Tribes of America" in the
November/December 2004 Columbia Journalism Review.

ISBN 978-1-59558-230-0 (pbk.)
CIP data available.

The New Press was established in 1990 as a not-for-profit alternative to the large,
commercial publishing houses currently dominating the book publishing industry.
The New Press operates in the public interest rather than for private gain, and is
committed to publishing, in innovative ways, works of educational, cultural, and
community value that are often deemed insufficiently profitable.

www.thenewpress.com

Printed in Canada

2 4 6 8 10 9 7 5 3 1

To Rachel, who brings life

CONTENTS

INTRODUCTION

by Rick Perlstein

In the fall of 1974, in Kanawha County, West Virginia, Christian fundamentalists enraged at the imposition of "blasphemous" textbooks in the public schools demolished a wing of a school board building with fifteen sticks of dynamite. When the board insisted on keeping the books in the curriculum, homes were bombed and school buses shot at. "Jesus Wouldn't Have Read Them" read one of the slogans of a movement whose leader, a preacher, would soon face charges of conspiracy to bomb two elementary schools.

Into this whirlwind stepped Paul Cowan, a shaggy-haired, bespectacled, left-wing New York Jew, trying to make sense of why he felt sympathy for the side that was laying the dynamite.

For people like Cowan, a thirty-four-year-old staff writer at *The Village Voice*, it was a boon time for existential drift. In 1970 he published *The Making of an Un-American*, the memoir of a raw and arrogant new-left punk who had taken a one-year leave from the *Voice* in 1966 for a stint in the Peace Corps that was supposed to be broadening, but ended up being wildly disillusioning. "When I read that the Viet Cong had attacked the American embassy in Saigon during the Tet offensive," Cowan concluded in *The Making of an Un-American*, "I was almost able to imagine that I was a member of the raiding party." But by the time Cowan began his next project, in 1971, life inside the new left had become an emotional burden for him: diminishing returns, dashed certitudes, "intellectual claustropho-

bia." That was how, "gradually, half-consciously, without any theory
or any plan, I decided to cross the sound barrier of dogma and test
my beliefs against the realities of American life." The twelve chapters of *The Tribes of America* were the felicitous result.

A person of Cowan's inclinations and background was supposed
to know exactly what to think about a howling mob gathered around
a crucifix-emblazoned flag and expectorating demands to burn
books of the sort the reporter would want his kids to study, books
with chapters by Norman Mailer and James Baldwin and test questions asking students to interpret rather than parrot what they had
read. It would have been easy to record the scenes of bonfires and
leave it at that; certainly that would have satisfied Cowan's readers
back in Greenwich Village. Instead, Cowan took the riskier step:
wondering whether these criminals didn't also have a point.

The people responsible for the textbooks were bureaucrats who
wrote blithely of pedagogy's power to "induce changes . . . in the behavior of the 'culturally lost' of Appalachia," and identified teachers
as state-designated "change agents" and schools as "the experimental center, and the core of this design." Nowadays the arrogance of
this formulation is as grating to us as a chalkboard screech. Not then.
It was an era when the language of universally applicable liberal en-
lightenment flew trippingly off cosmopolitan tongues. Which was
why it came as such a shock when the "culturally lost" proved to
have ideas of their own—that their culture had inherent dignity and
value, and that textbooks suggesting that Christian revelation was on
a par with Greek myth were, as protesters put it, "moral genocide."

It took a keen eye and an open mind to recognize that the cos-
mopolitans were pursuing a form of class warfare. Cowan noticed
how urban and suburban professionals in Kanawha County—
"Hillers," in local parlance—spoke nervously in private of how
familiarity with names like Mailer and Baldwin would get their precious darlings into Harvard and keep them out of West Virginia
Tech. The Hillers weren't about to risk having their upward climb
impeded by the "Creekers," poor residents in the hollows who
wanted "to protest corruption," as one suburbanite told Cowan, but
didn't "even know how to spell that word." But some Creekers were
motivated by similar dreams of upward mobility. Their version of it
was just incompatible with the Hillers' impositions—like the kid

who told Cowan "he wanted to go to West Virginia Tech, to be an engineer," and he felt he needed "a good basic education" to do it.

Dynamite wasn't the answer. But neither was a kind of cultural imperialism indifferent to the fact that 81 percent of the district opposed the textbooks. It was, in a word, complicated. Certainly more complicated than the portraits other journalists were creating for sneering consumption back home: death threats, double-barreled shotguns, Onward Christian Soldiers. The futile last stand of yokels against the inevitable march of progress.

It was at a time when, certainly to the left, local cultures were of keenest interest as obstacles federal judges eradicated in order to deliver social justice. But what Paul Cowan understood long before anyone else was that there was a new kind of story to tell about such conflicts: that attempts to "coax people into the melting pot" had costs as well as benefits, and campaigns to replace "our periods with your question marks," as one Creeker put it with aphoristic intelligence, must not simply be imposed by fiat. Cowan understood how "often, people I might once have written off as reactionaries were fighting to preserve their culture and their psychological and physical turf," and that this new argument over the meaning of democracy was defining the next frontier of political conflict itself. That America had tribes, and that sometimes—often—they would come to blows.

We call those fights the "culture wars" now, and we have a more richly variegated vocabulary to describe the Hillers and the Creekers: red state and blue state. Redneck and yuppie. New Class and white working class. "Evangelical" and "liberal." We describe our nation's dueling dreads over such concepts with a casualness that once marked cocktail party chatter about the inevitability of consensus liberalism. Writing in the 1970s, however, Cowan had no such clichés to lean on. He had to figure it out for himself. He did so brilliantly—eyes open, with a courage I can scarcely believe. He traveled all over the country: to Boston during the busing wars; to Forest Hills, Queens, where he was shocked at the racism of immigrant Jews fighting the construction of a low-income housing project; to the southernmost border of the United States, where the sacrifices Mexicans were making to preserve their families looked like anarchy to the Americans patrolling the border with shotguns. Cowan's reporting from these places left him "with a profound respect for the stability of religion, of ceremony, of family life: of customs I'd once regarded as old-fashioned and bourgeois." His travels also found him realizing that "those same longings, translated into political terms, have produced the vicious fights I've witnessed for the past seven years and recorded in this book." His agonized sensitivity to battlefields then barely emergent makes for one of the most remarkable books I have ever read by any journalist.

It was courage that allowed him to achieve it, though courage of a certain sort. Paul Cowan was a journalist who threw himself into situations that might just change his mind, and how many of us dare to do that? In the deeply humanizing portrait of illegal aliens, he notes how "I'd always included braceros"—Mexicans who traveled back and forth on legally sanctioned work contracts—"in my private litany of the oppressed." Instead, he found "they talked nostalgically, not bitterly, about their adventures" north of the border. He calls the chapter "Still the Promised Land"—a self-reproach to someone who once proudly called himself an "un-American." In a profile of Jesse Jackson, he encounters a man on the verge of apostasy from the left: Jackson, who was then deeply opposed to abortion, was the keynoter at the 1978 meeting of the Republican National Committee. Cowan sat and listened, relegating his own voice to the background. That quiet and reflective voice may account for a mystery regarding Cowan, whom I had never heard of at all when I encountered this book by accident last year. Flashier contemporaries went on to greater fame. Cowan's willingness to play down his own ego—indeed, to mock his own ego—accounts for some of his obscurity.

The more famous names often seemed more macho; there is something about the male journalist and the trope of physical courage. Though Cowan was no chicken. Covering a nationwide transportation strike, he thumbs a ride with a trucker through Ohio where strike supporters are shooting scabs from overpasses. But then comes the characteristic Cowan move: the introduction of a discordant image. He describes a group of college students goofing around in a truck stop's game room, himself "oddly envious, as they chatted cozily about the plays they planned to see during a weekend in New York." He would rather be with them. It is a meditation on a deeper meaning of courage. What journalist, reporting a story, forcing yourself on strangers, attempting to convince yourself that you have something worth saying about a world not your own, hasn't felt the desire to be somewhere else—anywhere else? And what, really, is more difficult: admitting that to yourself (and the world: Cowan wrote of his "fear that I'll appear a fool"), or placing yourself in the way of a "dangerous" situation that renders moot the question of whether what you're doing is worth writing about? The latter course is a way to banish the real fear. Sometimes you realize, reading *The Tribes of America*, that physical courage and psychic courage are inversely proportional.

The book is not just a collection of published articles. Cowan revised and extended the articles by revisiting the places where he'd reported them. You want scary? Imagine catching up with the people you originally thought you'd turned into heroes with your stories, and who you now know think you've sold them out.

In 1974 Cowan was among the onslaught of outsiders—students, politicians, scribblers, filmmakers—who descended on Harlan County, Kentucky, to chronicle a coal miners' strike. He arrived bearing fantasies. The locale was legendary: "Bloody Harlan," site of the Depression-era strike that inspired the song "Which Side Are You On?" "Some of the journalists I admired most—Theodore Dreiser, Sherwood Anderson, and John Dos Passos—had been part of a committee that investigated working conditions in Harlan in 1931," Cowan explained. They had left as heroes, or so he thought. Why couldn't he? He overlooked the arrogance of some of those earlier reformers, who had distributed copies of the *Daily Worker* to miners and then stood by as those very possessors of the *Daily Worker* were removed to jails in remote hamlets reachable only by mule. In Harlan, Cowan partnered with a young miner with leadership ambitions, Jerry Johnson, who seemed more cosmopolitan than all the rest: "I began to fantasize that we were a latter-day version of Butch Cassidy and the Sundance Kid, pledged to cleanse the mining town of its heritage of corruption." Sure, some of Jerry's values were different, such as his devotion to the land and his traditional marriage. His motivations were different, too. Jerry was moved less by abstractions of justice than by a passion to recover the folkways of his ancestors' Appalachia, before it was commandeered by the greedy overlords of coal. Cowan, the left-wing universalist,

emphasized their commonality and romanticized the differences. "I
began to think of them as the lost tribe of the working class," he
wrote of the miners—arrogating himself, dangerously, a role as their
anthropologist.

It couldn't end well.

Jerry hated the story that was meant to lionize him and ended up
hating its author, too—who Jerry thought had rendered Harlan's tra-
ditionalism in the *Voice* as titillating local color incidental to the political struggle, when to many in Harlan their traditions as they
understood them were the point of the political struggle. Only upon
returning did Cowan realize that these friendly people "felt a smoldering resentment toward outsiders"—even, or especially, outsiders
who parachuted in and styled themselves as saviors. He had made a
terrible botch of things. "Harlan County: The Power and the
Shame," he titled this chapter. Part of that shame, he suggested, was
his own. He had "indicated a set of commitments—and an unquestioning acceptance of Jerry's view of the strike—that my articles
didn't really reflect."

That, he says, "helped me distill the argument that was the genesis of this book": that the passions of reformers can sometimes betray
a contempt for the common sense of ordinary people, leading in
turn to a dangerous narcissism that could transform someone like
him into a close kin of those arrogant school bureaucrats in West
Virginia.

Cowan reckoned with that danger most explicitly in his book's
concluding chapter. In 1972 "the urban journalistic and political
elite"—a tribe in its own right—had flooded another parochial locale, the Middle District of Pennsylvania, where Richard Nixon's
Justice Department had staged a politically motivated conspiracy
trial designed to neutralize the bands of Catholic radicals trying to
end the war in Vietnam by disrupting the draft system. Cowan's tribe
came with "visions of jurors lifted from the pages of Sinclair Lewis's
Main Street." So did the tribe of John Mitchell, Nixon's attorney
general, whose Justice Department was counting on these terrified
Silent Majoritarians to sentence the defendants to an eternity un-
derneath the jail.

Well, the yokels saw that the government's case was patently absurd, so the yokels had no trouble acquitting. "How stupid did

those people in Washington think we were?" one juror later asked Cowan.

That was how Cowan ended the book. The Harrisburg experience, he concludes, "left me feeling that my attitudes toward that group of Americans (like the attitudes of most lawyers, reporters, and defendants—members of the urban elite who were connected to the case) were just as narrow and parochial as their attitudes toward us." He vowed to do better.

By the time I read that, around Christmas in 2003, I had an aching question I wanted to ask Paul Cowan. I wanted to know what had become of him ideologically. After all, in the mid-1970s, other writers were also raising criticisms about the urban journalistic and political elite and their self-serving condescension toward "heartland" people and their values. These writers were also discovering a newfound "respect for the stability of religion, of ceremony, of family life." They recognized the habits of a former radicalism as a set of blinds, just as Cowan had, and embraced what Cowan called "the more primal part of oneself" and the conviction—as Cowan wrote—that "cultures aren't clay that you can sculpt to your liking." These writers called themselves neoconservatives. Had Paul Cowan become one of them?

I couldn't ask him that question; he died of cancer in 1988. So I called Paul's widow, Rachel, his frequent companion in many of these chapters. What Rachel Cowan told me was that her husband was just as proud to write from the left at the end as he was at the beginning. He continued to work for *The Village Voice*; one of his last big stories was a profile of the victims of the Three Mile Island nuclear accident, also in the Middle District of Pennsylvania.

Politically, the answer made sense to me. It shows in Paul Cowan's ultimate judgments—for example, that the border guards whom he also deeply humanized in his portrait of illegal aliens, otherwise decent men and professionals, ultimately suffered from a racist inability to recognize the full humanity of the "wets" they hunted. It shows in his conclusion to the West Virginia chapter, in which he faces a moment of truth with the Creekers' charismatic leader: he has to grant her point that "maybe there is no school system that can provide for your kids and mine," but concludes, "I would like to think there is room for fundamentalists in my America. But I'm not sure there is room for me in theirs."

The answer also made sense to me as someone on the hunt for good writing. His ability to probe where those he disagreed with were coming from while still understanding why he disagreed with them—he knows which side he's on—was a token of his moral seriousness and his comfort with moral complexity. He was equally allergic to moral relativism as to moral dogma, which is exactly what made him a great journalist. I came to this realization while thinking of another book published in 1979. It was written by a bad journalist, who in his previous book had proved himself to me a very a good one. That previous book was called *Making It,* and its descriptions of subterranean social forces that no one had described before—in this case those shaping the New York literary world—were in their way as astonishing as the journalism in Cowan's *The Tribes of America.* But Norman Podhoretz's next book, *Breaking Ranks: A Political Memoir,* one of the most famous and influential books of neoconservatism, was a very lame one. Podhoretz told "the whole story of how and why I went from being a liberal to being a radical and then finally to being an enemy of radicalism in all its forms and varieties." Podhoretz had picked the wrong side. So he rejected it root and branch, right down to its core principle: social solidarity: "The politics of interest," Republican-style: that, he wrote, was "the only antidote to the plague" of sixties radicalism.

You can agree or disagree with the politics. I think it's hard to disagree that Podhoretz became a much worse writer, much less skilled at describing the world. In *Making It,* self-examination was the taproot of social observation. In *Breaking Ranks*—and his subsequent work—Podhoretz recognized only demons that existed outside himself. The left left him; he always stayed the same. Podhoretz claimed a courage—he called it moral courage—that was inversely proportional to his actual courage, which was sorely lacking. For perhaps it wasn't the left that was dogmatic, but himself—and dogmatists make terrible journalists.

Paul Cowan took a different course, and that is the meaning of his work. He looked inside himself. He found sins—his own sins, not the sins of some abstraction called "the left," to be rejected as such—and he reckoned with them. Which is hard work. He tested his prejudices against reality, about as deeply as anyone could test them; he embraced new principles, cleaving to the ones worth keeping. He saw virtues in bourgeois virtue. But that didn't paralyze his conscience. He saw that America had tribes, and that the left-leaning Ivy League professionalism he inhabited was one of them, with its own characteristic inanities. That wasn't the end of the story for Cowan, but rather a new, richer beginning.

ACKNOWLEDGMENTS

Ken McCormick, senior consulting editor of Doubleday, is one of the legends of book publishing. His faith that my *Village Voice* pieces could be transformed into a coherent book and his attentiveness to the particular themes and details of each chapter encouraged and inspired me.

Susan Schwartz, associate editor of Doubleday, worked on this book chapter by chapter. She never failed to return my worried writer's phone calls or listen patiently to the ideas I was formulating. She is generous with her praise and stubborn in her insistence that a passage or set of themes is unclear. Those two qualities are extremely welcome ones.

In 1974, Clay Felker took over *The Village Voice* from its founder, Dan Wolf. In 1977, Rupert Murdoch took the paper over from him. Tom Morgan and Marianne Partridge, who edited the *Voice* during much of that period, managed to protect the writers from owners who—to an increasing degree—treated the *Voice* like a piece of real estate. Both of them gave me the support I needed to continue the explorations that are in this book.

Alan Weitz, managing editor of the *Voice*, worked on about half of these chapters with me when they appeared in the paper. His eye for the detail that clutters up a scene, for the precise rhythm of a sentence or a quote, his respect for the uniqueness of a writer's style and working methods, haev been blessings for me during some very difficult times.

Linda Perney, copy chief of the *Voice*, has worked with me on this entire manuscript. Her commitment to accuracy never fails to amaze me. She represents the very best of a department of journalism whose importance is too rarely stressed.

INTRODUCTION

This book represents a seven-year effort to learn more about America and about myself, and to develop a way of writing about my discoveries.

I've been a political radical since the Sixties. But by late 1971, when I began these explorations, life inside the New Left had become an emotional burden. By then, we'd helped end legal segregation in the South and were helping to stop the war in Vietnam. But we didn't act like people who had triumphed. Now I look back on those years as a time of a collective nervous breakdown, when most of us—youngsters, really, in our teens and twenties—could no longer cope with the strain of combating the evils we saw in America and in ourselves. Most of us survived that breakdown; many became activists again. But, back then, in the early Seventies, our world seemed like a nightmare of intellectual claustrophobia. So, gradually, half-consciously, without any theory or any plan, I decided to cross the sound barrier of dogma and test my beliefs against the realities of American life. I described my findings in pieces I published in *The Village Voice*.

It was thrilling—and terrifying—to read a *New York Times* article about a fight over some textbooks in West Virginia, or about some coal miners who were striking in Harlan County, or truck drivers who were closing down America's highways, and know that the *Voice* would assign me to discover the human feelings behind those stark facts. I could spend weeks or months in cultures I'd always regarded as remote, mysterious, even mythical—with Mexicans in the border town of Juarez, or fundamentalist Christians in Campbell's Creek, West Virginia, or European-born Jews on New York's Lower East Side. My profession and my passion coincided. I could immerse myself in the lives of unsung people, and learn so much about their communities that I became almost fluent in their private language: in the details of their work, their faith, their manner of speech, their attitudes toward one another. I tried to see them, and America—and my own presence among them—from their point of view. That was the best way to unlearn my own prejudices, and to challenge those of my readers.

Over the years I found myself changing. I am very much a product of the highly mobile urban elite. My parents, who were successful in show business and politics, sent me to Choate and Harvard; my politics, which they influenced greatly, sent me South during the civil-rights movement and to Ecuador during the heydey of the Peace Corps; my desire to write experimental, personal journalism for a highly educated audience sent me to the most freewheeling of all newspapers, *The Village Voice*.

Those things were all blessings. Still, I always felt that something substantial was missing from my life. The flip side of privilege, American-style, was the disturbing feeling that one lived outside of history. That sense subsided when the New Left was strong: when politics was a creed, when it furnished an identity one could be proud of. But that was over by 1972. Besides, I was married and had two children. I wanted something more nourishing, more permanent, than the political struggles, the cultural fads, the journalistic assignments, that seemed to eddy randomly through my life.

I sensed what it was as I got to know Orthodox Jews on New York's Lower East Side, churchgoing blacks in Chicago, coal miners who had left safe, well-paying jobs in the Midwest for the dangers and insecurities of their Appalachian home, Mexicans who cared deeply for their community in Juarez. The stories I wrote about them turned out to be dialogues with experience, with my own private dissatisfactions. As a whole, they left me with a profound respect for the stability of religion, of ceremony, of family life: of customs I'd once regarded as old-fashioned and bourgeois. They pushed me toward an increasingly deep interest in my own religion, Judaism, and a desire to organize a part of my life around that rich heritage.

I know now that I want an emotionally satisfying faith; an enriching family life; a secure, peaceful neighborhood for my kids. Yet those same longings, translated into political terms, have produced the vicious fights I've witnessed for the past seven years and recorded in this book. How can one embrace them and still be an integrationist, still be a political progressive? Some leftists—including many who have chosen popular journalism as their profession—maintain their purity by heaping scorn on those values. But how can one do that without disowning most people in this country, without disowning the most primal part of oneself?

Those personal questions underlie most of the journalism in this book.

The Tribes of America is a metaphor for my way of seeing this country. And it is a political statement.

I was raised to believe that the United States is a melting pot, and since I'm a confirmed racial, sexual, and cultural integrationist, I'd still like to think that was true. But I don't. The last seven years have convinced me that the melting pot—with its dream of a single, unified America—is largely a myth.

We are unified during times of crisis like World War II, like assassinations. We're united as consumers. We vote in the same national elections. We have a mass culture in common—most of us are aware of Elvis's death, we can imitate the Fonz, we argue about Muhammad Ali or the Yankees or the Dallas Cowboys.

But, to an unrecognized extent, we're a nation of professional, religious, ethnic, and racial tribes—the Tribes of America—who maintain a fragile truce, easily and often broken. We had to conquer this continent—and its original tribes—in order to exploit its resources. But we were never able to conquer our atavistic hatreds, to accept our widely diverse pasts, to transcend them, to live together as a single people.

Of course, if you transform that insight into a generalization, it dissolves immediately. There is probably more mingling of cultures here than anywhere in the world—a greater acceptance of mixed marriages, say, a more genuine interest in unfamiliar customs and beliefs, a relaxed acceptance of diversity on the assembly line or the ball field. Nevertheless, the currents of tribalism run deep. And, when political or social pressures are severe, they become floodwaters.

That's most obvious, I guess, in disputes involving race. Where there's a fight over busing or over jobs, blacks and whites inevitably see each other through the distorting lens of their own particular culture. Small details assume menacingly grotesque proportions. I saw that when I covered the 1971 battle over a low-income housing project in the Forest Hills section of Queens, and when I covered busing in Boston. It was hard for white people to see past the fact that a man was black and think about his character. Thus, to them, blacks "strutted," they never walked; they cursed and hollered, they never talked. If they dressed well, they were drug dealers or pimps, not honest, successful businessmen or professional people. The accretion of those stereotypes made them see blacks as "animals," and no amount of rational argument could change their minds.

Similarly, during the worst weeks of the busing crisis in Boston, it was hard for some of the blacks I interviewed to see that the presence of a few people who claimed to be members of the Ku Klux Klan did not presage the resurrection of that ancient foe. Even after the most severe tensions subsided, it was hard for them to see that whites were just as frightened, just as hungry for economic and emotional security as they were.

The interaction of stereotypes made peace nearly impossible.

But race isn't the only tribal banner. In Kanawha County, West Virginia, the "creekers"—working-class whites, mostly Baptists—were at war with the "hillers"—professional people, mostly Congregationalists and Episcopalians. The immediate issue was the textbooks that would be used in the schools. But the battle was really a cultural civil war between fundamentalist Christians and secular humanists over the kind of nation their children would inhabit.

All along the Mexican border, Anglos are terrified that Hispanics—particularly illegal aliens—will steal their jobs, enjoy special privileges, and smuggle a new kind of separatism—the separatism of language—into American life. On the Lower East Side of New York, a Puerto Rican who disperses poverty funds can ignore the stark fact that hundreds of thousands of elderly Jews live below the poverty level of $3,500 by echoing the old tribal myth that "there is no such thing as a poor Jew."

Of course, tribalism has its advantages, too. These days they're most often suggested by phrases like "my search for my roots." I've tried to show how that attitude affected me when I wrote about the unexpectedly strong links I felt to the poor Jews I met on New York's Lower East Side or my unexpectedly close, almost filial relationship with the Polish-born Orthodox Rabbi Joseph Singer. There's no question that my deepening awareness of being Jewish has given me a more secure sense of my own identity. It has eased my loneliness in America by teaching me that I do have a home in a tradition I love.

But the tensions of tribalism have haunted me throughout most of this journalistic journey. I keep trying to find a political language, a journalistic language, that will help people form alliances based on economic needs rather than ethnic stereotypes; that will help us affirm what's richest, most special about each specific tribal heritage instead of denying those qualities in the name of some bland idea of America; that will help us learn from one another instead of fighting one another. Often, as I've written about the situations I've witnessed, I've doubted that could happen. Yet it is one of the obsessions that dominates this book.

When I was a teenager I loved to read the novels of John Dos Passos, Theodore Dreiser, Upton Sinclair; journalism by James Agee and George Orwell. My fantasy, in those days, was to write about the contemporary counterparts of the people who inhabited their books. That fantasy continued to correspond with my tastes. Once I became a reporter, I discovered it was more pleasant and interesting to spend time with people who had never been written about, who were often spontaneously warm and unpredictable, than with famous people, who were always performing, who regarded me as a vehicle for polishing their carefully sculpted self-images.

Over time, I usually developed a deep emotional commitment to the people and communities I was writing about. They were friends, not subjects of articles, and they taught me a great deal. They inhabited my dreams, my imaginative life, my conversations with my friends and family. I began to think of my method of reporting as total-immersion journalism.

Still, when I start out on a story, I'm usually consumed by an almost paralyzing nervousness. I postpone plane trips for days or weeks at a time, try to drown my self-doubts in late-night booze, rack my life for excuses to cancel the assignment altogether. It is not a physical nervousness. It's a fear that I won't get the story— or even discover what the story is. And it's a fear that I'll appear a fool.

In Harlan County I couldn't visualize the coal-mining scenes people described. I was constantly tempted to let the people I was meeting assume that I grasped the terms they used so fluently: to nod my head when I heard about an incident at the tipple, or when someone talked about the dangers of operating a roof-bolting machine or working in a tunnel a hundred feet wide instead of twenty-five feet wide. That way, perhaps, I'd appear to be one of them. The trouble is that those disguises never work. The only way to cope with unfamiliar situations is to swallow my pride and ask dumb, direct questions about things that baffle me. It often turns out to be a surprisingly effective way of forming relationships, since most people love to discuss the details of their work.

When I first went to the Lower East Side to research "Jews Without Money, Revisited," I was so ignorant of my heritage that I didn't know you were supposed to wear a yarmulke in a yeshiva. I couldn't understand why people answered my friendly questions so curtly, why they stared at my bare head with such disapproval. Soon I made friends with some Orthodox Jews, but it was weeks before I mustered the courage to accept their invitations for dinner. I was vaguely aware that you had to say blessings and perform hand-washing rituals, but I didn't have the slightest idea of how to do these things. I was afraid my new friends would shun me when they discovered the extent of my ignorance. They didn't, of course. They treated me as a prodigal, not a heretic.

Still, sometimes my fears have been well-founded. The people I've set out to cover have perceived me as an alien or as a stereo-typical member of the media—a hurried, half-interested urban so-phisticate who was only out for a few juicy quotes.

When I began to interview truck drivers, I saw that they were talking to my tape recorder, not to me. They used the machine to issue the sort of sterile rap you hear on the seven o'clock news. But, when I began to hitchhike with them, hoisting myself into the cabins of their rigs, chatting quietly against the squawk of their cbs, our conversations became more intimate. Their deeply felt complaints about the soaring costs of fuel, the wretched con-ditions of the roads, the time they wasted at loading docks, began to blend in with the more intimate details of their family prob-lems, their ambitions, their lonely thirst for adventure.

Still, there are ethical and emotional problems with my ap-proach to journalism. What happens when someone you're writ-ing about begins to trust you too much? When he or she forgets your tape recorder and your notebook and begins to disclose infor-mation that fascinates you, but that will embarrass your subject once it is in print? When public figures do that a reporter doesn't have to worry so much. They've chosen a way of life that involves this risk. But what about a coal miner, a truck driver, a border pa-trolman? They might hate the media, but it is also Holy Writ to them. Your choice of quotes, of details might determine the way the public—and their neighbors—see them for a very long time.

Often I avoid that problem by changing the names, the occupa-tions, the residences of people who might be unsettled by the in-formation I disclose. For example, even though I had the tape re-corder on when I traveled with the truckers, I doubted the driver I called the Pilgrim expected me to describe his fears for his sister's health, or that the man I called Ringo thought I'd reveal his method of hauling cargo illegally. So I disguised them, as I dis-guised the Mexicans and border patrolman in "Still the Promised Land," the itinerant workers in "The Lower Depths of American Labor," the black family I wrote about in "A Return to the Fun-damentals."

But I had to face the problem when I wrote about Harlan County. Before I set out on that story I had asked people at the

United Mineworkers union to find a striker I could stay with. The miner, who became my friend, said that I could use his name, and any portion of his life I thought was suitable. I guess it never occurred to him that I'd be interested in the Appalachian religions, the patterns of violence, the relationship between a male-dominated work world and a male-dominated household, which he and his wife and their friends discussed so often. That information fascinated me. In fact, by the time I left I was convinced that one had to understand Harlan's people and its culture in order to understand the strike.

I thought—and still think—that the piece I wrote was a fair one. But he felt that, in some places, I had extracted colorful bits of information from his complex life simply to interest *Voice* readers. (His complaints were about specific details, which seemed inconsequential to me but embarrassing to him. I have omitted them from this book.)

I liked him very much. He felt I had betrayed his hospitality— and betrayed him.

That was an especially painful experience, but it wasn't an isolated one. There was a teacher in Forest Hills who allowed me to spend time in her classroom, then complained that I was violating a trust when I described it as a microcosm of the xenophobic attitudes that were engulfing the neighborhood. There was an old woman on the Lower East Side of New York who allowed a photographer and me to enter her apartment, to take her picture, and then telephoned, enraged, when her tormented face appeared on the front page of *The Village Voice*.

Every reporter has to deal with problems like that. Misunderstandings are inevitable. So are sharp disagreements over judgments and interpretations. Still, cumulatively, such episodes sometimes made me wonder if I were becoming a sort of Typhoid Mary of journalism, who wangled my way into other people's lives, then caused unnecessary hardship by the simple, unavoidable act of recording their words and my perceptions accurately, who would then leave the communities that had temporarily seemed so important and return to my own comfortable life in New York.

But what else could I do? Studs Terkel—whose work I admire

greatly—shows people the transcripts of their words before he publishes them. But Studs is an interviewer; I'm a reporter. His solution is not a satisfying one for me since, in effect, it allows the people I write about to censor my work. It can rob me—and my readers—of a crucial insight, a telling remark, a physical detail that furnishes a vital clue to a person's culture or character.

I have learned to make my verbal contracts as clear as possible. For instance, I tell people whom I plan to spend a great deal of time with (as opposed to those I interview for an hour or two) that if they fear embarrassment or reprisals, they should ask me to disguise their names or not write about them at all. Sometimes I read back notes I've taken so that the person I've just interviewed can explain or amplify a point. If I'm working in a culture that's alien to me or my readers, and an anecdote seems jarringly exotic (or requires a careful, patronizing explanation), I'll ask the subject if he or she wants it used. And I've decided that certain situations—like a conversation between a husband I'm writing about and a wife I'm not, or a family quarrel I see because a person has invited me home for a meal—have got to be off limits. But the only external restraints I recognize are those that are imposed by my private sense of honor and fairness. For I'm trying to explore the Tribes of America, not present them in pretty little friezes. It's an emotionally complicated form of journalism. I believe it's a vital one.

During the winter and spring of 1977 and 1978 I revisited most of the places I'd written about in the *Voice*. I was personally very eager to know what had happened to the people I'd met over the last seven years. Furthermore, I think one of journalism's biggest flaws is its failure to follow up on stories that seize the public's attention for a month or two. My own follow-ups were extremely important experiences, for they reminded me that communities continue to evolve, and people continue to grow, long after the last media image has frozen itself in the public mind.

I have written most of these chapters as if the *Voice* pieces were first drafts, adding new information, reexamining earlier conclusions, omitting material that seemed irrelevant or insubstantial when I reread it.

I have not arranged the chapters chronologically (if I had, the one on Forest Hills would be first), but according to the themes they have in common and the effect they had on me. From time to time I stand back from the chapters with interludes, where I summarize my arguments or describe self-discoveries that emerged from a particular journalistic experience.

During the seven years I was developing the themes that are in this book, the *Voice* had three different owners and four different editors. But my work grew out of the fertile journalistic soil that existed there before June 1974, when Clay Felker took over the paper from Dan Wolf.

In those days, the *Voice* really was a writers' paper, in which Wolf edited character, not copy. He would choose five or six totally unknown writers as his proteges, and spend hours alone with each of us in his silent office, chatting with us, probing our psyches, questioning our certainties in his disconcertingly sardonic way, using every device he knew—not to dominate us (though that happened to a few people) but to help us find our own special voices.

There were problems with his method, of course. His sardonic style sometimes shaded into a cynicism that made you wonder if your ideas, your activities, were worth anything at all. Still, that quality, painful and infuriating as it could be, usually prompted self-examination, not paralysis.

I benefited enormously from my relationship with Wolf. He was an ideal reader—curious about everything, intelligent, skeptical of any attitude that sounded inauthentic; and (perhaps because he paid such low wages) he gave us all more freedom to experiment—and fail—than we'd ever again find in the gaudy, fast-paced world of commercial journalism.

Dan showed me that journalism could be a way of sustaining a search, not presenting prepackaged perceptions or conclusions. He helped me evolve a form of writing where I could draw on my instinctive respect for other people. By doing that, he helped me develop respect for myself.

The *Voice*'s Ross Wetzsteon, who text edited my pieces for years, helped me almost as much as Dan Wolf. He was thoroughly committed to an environment where all ideas—all risks—are potentially valid. In the early Seventies, when I started experimenting with the journalistic forms that are in this book, I had terrible self-doubts about my own skills and about the worth of what I was doing. Ross helped me overcome them by making me feel I was part of literature, not just of the media.

My wife, Rachel, is a professional photographer, a writer, an environmentalist. For the past fifteen years she has been my lover, my companion, my co-worker, my pal. I'm a very difficult person to live with, especially when I'm working. Her patience and her generosity—and her skill as an observer and an editor—constantly amaze me. She has not only helped me shape each of these chapters, helped me to observe physical and emotional details that my hasty eye would have overlooked; she has also taught me, by her example, how to empathize with people I might once have dismissed. Certainly, this book would not exist without her.

THE TRIBES OF AMERICA

CHAPTER 1

The Vigilantes of Highway 80

Truck drivers are America's gypsies, with their own secret language and culture.

I traveled with them one freezing December week in 1973, when owner-operators—small businessmen, not company drivers or Teamsters—led a strike that half-emptied America's highways. I hitchhiked from Jersey City to Dayton, interviewing diesel drivers in their noisy, trembling cabins or in the gadget-filled fluorescent-lit truck stops where many of them idled away their time until the roads were safe again.

The drivers are latter-day cowboys, rootless men with giant mechanical toys—men who know more about the new dispatcher in Salem, Washington, the new hooker at the truck stop in Akron (she charged twenty dollars for an hour's work and supposedly made more than five hundred dollars a week), about the relative merits of the newest 1973 Kenworth and Peterbilt rigs—they call them their "horses" and pay up to forty thousand dollars for them —than about their neighbors and families in towns like Henry, Illinois; Kearney, Nebraska; Waterford, Iowa; Artesia, New Mexico; Tempe, Arizona; where many of them live.

You can hear their frontier dreams in the handles they choose, the monikers with which they identify themselves over their citizens'-band radios: Covered Wagon, Pioneer Outlaw, Indian Man, Colorado Wild Man, the Jewish Hillbilly, the Tennessee

Muleskinner, Whiskey Charlie, Saddle Tramp, Pecos Bill, the Polecat. You can hear it in the pride with which a trucker who's not confined to a single product, who will haul anything, refers to himself as an "outlaw." You could hear it in the songs that poured out of the truck stop jukeboxes endlessly that winter, ballads about the road, about fleeting glimpses of nature, about far-flung American towns: "Delta Dawn," "Abilene," "Blue Ridge Mountain Turning Green," "Rambling Man," "City of New Orleans," "Riding My Thumb to Mexico," "Saturday Night in Hickman County," "Country Roads," "Rocky Mountain High."

Trucking is a lonely, punishing life. Drivers have to haul heavy, dangerous cargo across the country in just three or four days. Their trips are punctuated by meals at truck stops, where they bloat their already paunchy bellies with overpriced dinners of tasteless processed foods; by a few hours' sleep at a rest area, or a night's sleep in a truck's cabin—they call that "dying"—or in the tiny, narrow eye slit of a room truck stops rent them for eight dollars a night; by wasted hours at the loading docks, where they have to sit in their semis for as long as a day, waiting for cargoes of beer, steel, lettuce, cardboard. They're treated like machinery or portable warehouses. They rarely get paid for their waiting time. They usually have to do the unloading for themselves.

Still, they can't stand the idea of settling down. When they thought of me as a reporter they'd complain about how their work forced them to be away from home—how they'd missed their babies' first words, their first ten birthdays, their first dates. But then, when I put my note pad or my tape recorder away, when an interview became a friendly, introspective discussion, they'd described how restless they'd get after a few days with "Mama and the kids," how they're ready for the road long before the dispatcher calls to tell them about their next runs. Sometimes the only substantial comments they make about their stints at home are quick sexual boasts. It's as if their long half-willed absences fill them with a special need to be sure they are satisfying their abandoned mates.

High Flyer, a trucker from Columbus, Ohio, who was hauling meat from St. Paul, Minnesota, to Kingston, New York, told his friend Covered Wagon, from Kearney, Nebraska, that he'd only been home forty-five minutes in the last week. "What did you do?" I asked naïvely. "My homework," he said with a quick wink.

A trucker who goes by the handle Double Clutcher tried to be candid about his feelings. He's a forty-year-old from Waterford, Iowa, who looks a decade older since he's missing most of his upper teeth. His wife had threatened to divorce him after he'd first gone on the road, fifteen years ago. He'd tried to quit, to appease her—once he went to work on his dad's corn farm; the other time he got a job as a security guard—"but trucking was in my blood. It was the only way I could be my own boss. My wife had to learn to live with that. Now she's able to wake up at three in the morning and sit with me for hours on end while I unwind. She's had to learn that it's her job to make all the decisions in the family. It takes an extraordinary woman to be a trucker's wife."

I met him at the Bartonsville, Pennsylvania, truck stop on a snowy night shortly after the strike had ended. He was driving for the Emory Packing Company, hauling swinging meat, a particularly dangerous cargo that could topple his thirty-five thousand dollar Peterbilt rig if he swerved too fast. What did he mean when he said trucking was in his blood? "Well, the job is always a challenge. You're always fighting the elements. Take this snowstorm up yonder. What are my chances of getting my rig through her? Oh, we'll make it, I guess. We always have. But, still, I know that good men are killed every day. I've trained my body to endure a lot—I can drive forty hours at a stretch if I have to, then I take out my pillow and sleep for two hours that are as refreshing as most people's eight. But there's always danger up ahead. And I always want to know if I'm man enough to make it."

Then there is the machinery—the truckers' great love. Their rigs, sure, and their cbs. "Ratchet mouths" are people who love to talk through the American night. When they speak cb, it sounds like their special language—if they're America's gypsies, then it's their Romany. It is truckers' hard-boiled, foul-mouthed talk, processed through the rigid laws of the FCC, which forbids swearing or any mention of the human anatomy ("Mercy" and "cottonpickers" are coded profanities; the drivers' word for tits is "seat covers"). Voices that, in normal conversation, are flat and slow become energetic, almost imploring as they seek to make mid-

night contact with their fellow drivers. There is a rhythmic litany
to talk over the cb that reminds you of a priest saying mass or a
rabbi saying kaddish.

All over America, truckers' special messages crackle through the
night. "Breaker, breaker, this is Pennsylvania Thunder on the
horn over by exit 23." "Come on, breaker." "Smokey the Bear is
heading West on Interstate 80." "Ten-four, guy. Mercy sakes,
those cottonpickers have already given me one ticket. Three's on
you, you old ratchet mouth" (the blessings of the road). "I'll give
you a holler on the flip-flop—the way back."

After midnight, especially, the talk turns from simple matters
to denser subjects—the oil companies' corruption, the huge reserves of fuel that are supposedly stashed underground in New
York or New Orleans, the couple making out at exit 9. Any subject that will help a weary trucker make it through the night.

But in November 1973, thousands of owner-operators were worrying about their own economic survival. The soaring price of diesel fuel had cut deeply into their profits. Since they could buy
only fifty gallons at a time—and often had to wait on long lines
when they did so—they wasted precious time making fuel stops. In
November, some of them had organized an impromptu blockade
on Interstate 80, near the Delaware Water Gap, an act that had
generated unexpectedly broad national publicity. The pre-
Christmas nationwide truck strike seemed like the most effective
way of maintaining their momentum, of getting Congress to ease
their economic burdens.

That December week the strike turned many drivers into vigilantes and transformed America's highways into concrete
minefields.

I met Bob Zerba, thirty-four, a burly, baby-faced, cigar-smoking
company driver, over breakfast at Bartonsville the morning the
strike began. The day before he'd dropped off some cardboard at a
plant in Brooklyn. Now he figured that if he drove by day he'd be
able to load twenty-one tons of cardboard at the Watertown
Building Products factory in Laurel, Pennsylvania, and deliver
them to his terminal in Lorain, Ohio. His act of courage would
impress his employers, who had no use for the independent

truckers who'd started the shutdown. He agreed to take me with him.

Our departure was a hasty one. As Bob walked to his truck he was pummeled by some strikers who kneed him and elbowed him until calmer people told them to stop. They did, but one warned him that the next time they met, in some other part of the country, he'd pay for his disloyalty.

Actually, he agreed with the strikers' complaints about the skyrocketing price of diesel fuel. But he hated the thought of losing a day's pay. His truck was the shabbiest one I drove in—a 1967 Mack with flaking red paint, hauling a battered flatbed trailer. The cabin was decrepit. The padding around the foot pedals was worn with time. Though there was space for two people, there was just one seat, the driver's, and I had to prop myself up with my suitcase and his briefcase. His heating system had broken down, and the company hadn't invested in a replacement. Despite my heavy sweater and Antarctica parka, I kept shivering as we talked. His company hadn't given him decent mufflers either. The engine roared so loudly that I couldn't hear his answers to most of my questions. He didn't have a cb (which was why he didn't have a handle), or a regular radio. He was completely alone in that vibrating, freezing compartment.

He'd grown up on a farm in Rockville, Ohio, and gone into trucking because it paid better than farming or a job in the steel mills at Lorain. He'd quit school in sixth grade and worked as a mechanic until he went out on the road. He could only read and write well enough to fill out a log book and struggle through the little red book of safety regulations the American Truckers' Association puts out.

George Wallace was the only politician he respected: "He's the only one in this country who knows what it's like to hold down a job." He was sure America would fall apart "unless a strong man comes along to lead us."

Sometimes he seemed to be on the verge of falling apart himself. He was riddled with fears—of his company, of his fellow workers, of poverty, of anybody who sat behind a desk and seemed to occupy a position of power. While he was waiting for the Watertown crane to load up his rig he requested that the personnel manager give us a tour of the plant. He'd been loading there for three years, and he'd always wondered how scrap paper was recycled into wallpaper. But he'd never had the courage to ask. Now my presence buoyed him until he got through the office door. But when he saw the middle-level executive, who looked pudgy and unctuous to me, he reflexively put his cap in his hands and began to blush and stutter deferentially. Actually, he had forty pounds and twenty-five years on the guy, and unthinkingly blew great puffs of cigar smoke in the executive's face as he tried to muster the courage to make his harmless request.

It was refused. Once the truck was loaded and the dispatcher was filling out Zerba's receipts, there was another crop of people to ingratiate himself with: He asked the dispatcher, please, to tell whoever called him from the terminal at Lorain that he'd been one of the few truckers who had been brave enough to travel that day. "I'll bet they remember that for a long time," he told me proudly. That prospect more than compensated for the shame he'd felt in Bartonsville.

At least it did until we approached the truck stop in Lamar—one place the boycott leaders had chosen for their headquarters. Then he began to mutter frightened reproaches to himself. He should never have left Brooklyn. His bosses would have allowed him to shut down: He was only on the road because he knew it would impress them. Hell, the company had 150 trucks, and only seven were operating during the shutdown. Maybe he needed the cash more than the other guys; maybe that was why he was crazy enough to be driving into this mess. He was single, thank the Lord, but his father's farm was doing badly, his brother was laid off work. If the fuel shortage kept up, his company might have to let him go, too. So he was hauling as many loads as possible while the money was available. The ICC says truckers are supposed to drive for ten hours, rest for five, but for months he'd been running twelve or thirteen hours at a stretch and falsifying his books. He rarely slept more than six hours a night. If he were laid off, though, "I'll go on welfare. Where else can I find a job like this one? I'll let the government support me."

There was no reason he had to go to the Lamar truck stop, no reason he had to mingle with the strikers. He'd planned to drop me there, then drive on to a more peaceful one at Kylertown, thirty miles down the road. But when we got to Lamar, he decided to walk inside with me. He sat down at the half-full counter and ordered a cup of coffee and a bowl of homemade vegetable soup. Near us, several drivers were talking about Ohio's cops— truckers called them the Gestapo because they enforce the state's exorbitant road-use tax, which, drivers feel, is part of the railroad interests' plan to cripple their industry. They warned each other not to drive on to Ohio. For steelhaulers out of Youngstown— some of the most militant truckers—were allegedly arming themselves for a showdown with the Gestapo.

That conversation was several seats away from us, but Zerba leaned toward the men and tried to wedge his way into it. They didn't pay much attention to his mild observation about how quiet things were on the road, so he made increasingly strident remarks about how he hoped the steelhaulers would "take care of those Gestapo boys tonight." It was as if, after the episode at Bartonsville, after a day of scabbing, he had to talk tough to reassure himself that he really was part of the fraternity of truckers.

Still, he was parceling his time cannily, eager to arrive at Kylertown with at least an hour of daylight to spare. The thought of driving that night terrified him. So he left the counter and paid his check after just one cup of coffee. But he halted as he walked toward the door. There was a can with the label BULLSHIT near the cash register—some sort of truckers' gag.

He picked it up and carried it over to the group of men, who were now chuckling over rumors of violence on Ohio's roads—the warnings had been passed along the drivers' grapevine that a scab could get killed there at night. Laughing nervously, Zerba pointed to the BULLSHIT label and said, "I'm going to mail this to the Gestapo." One of the men nodded slightly, then they went on with their conversation. He repeated himself more loudly. They ignored him, scorning his last-minute offering. Obviously disappointed, he hunched his hulking frame slightly and walked out the door.

Everywhere I'd been in New Jersey and Pennsylvania, I'd heard about the legendary Lamar truck stop—one of the headquarters of the shutdown. I'd expected the strikers there to be a lively crew. But most of them were listless. From dinnertime, when Zerba and I arrived, until eleven that night, when I left, most stayed holed up in the small TV room of the truckers' lounge, watching *The Brady Bunch, Beat the Clock, The Waltons,* and a movie called *The Great Escape,* with stupefied expressions on their faces.

In one room off the truckers' dormitory, five men were playing seven-card stud. They'd been at it since the strike had begun. In the game room, a young man and woman—students, driving east for the Christmas holiday—were engaged in a marathon bout of electronic Ping-Pong. I listened, oddly envious, as they chatted cozily about the plays they planned to see during a weekend in New York.

Next door, in the commissary, someone was leafing through *Overdrive,* the truckers' magazine, and another was chuckling over the cartoons in *Sexty-Sex,* a publication that was displayed in every truck stop I visited.

I went into the restaurant and asked a middle-aged couple if I could join them for coffee. They were a husband-and-wife team, trucking out of Louisiana. She was part Cherokee; he was part Cajun. As they talked, the woman, who was hefty but pert, kept snuggling up to her husband, patting him fondly on the knee, kissing him on the neck. They talked about their six kids, who stay with a babysitter while they're on the road, whom they see about four days a month. They looked like the Waltons, but talked the *National Enquirer.* They insisted that Lyndon Johnson had arranged for John Kennedy's assassination, but that JFK had lived for three years after the bullets lodged in his brain, years when Jackie had paid ghoulish visits to Parkland Hospital.

I began to talk with Minnesota Wilderness, a steelhauler who had been helping to direct protest activities ever since the blockade near the Delaware Water Gap. He combined the rage I had expected to find at Lamar with the mood of glazed boredom that had pervaded the truckers' lounge. His blue KEEP ON TRUCKIN' sweatshirt was gamey from overuse, and his round, sad face was ringed with the beginnings of a ragged beard. He'd been up for twenty-four hours, answering long-distance phone calls from drivers, reporters, and truck dispatchers across the country. But he still had enough energy for an animated conversation.

He was a huge, violent, raging man who hated the Jews and Dagos who ran the loading docks in New York as much as he did the oil-company executives. During the steelhaulers' strike of 1967, he had demolished a car belonging to the head of the company he drove for with a pick ax and his bare hands. He'd been fired for that, of course. He'd do it again, though, "since it taught that scab boss a lesson he'll never forget."

It was 10:30 P.M., and a few trucks were still running on Interstate 80, just beyond the gorge in front of us. Minnesota Wilderness looked out at them wistfully.

"This fucking strike," he said suddenly. "I feel dead in this place. All the guys who are here do. Every time I see one of those diesels I just want to go back on the highway. Where else can a man be free anymore?"

Creampuff, his comrade, a young woman trucker, was the most energetic person at Lamar. She was much younger than Minnesota Wilderness, a lithe, attractive woman with pale blue eyes, a very slight patina of freckles on her face, and auburn hair that might have billowed in the city but had gone slack and stringy during her time at Lamar.

She answered reporters' phone calls with a cheerleader's gusto, stood outside the truck stop to greet visiting drivers who lived nearby, sat out in Minnesota Wilderness's rig, using his cb to chat flirtatiously with drivers who were still on the road as she urged them to shut down and join the strike. She wore four bracelets on her thin wrists, commemorating men who were missing in action in Vietnam. She appeared to be a truckers' La Pasionaria, totally committed to her cause.

A year ago, she said, she'd been taking a six-month course in "Mixology," the art of making Singapore Slings, Bloody Marys, and Rob Roys. She'd liked her classes but not the profession. So, after graduating with high honors, she began her career as a truck driver. She'd been at it for four months. Then during the blockade, she'd happened to get stuck in Lamar and, because she was a woman, to be interviewed by a newspaper reporter. When she expressed sympathy for the drivers who had shut down, her company fired her. She decided to stick around.

Was she enjoying the action? "Hell, no. I'm bored out of my mind. I'd go home to Akron in ten minutes except I'm scared of getting shot out there on the road." Minnesota Wilderness, who was sitting at the table, drinking coffee with her, nodded his shaggy head in doleful agreement.

As I listened to them and thought about the men in the truckers' lounge, watching *The Great Escape* through those glazed, deadened eyes, I realized, for the first time, that not only the ordinary drivers, like Bob Zerba, but even strikers who seemed as committed as Creampuff, were acting out of personal fear as well as economic necessity.

They were all convinced that the "energy crisis" was a fraud the oil companies had concocted to increase their corporate profits; they all felt that lower fuel prices were essential to their survival. They hated the haphazard system of laws that existed on America's highways. For example, you could be licensed to carry eighty thousand tons of goods in one state, then enter another that only allowed drivers to haul seventy-two thousand tons and that penalized those who were overweight. You could be fined for that. So, one of the first things a young driver had to learn was how to skirt the weight scales that would greet him as he crossed state lines. He had to learn to break the law.

Many drivers felt hurt and betrayed by the institutions they'd been taught to respect—the government and the union, which failed to protect them. They all despised the oil companies, which gouged them.

But how could they fight back? It wasn't as if they were a group of dissident steelworkers, who saw each other at the same plant each day, or coal miners, who lived in the same rural holler. They had no common base—only the truck stops, the loading docks, and the road. The Teamster apparatus was determined to suppress dissent, especially when it came from owner-operators. No truckers' Jock Yablonski or Ed Sadlowski had taken regional power, sought to define new workers' issues, to forge alliances between union drivers and the independents.

But who were the vigilantes hurting? Not the government, the Teamsters, or the oil companies. So far, those institutions had escaped unscathed. It was the drivers, holed up in truck stops, who complained they were losing more money than they had before the shutdown. Many of them wanted to end it.

That night at Lamar, it seemed as if the militant truckers had devised a new, uncontrollable monster—this strike—to destroy the older uncontrollable monsters—the government, the oil companies, and the Teamsters. Now the monster was filling some of the people who had created it with an unexpected terror of their own faceless, nameless people "out there." Why, even Creampuff or Minnesota Wilderness could be killed if they followed their impulses and went back on the road.

I wanted to find the source of that terror, and there was only one place to do that—on the highway. So, at about 11 P.M., I decided to thumb a ride to Ohio: to visit cities like Youngstown, Akron, Dayton, which the drivers talked about with dread.

I walked into the truck-stop parking lot and asked the few drivers who were stopping for fuel or coffee if one of them would give me a lift. Most of them were shutting down for the night. Then, after an hour, I met the Pilgrim, thirty-two, stocky, and bearded, hauling ball bearings from his hometown of Framingham, Massachusetts, to a Goodyear plant in Akron, where he'd pick up some tire rims and take them on to Indianapolis. I asked him for a ride. He hesitated for a minute, muttering how this was a dangerous night to be on the road and I wasn't covered by his insurance; then he decided, what the hell, he'd take me after he drank some coffee.

Inside, Creampuff and Minnesota Wilderness were still sitting together, drinking more coffee and staring out at the highway. When I told them I was leaving, Minnesota Wilderness drawled, "Look, it's your life, neighbor, but I certainly wouldn't do that." So I muttered something like, "Well, you have your job and I have mine," walked outside with the Pilgrim, and headed west.

It was beginning to snow as we boosted ourselves into his fastidiously neat cabin. In the December moonlight, the Pilgrim switched on his diesel and turned his cb to channel ten, the truckers' station; reached for a Life Saver from the candy and gum packages that lay in a row on his dashboard next to his atlas, his cigarette lighter, and a picture of his two kids; put a new carton of

Kents beside the chess set in a curtained-off sleeping compartment behind him.

When I asked him about the chess, he said he often traveled with an eighteen-year-old nephew and they played at every truck stop. "But he was scared to come this time," the Pilgrim said. He rubbed a finger back and forth over one of his sideburns. "One thing I better tell you. In there"—in the truck stop—"I heard some guys saying that if anyone shoots at them from an overpass, they'll shoot back. Well, I can't do that. I guess I'm one of the few truck drivers in America who doesn't carry a gun."

The snow worried the Pilgrim even more than the rumors of violence. Bad weather always did. When he began to make solo runs cross-country, two years ago, his palms would get so soaked with sweat he could barely grip the steering wheel. He still said his rosaries before every trip. He was more confident now though —he'd even learned to love driving on clear summer nights. But, still, when he saw a truck jackknifed by the side of a road or read about a collision between a semi and a car, the scene would trouble him for days. Back home in Framingham he'd have nightmares about those Pennsylvania roads, especially about the windy, dangerous, trip over the mountain truckers call Snowshoe. Then his wife would have to soothe him back to sleep.

He was eager to talk, though our seats were separated by a sleek, wide leather console (one of the hallmarks of his rig, a Kenworth, the Cadillac of trucks), and we had to strain to hear each other over the motor and the buzz of the cb.

He'd hated the thought of making this trip. But his dispatcher at the American Packing Company had insisted, saying that if the ball bearings didn't arrive in Akron on time, the Goodyear assembly line would slow down. If that happened, the Pilgrim's lucrative contract with American Packing—which guarantees him fifty cents a mile, full or empty, for at least 100,000 miles a year— would be jeopardized. It's the only contract he has, the only thing that allows him to make his $550 monthly payments on the forty-thousand-dollar Kenworth he'd bought two years before. That contract allows him to remain an owner-operator—an independent businessman—not a hireling, like Bob Zerba. Even accounting for fuel, for overhead and payments on the rig, for food and lodgings, he still nets more than twenty-five thousand dollars a year. His father, a mechanic, an immigrant from Portugal, never grossed more than ten thousand. By the time the Pilgrim is forty he hopes to have his own fleet of at least seven trucks.

But that wouldn't happen if he were blacklisted by American Packing. So he ignored the strike, ignored his wife's pleas to stay home and carefully picked his way past the strikers at the truck stops at Bartonsville and Lamar, under the overpasses—the vigilantes' hideouts—toward his rendezvous at the loading dock at Akron.

Now that he was driving he was determined not to be stopped: He wanted to get home as quickly as possible. Unlike Minnesota Wilderness, who likes to be on the road for weeks at a time, the Pilgrim makes a point of spending Sundays with his parents, his wife, and his kids. He's determined to be a family man, despite the itinerant nature of his work. This week it was particularly important for him to be back in Framingham since his sister, a twenty-six-year-old divorcee with her own two kids, was in the hospital with cancer. "It really hasn't hit me yet, but the doctors say she may be dead before New Year's. My father has been crying about her for days. My mother is a little stronger, but I want to be with them to help out."

The Pilgrim is six years older than his sister, and he'd always taken care of her. He'd helped pay her way through secretarial school. When her husband came home a junkie, after service in Vietnam, he'd helped arrange the separation. Now he'd ordered the doctors not to tell her that the disease might be terminal because he didn't want to spoil her last, peaceful Christmas. Anyway, he said wistfully, maybe there really were miracles. One might save her.

It was one in the morning, but Interstate 80, usually filled with trucks until dawn, was practically deserted. We were just beginning our descent from Snowshoe and we hadn't seen another semi in about ten minutes. The Pilgrim had his cb on, very low, and there was a droning silence for miles at a stretch—a sure sign that most of the ratchet mouths had been frightened off the road. The radio's silence and deserted highway troubled the Pilgrim, but he mentioned them only hastily and then returned to the subject of his sister.

He asked me if I believed in an afterlife. I told him I didn't really know.

"What religion are you?"

"Jewish."

"I thought so. I don't mean to hurt your feelings, but, you know, people always say nasty things about Jews. But I used to work for them and they treated me pretty well." A pause. Then, anxiously: "Do your people believe in an afterlife?"

There was no malice in his voice, just concern for his sister's celestial future mingled with friendly curiosity. I decided that the most soothing, accurate response I could make was that sometimes I believed there might be some kind of reincarnation.

He leaped at the word. Before he'd married he'd dated a girl who knew something about those Eastern religions. (He didn't remember which one.) She used to talk about reincarnation, and he'd liked the idea that the next existence might be better than this one. "I believe that life here is hell."

It was becoming the sort of mystical conversation two sailors might have as they stood watch on a crisp night. But then, as I began to tell the Pilgrim why I believed in reincarnation, an urgent, scared voice came over the cb. The Pilgrim turned the volume up.

"Breaker, breaker, the handle here is Poker Chip, and I'm heading east. Those cottonpickers are throwing things at us from the overpasses out by exit 4. Do you copy me?"

"Ten-four, guy. This is Pilgrim, heading west. Mercy, we've been hearing rumors like that ever since we left home, but we haven't seen much of it yet. How do you know? Come on, come on."

"One of the trucks we're running with just got hit on the roof. We're closing down for the night."

It was raining now. We'd crossed Snowshoe and were on flat, Midwestern roads, about twenty miles from exit 4, three hours out of Akron. The Pilgrim didn't want to shut down unless someone forced him to. The ball bearings were due at the Goodyear plant at seven, and he was determined to keep on schedule.

We lapsed into a concentrated, intense silence. The Pilgrim was driving at about seventy, fifteen miles over the speed limit, much faster than he usually traveled in the rain. His body was cocked tensely over the steering wheel, his eyes swept back and forth over the road. The overhead light was our only beacon, but he had to use it sparingly, for fear of making the truck more visible.

Once, as we neared exit 5, the Pilgrim thought he glimpsed someone at the overpass. But nothing was hurled at us. Probably just a shadow. A pickup truck kept passing us, then dropping behind. The Pilgrim thought the driver might be luring us into a trap. Then he speeded up, pulled ahead of us, and drove out of sight.

Suddenly, the cb, which had been silent again, crackled with an argument. Someone at a base station off exit 4 contacted a driver heading east and ordered him to pull over. The driver, whose handle was Aardvark, said he was running in a convoy and had no plans to shut down. "Give me your handle, neighbor," Aardvark said.

"Negatory, guy," answered the man at the base station. "Just shut the cottonpicker down."

"How about that," Aardvark asked with angry irony. "The cottonpicker talks tough when no one can see him, but he won't even give us his handle. Hey, guy, why don't you tell us where your base station is? Mercy sakes, I'll come in there with some of my boys and we'll beat you so bad you won't ever talk out of that cottonpicking machine again."

"Come and try it. My boys are waiting for you." But the anonymous ratchet mouth didn't give Aardvark his location.

"You know, you sound like a nigger," Aardvark said. "Now, wouldn't it be just like a nigger to hide in the dark and scare a fella like me."

"Listen, guy, I'm going to let you go this time. But you remember this. I've had a cb for ten years, and I don't forget voices. If I'm ever on the road and I meet someone who talks like you, I'll make you wish you'd stayed in bed with Mama tonight."

We were passing exit 4, and everything was silent. Then, a few hundred yards down the highway, we saw a line of trucks—Aardvark's, we learned from the cb. They'd just pulled in from Dayton. The sight of a convoy that had actually made it through the terrors of Ohio was unexpectedly comforting.

After we'd passed the state line and driven within range of the

bright lights of Youngstown, I asked the Pilgrim how he felt.
"Still pretty tense. How about you?" I knew I should be scared,
but in fact I was on an adrenalin-filled edge of excitement. War
must do that to a soldier—though it seemed ironic to me that I
was watching this battle through the eyes of a scab. I told the Pilgrim I was glad we hadn't shut down because I didn't like being
stopped by the kind of threats we'd heard. "Maybe that's one
reason I kept on driving," he said. "I didn't really think I'd lose
this contract if I was a couple of hours late with the ball bearings."

Once we were at the Akron truck stop, eating a 5 A.M. breakfast of ham, scrambled eggs, and home fries, the Pilgrim told me
that "Back in Lamar, when you asked me for a ride, I thought
you were one of the strikers, setting me up. That's why I had to
think before I gave you this lift. I was afraid maybe we'd go about
a mile down the road and you'd shoot me for scabbing or something like that. Then I decided you didn't look like a trucker—
I've never seen one with glasses like yours—and I wanted company. So I decided you must be okay."

In my motel room I made some notes and tried to relax myself
with a stiff shot of the scotch I was carrying in my suitcase. But I
only slept a few fitful hours. Then I walked back to the truck
stop.

I had to hang around for hours before I found anyone who was
willing to take me further down Ohio's violent highways. But
finally, near the fuel pump, I met a long-haired, twenty-four-year-
old owner-operator whose handle was Ringo. I convinced him to
give me a ride to Columbus, where he had to load some paint.

Ringo was Pilgrim's opposite—a carefree, reckless driver. You
could tell that just by looking at the unkempt, decaying equipment in his rig. His cb only worked if you twisted the bolt behind
the knob with a tiny wrench. His windshield was so dirty he could
barely see out of it. Inside the cabin there were huge strips of tape
around the windows, to keep the cold air out. One of the head-
lights was damaged. Ringo boasted that police in five states had
given him tickets for that.

He was an ex-GI out of Tempe, Arizona, where his dad had
been a trucker, too. He'd just hauled a load of lettuce from Yuma

to Akron, and told me he hadn't slept since he'd left El Paso. I believed it. He acted as if he were high on dex or bennies or speed. His hands trembled whenever he lit a cigarette or loosened his grip on the steering wheel or put a new cassette of Country and Western music in the tape deck. It was particularly noticeable because his fingernails were coated with grime. He didn't shake his head in agreement or disagreement—he snapped it, and his black hair cascaded over his eyes. His body temperature didn't seem to bear any relationship to the temperature outside—he kept putting his jacket on, taking it off, sweating a little, shivering a little.

A few years earlier he'd earned a great deal of money smuggling contraband goods. I'd heard stories like his from other drivers, but his tongue was unusually loose since he'd been drummed out of that lucrative business.

There are certain well-known truck stops, he said, where someone posing as management hands you a phone number. When you call in, a broker—a middleman—tells you where to rendezvous on some deserted side road. Once you've arrived, there's an unspoken understanding that you'll leave the makeshift loading dock while whatever it is you're carrying—guns, pills, heroin: Ringo never asked—is placed in your trailer. You're given a cash advance and a road map that shows you how to avoid weight scales and police on your way. Of course, you're the one who goes to jail if you're caught. If you arrive safely, you're met by someone with a gun who makes sure you stay in your cabin while the goods are unloaded. Then you're paid—two or three times the amount you'd make carrying legitimate freight, according to Ringo. "But the people you work for are very careful. Once I began to pile up all those traffic tickets, there was no way they'd trust me."

It was dark when we arrived in Columbus, and Ringo spent about fifteen minutes trying to wedge his rig into the narrow, ill-lit entrance of the rundown paint factory. The only person who met us there was a tiny, garrulous old man who kept shouting about how much he hated Columbus, how he'd love to assassinate Richard Nixon, as he helped load the barrels of paint into Ringo's truck. Afterward, we went into his office to get the receipts. Every corner of the wall was filled with pinups from *Penthouse*. "Yes, sir," he yelled as he handed the papers to Ringo, "I've been working here twenty-five years and I've hardly missed a day. The only

thing that keeps me going anymore is the idea that I'm surrounded by so much pussy."

Ringo insisted that we eat at a White Castle. He drove through
Columbus's back streets, sounding the loud diesel horn whenever
he rounded a corner. "I like to tell people I'm here," he said. We
parked the rig across from the tiny restaurant and, while I sat
watching, Ringo wolfed down eight White Castle hamburgers in
less than ten minutes. He was supposed to spend the night with a
girlfriend in town—he'd already phoned her from the paint factory—but another call to a driver he knew told him that militant
truckers were gathering right then at the Union 76 truck stop in
Dayton, where I was supposed to meet the Pilgrim. He thought
that sounded like more fun than a night with a woman.

As we approached Dayton's truck stop we saw a crowd of husky
men outlined against a fire they'd started by putting wood in a
trash basket. They were much more angry than the men who had
pummeled Bob Zerba back in Bartonsville. Here in Dayton they
were forcing every trucker they saw to shut down.

The Pilgrim, who'd parked his truck at a nearby motel, was
drinking coffee when I entered. He'd called home that afternoon,
he said, and learned that his sister had improved a little. His wife
sounded so frightened for him that he didn't dare tell her what
had happened to us the night before. At first he'd hoped to hurry
home, to comfort her, but now the situation seemed too dangerous for that. He'd been waiting for me, he said, to tell me he
planned to spend the night in his motel and hope the state of
siege was lifted by morning. Now his sense of responsibility told
him to leave the truck stop as soon as possible, before the violence
became uncontrollable. When I said I had to stick around, to see
what would happen, he apologized for his caution. I told him that
was the quality about him I admired the most.

Ringo was over by the fire, eagerly agreeing with a group of
men who planned to get revenge on "those fucking scabs." Maybe
I had a slight edge on him since I was the only person there who
knew he was a fucking scab, too. Anyway, when I walked over, he
introduced me as a reporter, "but one of us."

It was freezing cold out. If you stood too close to the fire, your
eyes would tear from the smoke. If you stood too far away, your

head and feet froze. Yet there were about thirty men huddled around the flaming trash can, and maybe twenty more who were parked in cars nearby. Most of the men in the cars were steel-haulers who lived in the area. They'd brought liquor from home, and they shared it freely.

The men kept telling each other they weren't doing any good freezing their nuts off at the truck stop, with Smokey the Bear watching every move they made. Two strikers had been arrested that afternoon. The others didn't want to tangle with the Gestapo. But they were a small army: They'd fan out and park near the overpasses, waiting to hurl bricks at any scab trucks that came by. As they drank, their fantasies hardened into plans. They could avoid Smokey with their mobility. The rule was never to stop at an overpass for more than five minutes. The lumbering trucks would have no way of fighting back—not in the darkness. And if any of the men did get into trouble, they could call for help on the cbs they'd transplanted from their trucks to their cars.

Soon one man called out, "I've had enough of this. I'm going out to do some real business. Anyone want to come with me?" He left with a carful of men. Then a second pulled out, then a third. It was a very slow ballet—men would drift away from the campfire, take a swig of whiskey in the semidarkness, then ride off into the night. Finally Ringo left, too, glancing at me with his wild, reckless grin.

I stood by the fire with the few men who remained, too cold, and suddenly too tired, to think much or ask any questions. I had just watched a posse of vigilantes. Sure, some of those men would head home and bitch and booze some more, and others would spend the night swaggering through truck stops up and down the road. But some would carry out their plans. They'd get to the overpasses, drink more scotch, and ambush any rig that came along. I thanked God the Pilgrim wasn't on the road. Hell, I thanked God I wasn't there. I'd finally seen one source of the terror that had been faceless and nameless even when we rode toward Youngstown the night before.

Back inside the truck stop I began to talk with a thin, wispy-looking, fortyish, red-haired man who'd been standing near me by the fire. Then, I'd sized him up as part of the posse. He'd been griping and boasting just like all the others. But now, as we

ordered cup after cup of coffee, I realized that he was another
casualty of the strike.

He was trying to muster the nerve to telephone his wife, who
lived nearby. Two years ago she had insisted on a divorce because
she suspected him of having affairs on the road. He said he missed
her terribly—and he missed his two kids even more. He'd planned
to run a mobile home up to Chicago so he could earn enough
money to woo them back with expensive Christmas gifts. But
the strikers had slashed several of his tires. The couple who owned
the mobile home was paying fifteen dollars a night for their motel
room. They wanted their house delivered to Chicago, strike or no
strike, and they were threatening to bill him with their living expenses for every day he was late. He was so nervous he couldn't
sleep. He was so ashamed of his predicament he couldn't call his
wife.

He asked me to go outside with him—to see his truck. But before we got to the door he paused to talk to a young black-haired
woman who worked at the fuel desk. He asked her, casually, how
she was getting home. She said she didn't know. She was scared
to go anywhere with all that violence out there. Coyly, she said
she wanted a man with a gun to protect her.

"I've got a gun, sweetheart," he said, "and it's loaded for you."

"I'd like to take you home and shoot it off," she laughed teasingly.

It was nearly daybreak. He showed me his truck, slumping a
little with the punctured tired, and gestured toward the shiny new
mobile home attached to the rear. He wondered if he'd get it to
Chicago before Christmas. Should he call his wife? No, she'd just
hang up on him. Then, once again, he began to tell me how he'd
been unable to sleep ever since she'd left him.

As I stood there, listening to his whiny voice, looking out over
the snowy Midwestern dawn, a line from Arlo Guthrie's song
"The City of New Orleans" the hit of the truck stop jukebox, kept
echoing ironically through my brain:

*"Good morning, America, how are you? Don't you know me,
I'm your native son."*

CHAPTER 2

Still the Promised Land

Truckers are heirs to America's frontier dream. Illegal aliens—a very different tribe—are heirs to the age-old dream that the streets in America are paved with gold.

When you hear the phrase "illegal aliens," you think of strange extraterrestrial creatures that have no anchor in time or place. Certainly you doubt there could be anything American in the life of a carpenter named Lucho Martinez in Juarez, Mexico. Yet, when you meet the Mexicans who are tempted to sneak across this country's border, you see that their lives embody a vivid, contemporary version of the tensions that must have wracked every prospective immigrant.

For they have deep roots in the country—the tribe—they are leaving behind. But they are caught between an economic structure that can't support them and a community structure that can—and more effectively than any they'll find on this side of the border. These days, Juarez, Mexico; Bogotá, Colombia; Guayaquil, Ecuador, are the scenes of the same anguished family dramas that took place in the *shtetls* of Poland; in the *paeses* of Sicily; in the peat bogs of Ireland a century ago. The young men and women who journey to America in search of their fortunes may be lost to their families forever. They may also save the lives of the relatives and friends they've left behind.

For years now I've seen the drama of illegal aliens through the

eyes of the couple I call Lucho and Maria Martinez, who live in
Juarez's *colonia* Lazaro Cardenas, in the mountains behind this
gaudy tourist trap of a border town. They became friends of
Rachel's and mine when we lived with them for a month during
Peace Corps training in 1966, and we've written and visited them
ever since. They and their neighbors helped me see why a change
of culture can be terribly frightening, even if it offers the prospect
of material progress. But they've also shown me why, at a time
when many Americans despair of this country, millions of people
still view it as the promised land.

Maria Martinez, forty-six, never wanted to roam. Lucho, fifty-
two, who lives in a world where men are the adventurers, feels a
relentless urge to travel and succeed.

In 1960 they did uproot themselves—to search for work. They
moved from their native village of Zacatecas, in northeastern
Mexico, a seven-hour walk from the nearest bus stop, to *colonia*
Lazaro Cardenas, a twenty-minute bus ride from El Paso, Texas.

For years the transition was extremely difficult. In 1966, they
lived in poverty that was, if anything, even more harrowing than
the poverty they'd known growing up in Zacatecas.

They and their five children shared two rooms in an adobe-and-
tar-paper shack with cement on one floor, dirt on the other, and
only two beds for all of them to sleep on. There was no electricity,
no running water, no plumbing. Maria spent most of her days in
the kitchen, shaping tortillas out of freshly ground corn, then
cooking them over her kerosene stove. That, plus refried beans,
was the Martinez's staple diet. They ate their meals in a straggly
parade because there weren't enough plates or cups or chairs to let
them all sit at the table at once.

In those days Maria worried constantly about Lucho, whose
alcoholism, just a year or two earlier, had been so severe that she'd
had to support the family by selling fake flowers to tourists in
Juarez's fetid marketplace. By the time we met them, Lucho was
usually sober—but that didn't help him find work. Every morning
he'd wake up at five, take a rickety bus through the dusty streets
of their *colonia*, and try to get a day's labor at the slaughterhouse
or the icehouse. There was rarely any work; by noon he'd be home

for lunch. Then he and his adoring six-year-old son, Pancho—the third oldest child—would comb the city's lumberyards for the cheapest wood they could find. When they'd scavenged enough, they'd come home and Lucho would carpenter ironing boards, which he sold to his neighbors for a dollar apiece. During a good week he'd net about ten dollars.

The Martinez's second child, Josefina, nine, was a thin, bronze girl with giggly high spirits and a wild Indian beauty. Every few months she'd become uncontrollably ill. The family couldn't afford an adequate diagnosis, but Lucho and Maria suspected malnutrition. Maria, who complained a lot, was always steady during those crises. Lucho, outwardly stoic, became almost entirely withdrawn, morose with a relentless sense of his own failure.

One afternoon, Josefina became paralyzed with vomiting and stomach cramps. She only survived because of Rafael Benitez, the don of the *colonia*, a seventy-one-year-old man whose most cherished memories were of the 1920s, when he'd helped lay tracks for a railroad in Elgin, Illinois; don Rafael managed to persuade an acquaintance who'd been a doctor in the Mexican army to treat the child for free. The doctor stretched Josefina out in the Martinez's shabby, kerosene-lit bedroom, then found a nail and pounded it into a wall. He suspended a bottle of transparent fluid from the nail and injected her with the liquid. The intravenous feeding lasted through the entire terrifying night, until Josefina finally revived. The family never forgot the incident—or the sense of isolation, of powerlessness, that overwhelmed them that day.

Still, the Martinez's life was not an unbroken saga of sorrow. They were a very cohesive family who worked together efficiently and played together with gusto. Many nights, after the last person had been fed, Lucho became an entertainer. He'd put one of the three kerosene lamps on the kitchen table, use his fingers to project a jungle full of wild animals on the wall, and invent weird dialogues between them. Once, staggering drunk, he'd hollered that his hero was Cantinflas. The kitchen was his tiny stage, the kids his ardent fans.

After a few days I felt at ease with the Martinezes. That was surprising. It wasn't just that we lacked a common language. My Spanish was almost incomprehensibly clumsy at the time. We didn't share a single cultural reference point. They'd never met an American before, never heard of New York, looked at me uncomprehendingly when I said I'd worked as a journalist before I'd joined the Peace Corps. They weren't aware of the most rudimentary details of commercial America that some of their neighbors had picked up from the radio, or television, or trips across the border. One afternoon I told Maria that I'd eaten a *perro caliente*—a hot dog—on a visit downtown, and she winced with horror at the thought that I'd actually consumed a roasted canine. And they certainly didn't have any idea of what Rachel and I were doing in their house—of why two young married gringos would join something called the Peace Corps and choose to spend two years working with people like them. They'd only taken us in because a local self-help organization had told them they could make twenty dollars a month by boarding us.

But we improvised our own set of rituals. I sweat very freely, particularly when I eat hot food in hot weather, and the Martinez family doused its meals in chili. They'd challenge me to do the same. It was a small test of machismo. I had to accept. Within a minute, my face would redden and water would flood from my forehead to my shoulders. Finally, one of the kids, laughing uncontrollably, would rush off to get me something cool to drink. When I spoke Spanish, Lucho, Maria, and the kids would revel in my strange mispronunciations and impossible grammatical constructions. Yet they were never malicious. They made me feel like some odd, cherished cousin from the city, not like a buffoon.

Through them and their friends I was able to pick up the rhythm of life in the struggling *colonia*. It defied a stereotype I never quite knew I had, of Mexicans as tequila-drinking citizens in the land of *mañana*.

I spent several days working with Lucho and his brother, both of them fifteen years older than I, to repair the Martinez's adobe-and tar-paper roof, which had caved in during a rainstorm. Though they seemed poky, and I tried to impress them with my energetic industriousness, they always accomplished more than I did and were less fatigued. Their slow movements and frequent pauses bore no relationship to my mental image of the carefree peasant, sitting with his sombrero over his eyes as he took a siesta under a tree. It didn't take long to realize that they'd mastered an almost artistic method of conserving their energy.

You needed that skill during Juarez's scalding noontimes, when temperatures climbed above a hundred. Those were the hours when most of our neighbors were busy molding adobe bricks or repairing their yards. Some worked with scavenged old pipes and tires, building their kids jungle gyms and wading pools. Others watered the scrubby peach trees, grape arbors, or squash and corn they'd planted in their dusty, hilly back yards.

It was the year after Congress had ended the controversial *bracero* (contract-labor) program, which had allowed American businessmen to employ Mexicans as seasonal workers. I'd always included *braceros* in my private litany of the oppressed; always assumed that left-wing journalists and politicians were telling a simple truth when they railed against the exploitive wages the Mexicans were paid, the unhealthy labor camps they were forced to live in, the tyrannical bosses who hired and fired them on a whim.

Many of the men I talked to during those noon hours were ex-*braceros*, now unemployed. Their reminiscences twined with the details of the Martinez family's life to make me realize that the situation was more complex than I'd realized. For they talked nostalgically, not bitterly, about their adventures during the years when they'd been shipped from harvest to harvest throughout the Southwest, like old, rusty plows. They'd earned much better money than Lucho could in Juarez—enough, in some cases, to open small *tiendas* or build their families pleasant homes with comfortable furniture and indoor plumbing. Enough to buy their kids meat, fresh fruits, and vegetables so they wouldn't have to fight Josefina's constant, perilous battle with malnutrition.

Now their restless energy, like the Martinez's, was bottled up in the poor mountainside *colonia*. They talked endlessly about the past; they drank too much and idled hours away, reading tattered brown adult comic books—sex stories or soap operas—the only form of literature you find in Juarez's many *colonias*. They expressed their frustrations gently, not angrily, but their stranded, bored mood should have suggested the torrent of illegal immigra-

tion that Rachel and I would glimpse when we revisited Juarez
seven years later, in 1973.

J. B. Chapman, forty-seven, had been with the Border Patrol
for fifteen years when we met him in El Paso in 1973. He was a
little worried—deteriorating eyesight and a leg operation that had
laid him up for two months had made him wonder how much
longer he could keep chasing Mexicans who'd crossed the border
between Juarez and El Paso. But by then the problem of illegal aliens had become so immense and complex that he felt a patriotic
duty to stay in the Border Patrol and help solve it. Besides, he
loved his work.

"I've been an outdoorsman all my life," he said. "When I
joined the patrol I told myself, 'Chapman, it's deer-hunting season all year around. Only now you're dealing with people, not animals, and that's a much more exciting challenge.'"

Chapman was one of seventeen hundred Border Patrol agents
fighting the strange economic guerrilla war along the two-
thousand-mile Mexican frontier. That war had escalated dramati-
cally since Rachel and I were Peace Corps trainees. Between 1966
and 1973 about two million illegal aliens had been caught sneaking into the United States. Bootlegging them had become a lucrative business. In Mexico, immigrant smugglers—"coyotes"—were
charging their countrymen between one hundred and fifteen hundred dollars to outwit men like Chapman. A coyote's services
depends on his fees: For the right price he can provide false labor
documents or guides who know the safest route across the Rio
Grande or secure housing in El Paso or late-night rides on trucks
disguised as commercial carriers, which haul crowded cargoes of
Mexicans to Los Angeles, Denver, or Chicago.

It's hard for the Border Patrol to catch them since the coyotes
usually have time, darkness, and geography on their side. But
thousands of Mexicans can't afford the coyotes' rates. They seek
to cross the vast Texas desert on foot. And they're the ones who
usually get caught.

For Chapman, stalking "wets" (as all Border Patrolmen call
Mexicans) is an art. He is part of a dying breed of "old boys"
from the country, whose daddies taught them how to survive by
bagging any quarry that moves. Even with his eye problems, he

can scan a shrub-shrouded hut across the Rio Grande, and notice a telltale beer bottle, a half-open door, a faint trail of trodden cacti, that suggest it's a place where the coyotes hide the immigrants they plan to ferry north toward work.

Near daybreak one morning Chapman showed us how to hunt. He took us to a desolate area beside the Rio Grande. The night before, he said, a team of agents had used an old tractor to drag a wide swath of dirt near the river. The Mexicans would have left footprints on the smooth surface as they traveled cross-country, he explained. That was the only clue an agent needed. He could turn track marks into the equivalents of fingerprints by examining the patterns the early-morning sun made as it glistened off the ground. Then he could spot the same faint shoe mark an hour or two later, as he drove his jeep through the long, hummocky desert at thirty miles an hour.

When that happens, Chapman says, technology becomes useful: Two-way radios signal the spotter planes that hover over El Paso all day. The pilots, trained in Korea or Vietnam, fly about two hundred feet off the ground, helping the agents stalk their prey amid the desert shrubbery.

Chapman, who was an exceptionally skilled tracker before age brought astigmatism, retains a grudging respect for the Mexicans. "Those old boys from the country stay in much better shape than you or me. I've seen a man of sixty scale a twenty-foot fence in just five seconds. And they can last for a week in the desert with just a jug of water and a sack of tortillas."

He has some compassion for them. "I know they're poor people, just like my daddy's family. And that government over there doesn't give them much work. But I'm not paid to ask myself whether or not they should be caught. I'm paid to catch them."

Though he's worked the Mexican border for nearly twenty years, "the only Spanish I can speak is about immigrant business. I guess I've never been interested enough in those people to learn how to talk with them about anything else," he says reflectively.

Chapman no longer spends much time tracking immigrants. At his age, he says with a trace of depression, he's had to develop a less strenuous specialty—surveillance at the El Paso airport. He was completely cheerful and at ease when he took us out there, particularly when another agent told us how he'd captured a "wet" who was planning to fly to Chicago. The Mexican had panicked at the sight of a Border Patrol uniform—he'd begun to sweat, to stare at the ground, to twitch his feet nervously. When the flight was announced he remained riveted to his seat, too frightened to move. That was when the agent demanded to see his papers. He made the arrest on the spot.

The encounter encouraged Chapman to reminisce: "It used to be that I could always tell a wet out here," he says. "Those old boys must have sold everything they owned to buy their tickets and their clothes. They sure looked funny—like scarecrows with two-hundred-dollar suits hanging off them. But now that some of them have made it to the States once or twice they wear their clothes better and look more confident. I'm still pretty accurate, but I stop more legal residents than I used to. You should see how that gets their dander up."

Later, driving along the Rio Grande, Chapman spotted two Mexican-looking teenage girls and a much younger boy playing on the bank of the river. "See how they carry themselves?" he asked. "Something's not quite right." So he gunned his car over to them and asked a few quick questions in Spanish. Their answers, in flawless English, convinced him they lived in one of El Paso's nearby housing projects. The kids hurried away as quickly as they could.

A younger agent had driven up to help. When he heard Chapman had made a mistake he began to describe his triumphant day. "I caught twenty-six wets on El Paso Street in the last three hours," he said. How many people had he stopped, I asked. "About fifty. But the rest were all legals."

He seemed to realize that his boasts might hurt Chapman's pride. Soon, the older man might have to retire to the two-story house he'd just bought in one of El Paso's middle-class suburbs. So, as he drove away he told us that "this old-timer is one of the best we've got." And he left Chapman with a scrap of jaunty encouragement. "J.B., you're going to get yourself a lot of water today, too," he hollered over his racing motor.

Maria was waiting for Rachel and me when we went back for our visit in August 1973. It didn't take long to see how much the *colonia*'s life had improved since 1966. Clearly, the primary reason was the number of people who were working in the States *de mojado* (Spanish for wet, a term Mexicans apply to themselves). Many of the ex-*braceros* I'd known in 1966 were back in the States, working in factories in Chicago, on the docks in Detroit, in restaurants and ranches in California and Texas. They sent most of their earnings home. In the past five years, we were told, the money illegal aliens mail to their families had become one of the *colonia*'s biggest sources of income.

The roads were still rutted and unpaved. It still smelled of rotten fruits, from outhouses, from sewage buried in mud puddles. But everyone had electricity now. Most families—including the Martinezes—had old cars or pickup trucks. The houses, once a drab adobe gray, were now brightly colored. The shrubs men had worked on seven years before were peach trees or grape vines. Most kids had dolls or bicycles or baseballs and mitts to amuse themselves.

None of the Martinezes had ever worked *de mojado*. But they had been helped by the new immigration.

It was one indirect reason that Lucho no longer had to scratch out a living selling ironing boards. For a brother of Maria's, who had always lived in Zacatecas, had two cousins who earned four dollars an hour as longshoremen in Detroit and slipped in and out of Mexico undetected. The brother had transplanted himself, his wife, and his ten kids to Juarez with the hope that someday he could make it to Detroit, too. He hadn't taken that risk yet.

The entire crew had moved in with the Martinez family, but that was an opportunity, not an inconvenience. For it gave Lucho his own small labor force. He'd invested in an old electric saw and two workbenches and, with Pancho—now an energetic thirteen— his brother-in-law, and his three oldest nephews, he set up a family factory in the back yard. He produced small wooden stands for the plastic statuettes Juarez's hawkers sell to the hurrying tourists downtown.

Lucho no longer had to travel from lumberyard to lumberyard to gather up cheap wood. Now he could pay a middleman to do that, a neighbor I'll call Maximo Villa, who'd been caught working *de mojado* in Boulder, Colorado. Villa had used some of the

money he'd earned during his two years in the States to buy a large
white pickup truck that allowed him to service struggling tradesmen like Lucho.

The business was pretty good, Lucho said. He grossed about a
hundred dollars a week, though he had to pay about thirty dollars
of it for wood, fifteen dollars to his brother-in-law's family, and
five dollars more to Maximo Villa. Still, it was five times as much
as he'd netted in 1966—though, with food prices soaring, he
couldn't save anything.

Lourdes, the oldest daughter, had found a job, too, in a plant
that made air-conditioning parts. She got up at 5 A.M., six days a
week, and traveled to the factory in a car pool that cost her five
dollars a month. She never got home before 4 P.M. She earned
thirty-two dollars a week and brought home twenty-five. Girls
she'd gone to school with were earning three or four times that
much working *de mojado* in the garment factories that have come
to El Paso over the past ten years. She was very tempted to do
that, too. But Maria was adamantly against it.

Still, between her earnings and Lucho's, the Martinez family
had enough extra money to add two rooms to their adobe house,
to cement all the floors, and to build a sort of lean-to shed in the
back yard, where most of the relatives slept.

They had bought some conveniences. Four new beds. A radio
and a console model Philco TV, made in the 1950s. An ancient
air cooler, which had to be filled with water from the outdoor fau-
cet and hummed so loudly you could hardly talk over it. And, best
of all, Lucho's pride, his green-and-white 1957 Ford, which he
drove around the *colonia* every night while his children, nephews,
and nieces all crowded onto the bumpers and fenders as if they
were riding a team of horses.

The Martinezes had absorbed a great deal from the radio, the
TV, the tales of travelers who'd returned from the States—
enough to forge some of the shared cultural experience we'd
lacked when we'd stayed with them seven years earlier. Now,
when I said I was still a journalist, Pancho was able to explain my
profession to his parents by mentioning two newscasters they
knew from TV. I brought Maria a package of frankfurters: She
laughed at that earlier misunderstanding, and said that these days

her family ate "weenies" whenever they could afford them. One evening the entire family was watching *Plaza Sesamo—Sesame Street*—with as much enjoyment as they'd once watched Lucho's magic shows. We spent an animated half an hour discussing the antics of Big Bird and Oscar, Bert and Ernie, who gave Rachel and me and our kids so much pleasure in New York.

Josefina, no longer sickly, was now a flirtatious teenager who loved rock and roll. She'd tacked huge posters of stars like David Cassidy and the Partridge family on the bare walls of the bedroom she and Lourdes shared. Her friends greeted each other by flashing "V"s, and used "*paz y amor*" as a substitute for traditional phrases of farewell, like "*hasta luego.*"

At night, the Martinezes could go out, walk over to the side of the mountain where they lived, and look out over the Rio Grande at El Paso's factories, its comfortable houses, its stores like Woolworth's, Penney's, and Newberry's, which, for poor Mexicans, were museums filled with the most treasured objects the modern world offered. Then they could go home and see those products advertised on TV, see programs depicting the glistening, lavish way Americans live in cities like New York, Chicago, Los Angeles, which lay just beyond the superhighway on the other side of El Paso. What a constant, beckoning invitation: The U.S. was no longer the forbidding, mysterious land it had seemed when Maria and Lucho were growing up in Zacatecas. It was a garden of riches just a single risk, an emotional leap, away.

Mexicans who slip past J. B. Chapman and his fellow members of the Border Patrol are by no means safely inside the garden of riches. From then on they are economic outlaws, hunted by the Immigration and Naturalization Service (INS) in New York, Chicago, Los Angeles.

The INS is armed with extraordinarily broad powers. Its inspectors can stop anyone they suspect of being an illegal alien in the same arbitrary way as J. B. Chapman did by the banks of the Rio Grande. They can demand to see the suspect's visas, search his home for immigration documents, and rush those who can't produce the appropriate papers to detention headquarters for further questioning. They "sweep" factories, apartment buildings—even subway stations—in areas where illegals are supposedly clustered.

The whole thing is a paradox since the illegals who are apprehended get a free plane ride home, where they soon lay plans to cross the border again. They see the INS as an inconvenience, not a deterrent. The people who really hate the arbitrary searches and "sweeps" are the American-born Hispanics, whose civil liberties may be violated by the random raids.

Since 1968, Congress and the White House have been involved in a series of fruitless attempts to find solutions for the problem. Sometimes they propose methods of reorganizing the Border Patrol, or introducing sophisticated electronic devices that would cut the aliens off at the border. But the technology involved is impossibly expensive and unwieldy. Recently, the INS has toyed with the idea of issuing a work permit (which would resemble a Social Security card) to every American national or immigrant who is in the country legally. But politicians and citizens' action groups have denounced it as an American version of South Africa's "pass card." The plan hasn't been put into practice.

Congress has spent years debating the Rodino Bill, which would levy fines against employers who consciously hire illegal aliens. That way, its authors argue, the main incentive to slip into the United States—jobs—would vanish. But, its opponents insist that, as a byproduct, some employers would be afraid to hire anyone with a Spanish surname—American-born or not—because they'd be scared of getting into trouble with the government.

Meanwhile, the migration continues to swell. Now, sometimes, you hear people talk about it with fear.

In 1973, J. B. Chapman's boss, David V. Blackwell, Chief Patrol Agent in El Paso, Texas, summarized the spreading sentiment very succinctly: "If you compare Mexico's birthrate to ours, and their unemployment rate to ours, then you don't have to be a genius to realize what will happen if we just let them come here. They'll take jobs from our workers. Eventually, they may even change our ethnic composition . . . change our country as we know it."

The day Rachel and I returned to the Martinez house, Lucho had just gotten a rush order for his stands. It was the height of the tourist season, and 1973 was evidently a flush year for plastic statues. He and Pancho interrupted their work to talk with us, to gossip with neighbors who stopped by, but they kept returning to their back-yard factory. By nightfall, the father and son had completed an impressive number of hand-tooled stands.

Later, Lucho drove Maria, all five kids, and Rachel and me to visit old friends in the *colonia*. It was a night of reminiscences, of wild stories about our very different cultures, of hot political talk. Everyone served us spicy food and beer. Though Lucho had been on the wagon for several months he outdrank us all. By midnight, he was in a fog. The binge lasted through the next afternoon.

At dusk the next day he was sprawled out on the dirt yard in front of his house, snoring faintly. He woke up, drank a quick beer to blunt his hangover, and ate several huge green chilis, which he chased with gulps of fiery chili juice to settle his stomach. He challenged me to try some, too: I did, and when the sweat poured off my face he began to laugh affectionately and triumphantly. Then he grabbed a battered old golf cap I'd been wearing, and used it as a prop in a series of Cantinflas burlesques which had the whole family laughing.

The next morning he was up at six, completely sober, able to organize his crew of workers well enough to turn out a fresh batch of stands by noon. By nine, the back yard was alive with activity. Luz and Angelita, the youngest girls, washed their family's clothes in a tiny rectangular cement pool Lucho had fashioned. As they were finishing, five of their cousins came over to do another wash. Pancho, laughing gleefully, sprayed the children with a hose. After that, the eight kids took a long, giggly bath together. Maria and Josefina cooked lunch for the family. Then they spent an hour rounding up some baby chicks that had escaped from their garbage-can cage the night before.

In the midst of it all, Lucho worked with a silent, withdrawn concentration that was only broken by a quick, proud smile when Pancho earnestly displayed a stand he'd just made, to show me he was just as good a workman as his dad.

But Maria kept taking Rachel aside for private, fearful conversations. Lucho's binge had worried her. It brought her back to those desperate years when she'd kept him in liquor and her fam-

ily in clothes by begging tourists to buy her false flowers. "I know
we're still poor," she said. "But this place is a palace compared to
what we had. You don't know how scared I am that we'll lose it
someday.

She told Rachel that she's even more concerned about Pancho
than about her husband. Her neighbor across the street has a son
who is now in El Paso's La Tuna federal prison for crossing the
border once too often. Dozens of other boys in the *colonia* are involved in smuggling people, cigarettes—even dope—across the El
Paso border. How could she keep Pancho out of that kind of trouble?

Seven years before, when he was just six, Pancho had been
the most affectionate member of the family. He'd run to the
corner of the block whenever Lucho or Rachel or I came into
sight—then he'd grin broadly and lead us home by the hand. But,
even back then, Maria called him *el travieso*, the troublesome
one. Now, at thirteen, he was the anchor of his family's business,
the one child his brothers and sisters constantly relied on. But, at
some level of her mind, Maria must have identified the boy with
Lucho, his idol, and worried that he would lead the same sort of
stormy, half-satisfied life as her moody husband. For she insisted
that he was a wild, rude child, a far more difficult burden than
any of her daughters. She told us that in front of Pancho, while
he stared miserably at the floor.

She does have reason to worry about her son, for Juarez is a
difficult place for a thirteen-year-old boy to grow up. Down from
the mountain, in the whorehouse of a border town, some boys
pimp for their parents or their sisters or themselves. They sneak
into El Paso and steal clothes or money or cars. Some adults—
drug-runners and coyotes—encourage gangs of twenty or thirty
youngsters to engage in small-time smuggling operations so they
can spot the most skillful young criminals and recruit them as ap-
prentices.

And Pancho is more exposed to that part of Juarez than anyone
else in the family. Unlike Lourdes and Josefina, who quit school
in sixth grade, he decided to go to high school, even though it
bores him. He hopes the education will help him work his way
out of the *colonia*, but it also brings him into contact with tough,

savvy kids who are his classmates. When he talks about them—or about the gang members he knows in the *colonia*—there's a hint of respect mixed in with the disapproval he knows he should feel. Why shouldn't there be? After all, he's also part of his father's business life and that shows him how important it is to be cunning. For he's the one who bargains every week with the store owners downtown, since he already has a shrewder knowledge of Juarez's ways than his country-trained Dad.

How far out of the *colonia* can Pancho rise? There's not very much upward mobility in Mexico: It's unlikely that he'll get into a university, or find a business or a profession that will satisfy his agile mind or his ambition. Perhaps, when he grew older, he'd decide it was easier to leave for the States than to gamble his future on his country's calcified social system. If he did, some of his sisters and even his father might follow. If that happened, then, in Maria's terms, the bright, energetic Pancho would really prove to be *el travieso*—for the family cohesion, which she has struggled to forge throughout her adult life, would be shattered forever.

J. B. Chapman finally bagged him a wet, but it wasn't the sort of catch he could boast about.

It was midafternoon. For an hour he'd been playing a cat-and-mouse game with some Mexican teenagers who seemed to be sunning themselves on a cement embankment across the Rio Grande. "Look at their act," he said. "If I weren't around, they'd be over here, making trouble. You know, the fourteen- or fifteen-year-old kids are the roughest ones. When you catch one of the old boys from the country, they go along peacefully. But these street kids throw rocks at our cars, give us flat tires, even pull knives on us. They're a real menace."

My mind flashed to Pancho. I had a terrible fantasy that Chapman would capture him that afternoon.

The agent began to drive toward the river. "There's one, all wet and muddy," he said. I looked out the window and saw a middle-aged woman struggling up the embankment. Her pink dress was as dry as my clothes. She was carrying a pair of high-heeled shoes in one hand and helping her daughter with the other.

Chapman stopped the car and got out.

As he walked toward her, I realized that Rachel and I had seen her with her daughter just two nights before, at a birthday party for one of the *colonia's* children. The event had caused great excitement at the Martinez house. The girls had helped Maria bake a rich vanilla cake and used a bagful of jelly beans as decorations. Then, just as they were leaving, they discovered they didn't have a present for the kid so they decided to give him something he could really use—a new pair of underpants.

The woman crossing the river had been one of about thirty neighborhood parents at the party. She'd drunk beer, eaten frijoles and a peppery stew, and gossiped with her friends while her daughter—and the Martinez children—played with the presents they'd gotten from a giant *piñata* that had been set up in the dusty back yard. Now, she was a "wet."

When Chapman got back to the car he told us he'd decided not to arrest her. That would have meant calling Border Patrol headquarters for a matron who could take her to a woman's detention camp. "It would take an hour. I hate to waste the time. I just told her to get on back to Juarez." So, for the next ten minutes, he sat in his car watching her, sometimes racing his motor ominously, sometimes hurrying her like cattle with almost yodeled threats in Spanish. She never looked back at Chapman or Rachel or me.

"I know her type," he told us. "She was probably going to El Paso to get in an afternoon's begging. I'll bet that's why she brought her daughter along."

Begging? With high-heeled shoes and a new pink dress? It seemed more likely that she wanted to do some shopping and didn't have the day pass that would allow her across the border. It seemed likely, too, that despite the afternoon's mishap she'd be back again soon, easy prey for another Border Patrol hunter.

One night Maximo Villa, the man who gets Lucho his wood and carries his stands downtown, came over to the Martinezes to discuss the sudden rush order. When he saw Rachel and me he decided to stay: He tilted back on his wooden chair and, whooping with infectious laughter, began to tell the two of us, Lucho and Maria, Pancho, and Lourdes about his experiences working *de mojado* in Boulder, Colorado.

He described the way he and three friends had bought a forged American driver's license in Juarez for two hundred dollars, how they'd hid out in some shrubs near the Rio Grande from daybreak to nightfall, how they'd snuck across the river, through the high grass, past Border Patrol jeeps, and walked straight to a used-car lot in El Paso. There, according to a prearranged plan with the owner, they bought an old Pontiac with Texas license plates and registration documents for a hundred dollars. They drove through the night to Denver. But they fled the next day, when they heard that immigration officials were cracking down on wets.

So it was on to Boulder. Within a week, Maximo was earning forty dollars a day, working as a busboy during one eight-hour shift, as a dishwasher during another. He and his friends saved their money by finding six other illegals to share a three-room apartment, which they rented for seventy-five dollars a month. The arrangement lasted for almost two years, Maximo said. His bosses liked him, and most of the *mojados* they hired, because they worked harder than most U.S. citizens. His Anglo neighbors would never report him, he recalled with pride, because he mowed their lawns and repaired their cars for free.

He laughed when he told us how his luck had run out. A Mexican-American woman, a U.S. citizen, ate regularly at one of the restaurants where he worked. She was a sort of bounty hunter, he said, who claimed she earned twenty-five dollars from the immigration service for each alien she turned in. It didn't take her long to discover that Maximo and his friends were wet. When she did, she offered them a deal. She had to make payments on a new Porsche, she told them, so if each of them paid her ten dollars a week she'd be quiet about their status.

"Well, I'd already paid one man for my driver's license, another for my car, so I decided to pay her, too. But she was much cleverer than me. She taught me some things I'll use next time. After a month she began to charge us fifteen dollars. Then it was twenty dollars. Then twenty-five. I couldn't pay anymore. So she told the immigration who I was. Within a week I was on a plane, back to Mexico."

Maria has a classically beautiful Indian face, in which mischievousness and rage are just a shade of an expression apart. In the middle of Maximo's story she poked Rachel gently and said, "Watch. I'm going to give him the scare of his life."

"You may not know it," she told him, "but these two Americans are from the immigration service."

There wasn't a trace of fear on his face. Maria often joked that way. "It doesn't matter," he said, grinning at her. "The immigration knows me anyway. I'm still going back, though. Only this time I'll go back to Greeley, Colorado. I have a *compañero* there who says there are no immigration inspectors at all. Can you imagine that? Or maybe I'll go to—what's the name of that city? —Gary, Indiana. A nephew of mine says there are jobs for all of us in the steel mills there."

Then, expansively: "Every time I cross the border my heart fills with joy. I feel like a new person.

"Next time, Lucho, you'll come with me. You'll see how fine it is. You'll be able to buy a new house in a year. Just ask me and *le manda un coyote*"—I'll put you in touch with a coyote.

"My husband will never go," Maria said. For a dislocated second I heard the sentence as a suburban housewife's criticism of her husband's timidity. Then I saw the frightened expression on her face. "Lucho is going to stay here, where he's safe and secure," she said. But her voice was trembling: She was pleading, not asserting. "He's not smart enough for all of your tricks. He's going to stay under this roof, with the rest of his family."

Maximo just shrugged, laughed in a way that showed he considered Lucho a henpecked husband, and arranged to pick up some stands for the plastic statues later in the week.

When he left Lucho asked me, with his slight, guarded chuckle, how I'd liked his friend "*El Maximo Mentiroso*"—the Maximum Liar. For his part, he said, he didn't believe half the man's tales. But that was the night he'd started drinking. I was sure Maximo's invitation had merged with Rachel's and my return and the strain of the rush order to fill him with a fresh, frustrated rage at his turtle-slow progress toward security.

Pancho laughed, too, when his father described the visitor as *El Maximo Mentiroso*. But he'd listened intently to the whole tale as if it were an adventure novel and he identified completely with the wandering characters. I thought of warning him about J. B. Chapman's special hunter's rage against kids like himself, about the "sweeps" in New York, Chicago, and Los Angeles, about the fear of a "Latin peril," which may infect politicians and labor leaders throughout the United States. But anything I could have said would have sounded even more prissy than Maria's frightened lectures compared with the lucrative life of travel and excitement Maximo Villa had described with such infectious gusto.

The next day I heard Pancho and Lourdes talking very seriously about places you could cross the border safely. Where, they asked me later, was Greeley, Colorado? Where was Gary, Indiana? What was the fastest way of getting there from Juarez?

When Rachel and I revisited the Martinezes for a third time, in November 1977, many of their neighbors were following Maximo Villa's example. The number of Mexicans who'd crossed the El Paso border to live illegally in the United States continued to soar. In 1966, it had been 11,761, according to the Border Patrol's figures. In 1973, it was 96,000. By 1977, it was about 150,000.

But the Martinezes were still taking advantage of the economic opportunities that presented themselves in Juarez. They'd become even more close-knit as a family. They were all living in the house in *colonia* Lazaro Cardenas that Rachel and I had shared with them in 1966.

There is a stereo in their living room now. Pancho and Lourdes and their friends from the neighborhood dance to Grand Funk or Wings. They barely remember the evenings, eleven years ago, when Lucho had used his kerosene lamp and his fingers to entertain them with the shadowy cartoons he'd project on the wall.

The rock group Kiss had a concert in El Paso that week, and they were eager to go. They knew how to evade the Border Patrol and cross the Rio Grande in order to see the show. But, unlike scores of their neighbors, they didn't have to sneak across the border in search of work.

Ironically, some of the ugliest manifestations of America's economic system—border-town tourism and runaway industries— have enabled them to maintain their stability.

Lucho's back-yard factory is prospering. The tourists who cross the border in search of cheap, quaint goods buy the statuettes mounted on his wooden stands as souvenirs of their adventure in an alien culture. Lourdes and Josefina are both earning good salaries at the runaway plant that makes air-conditioning parts. (Their salaries, high by their standards, would be unconscionably low in the United States.) Lucho and Maria rev up their truck and drive them to work at 6 A.M., then pick them up at 4 P.M., so they'll be protected from the dangers of the border town. In the past four years their salaries, and Lucho's profits, helped the family buy the stereo, a three-piece living-room set—and a refrigerator and gas stove, which save Maria hours of drudgery.

Pancho, a lean, hip teenager, who wears aviator glasses and wants to learn English so he can translate Wings's lyrics, is in high school now. He has a fantasy of becoming a doctor. In his more realistic moments he plans to take a course that will enable him to become a computer programmer. He affects a studied cool. It is almost impossible to imagine him as I knew him in 1966, the adoring six-year-old who used to spend his afternoons hunting through Juarez's lumberyards for the old pieces of wood Lucho would use to make his ironing boards. It's even hard to visualize him as the thirteen-year-old who was so energetic, so enthusiastic, about working in his father's factory. Nowadays, his visits there are almost like the visits of royalty. For he's *el hijo de patron*, the boss's son, *el estudiante*, on his way to a higher education. His younger brothers and sisters will never have to scurry and scrounge around Juarez as Pancho once did. *Their* Martinez family—the Lucho and Maria of the 1970s—was able to feed them, provide for their health, put them through school, without feeling the old, desperate worry about the next source of income.

In 1966, Maria was convinced that she and Lucho were fated to remain on the very margin of urban life. In 1973 she was still frightened that the little she had would vanish, or at least seem pale and boring in comparison to the exciting world the ex-*mojado* Maximo Villa invoked. By 1977, she felt secure at last. She still worries a little, but now it's about others, the *"pobrecitos,"* the unfortunate ones, her friends and relatives who have just migrated from the country, who have to live as she and Lucho did when they first came to Juarez. (She still has some relatives near Zacatecas; the kids, who have visited them once or twice, talk about their rural living conditions with amused wonder.)

Listening to Maria talk I realized that, over the years, she'd forgotten some of her old peasant fears and gained some of the self-confidence that comes with a more durable place in the urban working class. She says she is very lucky, that the *pobrecitos*, her relatives, are more typical of Juarez's unstable population. For, from the vantage point of *colonia* Lazaro Cardenas, it is clear that the Mexican government would rather have millions of people like Maximo Villa sneaking across the border, living on wages Americans pay, than set up the sort of economic system that would enable the wets to stay at home. And, if Pancho doesn't become a computer programmer or if Lourdes and Josefina finally decide to risk working in an American factory for double the amount they earn in Juarez, the Martinezes may still be among them.

Still, now, by sheer strength of character, Maria and Lucho had managed to accomplish something I had once regarded as impossible: to help their family achieve its American dream while it remained within the safe, cohesive world of its own culture.

CHAPTER 3

The Lower Depths of
American Labor

When I was in the mountains of Juarez, listening to ex-*braceros* reminisce, listening to Maximo Villa boast, I'd half-accepted their nostalgic, romantic view of *mojados*, of migrant workers. From that vantage point, Maria's fears had sounded a little whiny and overprotective. Then, in September, 1973, I hired out as an agricultural worker myself. I was a day laborer, not a migrant, recruited on the streets of Philadelphia to pick apples and turnips in the fields of southern New Jersey. But that experience gave me a firsthand look at the life some of Lucho's counterparts must be forced to live.

I felt as if I were inside one of Maria's nightmares. Like Lucho, the blacks and Hispanics I worked with had been born in rural towns; they were overwhelmed by Philadelphia's ghettos. Like the Martinez family, they had no idea that there really were forces that could offer them some help—labor unions, federal laws, muckraking journalists. Instead of fighting their bosses or the work contractors who failed to protect them, most of them lived in a semi-alcoholic stupor and directed their rage at one another. They were a caste—a tribe—of untouchables in the lower depths of American labor.

Every summer and autumn morning at five, thousands of migrants pour out of the ghetto and throng Philadelphia's deserted skid row to wait for the rickety buses that will ferry them to New Jersey's farms. In the pre-dawn murk, the workers—mostly men and women in their fifties and sixties who learned to farm when they were children—munch sausage sandwiches or crumbling pastry. They stand in large groups on the empty street, gossiping noisily, sharing bottles of cheap wine or raw, smelly scotch. Each time a bus arrives, the labor contractor (who gets paid by the number of people he can deliver to each farmer) hustles up and down the block, hawking his particular farm and crop. He prods stragglers with loud jokes about their laziness.

The buses are too small for the number of people they have to carry. During the journey to the farms, they're cramped and dark. The passengers, indistinct shapes, drink or doze until they reach the farm. Or they complain about yesterday's frustration—a trip to Easton, Maryland, worthless because it rained before the apple picking could begin; a potato field near Camden, New Jersey, supposedly lush, which had yielded just three dollars for the workers, who were paid by the bushel.

I was the only white person on those rides. I presented myself as a drifter who needed some spare cash to get to California, not as a journalist. Even though most of the laborers accepted me, I was afraid that someone would get suspicious if I stayed on the street too long, so I usually boarded the first bus that came along.

One raw morning, I was among sixty men and women who were let out at a turnip field, where we'd do piecework that paid about forty-five cents per bushel picked. It was a slow, tiring job. You had to crawl around on the wet grass, searching for the biggest, ripest vegetables. Then you had to stoop once to pick them and a second time to put them in the basket. You had to make sure you worked within your own thin line of ground, for poaching on someone else's territory could—and often did—trigger a bloody knife fight.

It drizzled on and off all day. Many old people were worried that the damp would seep into their joints and aggravate their arthritis. Because the ground was so soggy, many of the turnips were filmed with dirt, which lodged grittily under your fingernails when you picked them.

The wet turnip stalks kept brushing across your mouth, your nose, your eyes. In May they'd been sprayed with tons of pesticides, organophosphates, which have replaced DDT, and which were initially created by the military for chemical warfare. Medical researchers now think that, over time, pesticides may erode agricultural workers' health in the same way coal dust erodes a miner's lungs—that they can cause anything from skin rashes to severe neuromuscular disorders. But the laborers I talked to weren't aware of these dangers, and there were no safeguards against the pesticides in the fields.

We had to cut the stems off the turnips with very sharp blades. The farmer gave us all fifty-cent paring knives, with the stern warning that we'd have to pay two dollars if we lost them. There were no facilities for first aid—not even Band-aids—even though the knives and turnips were slippery that day, and several people cut their hands.

The working day lasted nine hours (not counting the bus ride), from 7 A.M. to 4 P.M. We weren't given any lunch break. There were no stores nearby; there was no canteen to provide workers who hadn't packed meals—about fifty of us—with any kind of nourishment. The farmer didn't make drinking water available, though that was required by federal law. Nor were there any sanitary facilities though that, too, is a violation of government legislation. Most of the workers took those conditions for granted.

It was impossible to earn much money. I was averaging a bushel every forty-five minutes, and the best workers were only fifteen minutes ahead of me. They picked two bushels (ninety cents) an hour. By four o'clock on that lunchless, waterless afternoon many of them were so weary and discouraged they were dozing in the damp field or gathering turnips to take home for themselves. The most anyone earned that day was $8.55, well below the federal—or state—minimum wage. When I grumbled to the other workers, I realized that only a few of them had even heard that there was a minimum-wage law.

There is one part of the day the workers cherish: the stop at the "happy house," a bar near Glassboro, which we made on the way back to Philadelphia. When we got there most of the men and women hurried out of the bus to buy their liquor by the bottle.

They'd spend two dollars of their earnings on cheap wine, like Thunderbird, or five dollars on more expensive whiskey, like Seagram's.

I was so hungry and thirsty I took a bottle of Miller's and a pickled sausage, and began to down them before I'd paid. The bartender began to yell at me, accusing me of stealing. I fumbled around for my money, finally put it on the register, and left without saying a word.

Back on the bus, two high school kids asked me if I had really meant to swipe the stuff. Then two gray-haired men walked by my seat, pointing at me. They muttered angrily that "We should have never let that white boy come along. Now they'll run us out of that happy house, too. Where else do we have to drink?"

Soon, though, their anger was diverted. The woman sitting behind them was beginning to fuss. Earlier in the day someone had told me she'd stabbed her husband two years before and been insane ever since. She'd brought her own sharp blade to cut the turnips, and was toying with it when she began to yell at the men. They'd been staring at her! One had touched her! She'd get revenge! She hollered and threatened all the way home and only refrained from fighting because the people sitting next to her were ready to pounce if she made a single aggressive move.

When I worked at an apple orchard near Glassboro, New Jersey, I was able to experience some of the pleasure the ex-*braceros* said they'd felt when they harvested in America. But I was aware of a kind of disorganization and outright despair I'd never heard about in Juarez.

It is certainly better to pick apples than to pick turnips. You stretch all day instead of stooping, so your afternoon's ailments are those of an athlete who has tried too much rather than an inmate who has been cramped in a crowded cell. Besides, at the orchard we were paid by the hour, not by the piece. We were supposed to earn seventeen dollars for a nine-hour day, though, in fact, two dollars of that money was withheld, to pay for a lunch served in a canteen near the packing house.

I have severe acrophobia. While we were still on the bus, someone told me we'd be working on twenty-two-foot ladders, that there were no first-aid facilities in the orchard. I felt my stomach convulse with fear. I must have sounded terrified, too, because several people quickly assured me that, as a new man, I could work on a seven-foot ladder. And in the orchard everyone was especially protective of me.

Our gang leader, Shorty, who didn't look older than forty, told me he'd been working in the orchards forty-five years. He didn't supplement his income with Social Security or welfare, as most of the other workers did. He was too proud for that. He day-hauled on Monday through Thursday, rising at four each morning to catch the bus for New Jersey, rarely going to sleep before eleven at night; he helped distribute a community newspaper Friday and Saturday; and he partied every Sunday. Most years, he worked in the orchards past the first snows, stripping the last frosty apples from the trees and then cutting off the limbs. One winter, a decade ago, he sought farm work in Florida, but living was so expensive and jobs so precarious he spent more than he earned. Now he stays in South Philly all winter, surviving on what he can save during the summer.

He taught me to treat the trees with wary respect, for they can kill you. Besides, apple picking, like the roof repairing I did at the Martinez's house, is an art to be mastered.

It's crucial to know how to use the ladder. You have to be sure the legs are the right distance from each other, that they're planted on firm soil, so they won't buckle and topple you in mid-air. Each time you ascend the ladder you have to test its stability by hopping hard on the first rung. You're never supposed to stand on top of it, for fear of losing your footing. You must never jeopardize your balance by putting too many apples in the half-bushel basket strapped to your waist.

Then there's an art to positioning the ladder. You have to find a place where the stray branches won't prevent you from seeing the apples you plan to pick. And you're never supposed to risk your footing by reaching for a fruit. Even if you lean outward a little bit, it's best to have your hand on a sturdy branch so you can catch yourself if you fall. Meanwhile, there are men overhead on the twenty-two-foot ladders who might let clusters of apples drop on your head. Or you might get tangled up with their equipment, and knock them over. So you've always got to be aware of your footing, of the tree, and the position of the men you're working with.

I watched Shorty for an hour, trying to imitate his actions and absorb his rhythms. After that, we began to work as a team, starting with our backs to each other, then picking in a semicircle until we met halfway around the tree. Once I was on my own, in the branches, my tension vanished. I got a kid's simple pleasure from clambering around in the trees.

By early afternoon, though, the pace of work had slowed way down. Since the crew was paid by the hour, not the piece, they could afford to spend long stretches of time munching apples by the trailer and talking about UFO sightings or whores they'd known in Philadelphia or the best way to resell "groundhogs"— apples they picked up from the ground and carried back to the city. The white overseer, Ray, a Tennessean who hates the North and wants to go back home and open him a fruit farm soon, damn well wasn't going to push them hard enough to risk a fracas. Especially since some of them now had their sweetwater— wine—in the fields with them, and were chugging it down as they talked.

Soon the sky began to cloud. The wind shook the ladders. Most of the men climbed down from the trees and began to look around for groundhogs. I kept working until Shorty, who'd been watching me all day, said in a voice that was partly chiding, partly helpful, "Slow down, Sonny. The man's not paying you enough anyway. Why do you want to bust your ass for him?"

When we got back to the packing house, where we'd receive our money and wait for the bus, a fight flared between a thin old black man and the short, squat white man in charge of the farm. The black, who'd guzzled too much sweetwater to be prudent, carried a bushel basket full of groundhogs right past the farmer's office. Apparently that was more than theft; it was an unforgivable sign of insubordination. The farmer hurried over to the black, stood as close to him as possible, his belly poking into the gaunt laborer's waist, and hollered that if the man ever did that again he'd be fired. He seized the apples and brought them into his office. He warned the rest of us not to take any home.

It was an absurd gesture. Every other worker had filled sacks or shopping bags with their own groundhogs and they weren't planning to return them. They simply took their plunder inside the warm, darkened shed next to the packing house, and hid them there until the bus came.

When the farmer paid us we had to form a cramped line in the rain and file past him while he counted out the cash. Though it was five-thirty, the bus hadn't arrived. But the money gave some of the men an expensive pastime. Back in the shed a Puerto Rican took some dice out of his pocket and began fooling around with them. Soon some of the other workers smoothed out a wide tract of dirt, and most of us pulled up apple crates to sit around and watch the action.

About twenty of the forty workers got into a crap game, betting up to five dollars a pass. Shorty lost that much money, then had enough sense to recognize a solid streak and retreat to the sidelines. But the Puerto Rican who'd started the game barely knew the rules. He kept losing foolishly. Twice he threatened to quit. But the black who'd fought with the farmer knew a sucker when he saw one. Holding his sweetwater in one bony hand, his stained, tattered coat draped over his shoulder like a cape, he kept the Latin in the game by repeatedly calling him a coward. By the time the bus arrived, the Puerto Rican had lost his full day's pay.

The labor contractor was a thin, dapper black man I'll call Josh Thomas, who wore a Panama hat and a Hawaiian shirt. By law, the contractors are supposed to be the workers' representatives— to make sure they know their rights, that the farmer is providing them with adequate health and safety facilities, to furnish them with an itemized pay sheet at the end of the day. But they rarely comply. They put their energy where the profit is, into the number of workers they can produce.

Thomas's bus, when it finally arrived, was already full. Before we arrived at the happy house—a package liquor store owned by a man named Ted who gave Thomas a cut of every purchase his workers made—we'd picked up more loads of people at another orchard and a tomato field.

Thomas's bus had eleven rows, with seats broad enough for two people on one side, one person on the other. It could have held thirty-five workers comfortably, forty-five safely. On the way to the happy house I counted sixty-seven people on the bus—three people on the broader seats, two on the narrow ones, about ten on the floor.

It had begun to pour. On the Jersey Turnpike the water was so deep some cars had already stalled. Our windshield wipers barely worked. I overheard Thomas tell his relief driver the bus might give out any minute. The driver agreed, complaining that the brake shoes were wearing thin.

The passengers muttered, but they didn't protest. It was an ordinary experience. Besides, if they antagonized Thomas today, he might ignore them at tomorrow morning's shape-up. All agricultural workers know that farmers and contractors blacklist people they regard as troublemakers. So they joked and hollered at each other as they crowded into Ted's tiny happy house and bought the booze that would be their only comfort on the way home.

Near Philadelphia I realized that the man sitting across the aisle from me had been hiccoughing ever since we'd left Ted's. He was holding a bottle of Thunderbird in one hand, a bottle of Schmidt's beer in the other, and taking deep alternating swigs from each. It was still pouring. But the air inside the bus was stagnant with the heat of sixty-seven bodies. Yet every few minutes he shivered and his teeth began to chatter.

When his seatmate asked him what was wrong he whimpered a little and said he'd been to several hospitals but no doctors could help him. I didn't know whether that was the truth or a drunken excuse, so I asked about his symptoms. "Don't bother me with questions like that," he said angrily. "Can't you see I've been poisoned? They're all poisoning me." Then he buried his head in his hands, grinding his fingers into his eyelids whenever the hiccoughs came in prolonged painful spasms.

Later, Shorty told me the man had those spells quite frequently. Sometimes he was sick, sometimes he had the d.t.s. But he'd probably be back in the orchard in a day or two. Like the rest of them, he had nowhere else to earn a living.

INTERLUDE

Into the Cauldron

When I wrote about the truckers, about Mexico's illegal aliens, and New Jersey's intinerant workers, I had to get inside the tribes I sought to describe. That posed a difficult journalistic problem. But, once I had my information, I was able to present it from a point of view with which I'd always been comfortable. I was able to focus on the problems of people who were the traditional underdogs.

But the next four chapters—about the textbook controversy in West Virginia; busing in Boston; a fight over a housing project in Forest Hills, New York; and the traditionalist, churchgoing blacks in Chicago—come straight from the cauldron of social conflict. In those situations, I discovered that the perspectives I'd formed from the safe distance of liberal Manhattan were inadequate. For when I got to the scene of the stories—and became involved with human beings, not abstract issues—my sympathies were unexpectedly divided. I found that, often, people I might once have written off as reactionaries were fighting to preserve their culture and their psychological and physical turf. It became clear to me that those social conflicts could not be understood purely in ideological terms. Clearly, they were tribal struggles, too.

CHAPTER 4

A Fight Over America's Future

In November 1974, I went to Kanawha County, West Virginia, to cover a battle over some grade-school textbooks. It seemed as if there were tens of thousands of people who would go to any lengths to keep those books out of their schools. I wanted to understand who they were and what they thought they were fighting.

For the 229,000 people who live in the coal- and petroleum-rich Kanawha County, which contains West Virginia's capital city, Charleston, and some of its poorest rural areas, the fight over adoption of 325 kindergarten-through-twelfth-grade supplementary English textbooks was a cultural revolution, an effort by the rural working class to wrest the schools—the means of production of their children—away from the permissive technocrats who controlled them.

It was a holy war between people who depend on books and people who depend on the Book.

In West Virginia's terms, it was largely a fight between the relatively prosperous "hillers" and the less well-to-do "creekers."

The "creekers," who despised the textbooks, lived in Kanawha County's hollers—in rural settlements like Big Chimney, Cabin Creek, and Cross Lanes, which dot the sprawling windy valley. Many of them are fundamentalist Christians, who attend their small, white-framed Baptist or Pentecostal churches twice on Sundays and every Wednesday night. They work in the coal mines, or in factories like the Du Pont plant in Belle or, if they're lucky, as truck drivers and construction workers. Most of them have never been on an airplane in their lives. Many drove to places like Chicago or Dayton or Cleveland during the Appalachian migration of the 1960s, but they found the cities alien and hostile and returned to their own tight-knit communities.

They saw the books—with their essays by James Baldwin, Norman Mailer, Malcolm X, their stories about rock bands and street gangs, their frequent use of four-letter words—as reflections of the horrifying new culture they'd glimpsed during their brief urban sojourns, or which they see now when someone like David Steinberg or Richard Pryor or George Carlin appears on the Johnny Carson show. That culture is an infection that incubated on liberal college campuses in the 1960s, spread to the wealthier areas of Charleston—and now threatened to defile their children's small-town classrooms by way of the textbooks that parents feared would turn their young into atheists or sex maniacs or drug addicts. The fundamentalists want to cleanse America of its filth if they're strong enough; seal themselves off from the plague if that's the only alternative.

The hillers have a clear cultural and economic interest in supporting the textbooks. They are doctors, lawyers, mine managers, and engineers who live in Charleston's lush South Hills, who are familiar with the culture that seems so shocking to the creekers. They read *The New York Times*, *Newsweek*, and the *Wall Street Journal* just as avidly as they read the *Charleston Daily Mail* or *Charleston Gazette*. Many take the twice-daily United Airlines flight to New York so often it's almost a commuter trip. They take their vacations in Atlanta or Miami—or in Europe. They know that Norman Mailer and James Baldwin—and George Orwell and Ernest Hemingway—aren't voices many people hear in their isolated valley. They regard the books that include those writers as the crucial ingredients of a contemporary school system that will keep their kids abreast of their peers, that will help them get into Harvard or Haverford instead of West Virginia State or West Virginia Tech.

And the hillers hope the books will help their kids feel comfortable in the Ivy League culture that will surround them. For students from even the most polished, well-heeled West Virginia families often have emotional problems at Harvard or Yale. In those places, they aren't hillers; their classmates—preppies from Exeter or Andover, upwardly mobile kids from sophisticated urban high schools—often treat them as the anachronistic representatives of a backward, poverty-stricken culture: as creekers. They do so through jokes, or clumsy, ill-informed questions. Those remarks can have a searing effect. The students don't know whether they want to be West Virginians or Ivy Leaguers—or whether they'll be stranded between those two worlds. Sometimes it takes years for them to work through that identity crisis.

At least, the hillers thought, the textbooks might help their children function more comfortably in the cosmopolitan environment the creekers perceive as the pinnacle of corruption.

But why didn't they just introduce the new textbooks into the public schools their own kids attend? Why did the books become mandatory for every school throughout the valley?

In a sense, the answer reveals the story of an idea whose time never quite came.

The idea was that educational planners could reach into America's ghettos, its hollers, its tradition-bound ethnic neighborhoods, and coax people there into the melting pot by instituting "multicultural, multi-ethnic" programs in their classrooms.

The theory was plainly stated in a funding proposal for the training of teachers, dated 1970, signed by West Virginia's superintendent of schools. According to the document, teachers are supposed to "induce changes . . . in the behavior of the 'culturally lost' of Appalachia. . . . The setting of the public school should be the testing ground, the diagnostic basis, the experimental center, and the core of this design. . . . The most important ingredient of social change is the change agent"—the teacher.

You had only to look at the controversial textbooks to see how they fit in with the theory. Though I found many of them quite appealing—the kind of books I'd like my two kids, Lisa and Mamu, to study—I could see how even their appearance would shock parents who had been brought up on Dick and Jane stories, on the six-point type of the King James Bible, and on the rigid belief that education meant rote memorization. Now their kids were using paperbacks where cartoons, photos, and gaudily colored pages dominate the print, where you didn't read about Evangeline or the Courtship of Miles Standish but about Hank Aaron or the Beatles, where achievement didn't rest in a child's ability to repeat a lesson accurately, but in her ability to answer the provocative questions at the end of each section.

Reading them I could see, for the first time, how a theist, who was still embittered over the Supreme Court's decision to outlaw school prayer, could believe that relativism and humanism represent a dogma of their own whose very skepticism implies a set of religious values.

In one book there is an exercise that asks students to compare the story of Daniel in the lion's den with the tale of Androcles and the lion. To fundamentalist Christians the exercise itself is blasphemy, since it suggests that revelation is no more than myth. Similarly, the books include writings like Mark Twain's "Adam's Diary," which shows God's first offspring as a bumbling upstate New York householder. There is a *New Yorker*-style cartoon of a naked Adam and Eve peeping out over some bushes. One of the most controversial lessons invites students to invent their own gods, an exercise hinting that God himself might be an invention.

The idea behind the books is the classic liberal assumption that a child who learns to question himself and his environment will grow beyond the confines of his culture. But, apart from the religious heresies, that assumption means the books are also filled with notions many West Virginians regard as secular blasphemy. Some of the exercises encourage kids to tell each other about disagreements with their parents, to describe their battles with authority figures. They ask whether it is ever legitimate to steal. They contain a great many four-letter words. (In many Appalachian households, children who use those words would get spanked.) They suggest that standard English may be one of many dialects spoken in this country, that the rules of grammar are relative, that ghetto English may be a legitimate form of speech.

Now, it's easy to see how a professional educator who has

learned, almost as a matter of dogma, that schools are the vehicles by which working-class kids achieved success beyond the wildest dreams of their parents, could have thought that "multicultural, multi-ethnic" textbooks could bring kids into modern America.

But it is probably unjust to demand that a countyful of people make the spiritual journey from the holler to the Space Age in less than five years, especially when the trip forces them beyond the furthest frontiers of their belief. It makes them the victims of psychic overload. Sometimes they submit in confusion. But in Kanawha County they found leaders to articulate their fury at the annihilation of every value they revered. They fought back.

The holy war erupted in September 1974, as soon as the books were introduced into the schools. During the next months there were exchanges of gunfire, schoolrooms were dynamited, school buses were shot at, cars and homes firebombed. One night someone put fifteen sticks of dynamite under Charleston's Board of Education building and demolished part of it. It was clear that most of the county felt sympathy for the protesters. In November, the *Charleston Gazette* (whose editorials reflected the hillers' point of view) published a poll showing that only 19 per cent of the people they contacted wanted all the books in the schools. But the Board of Education held firm. The week after the poll was published, it voted, four to one, to keep most of the controversial material in the schools. The violence continued. And, as in any war, attitudes hardened.

Susan Bean, thirty-two, who lived in South Hills, was a member of the committee that reviewed all the textbooks. She's the wife of a landscape architect, the mother of three grade-school kids. She was born in Mount Pleasant, Tennessee, where her father was a member of the John Birch Society. In his small construction business he systematically underpaid all the blacks who worked for him. He whipped Susan whenever he caught her reading unorthodox books, whenever she disagreed with him. At seventeen, she ran away from home, got a job as a typist at Sears, and worked her way through the University of Georgia, where she was an English major.

Susan Bean's conservative background made her defense of the textbooks especially fierce. She was glad her children would study the ideas forbidden to her. One day, after I'd been talking with a politically conservative mine manager who told me frankly that he liked the books because they'd give his son a culture in common with his classmates at Princeton next year, I told her I thought we were witnessing a class struggle. She responded quite tartly, "She it's a class struggle, but not in the way you outsiders think. You come from a liberal background. You can't imagine how much the opportunity to give my kids unlimited freedom means to me. It's a way of making sure that I, and my kids, rise above my past."

Nelle Wood, forty-five, the English teacher who selected the textbooks, is the daughter of a fundamentalist railroad engineer from a rural county in West Virginia. She taught an honors English class at the prestigious George Washington High School, nestled in the midst of South Hills. Though most of her students were from wealthy, sophisticated families, she is still a practicing fundamentalist. She never smokes or drinks, feels uncomfortable when the Lord's name is taken in vain, and has to ask one of her colleagues to read whenever a four-letter word crops up in a text.

It is possible that her ardent support of the textbooks came from her special teaching experience. There are teachers at George Washington who argue that if she had to teach a classroom full of rural working-class kids she might feel more ambivalent about the issues. But she is a woman who loves books and wants to share that passion with her students. She thinks censorship—any kind of censorship—is a sin. You have no more right to conceal a piece of literature from a coal miner's son who comes from Big Chimney and attends Herbert Hoover High than you do from a lawyer's son who comes from South Hills and attends George Washington High. Why deny working-class kids the knowledge she thinks is so precious? Why patronize them? She refused to weed out stories other fundamentalists find blasphemous because, "I can't stand the thought of telling lies by omitting ideas I know exist. " Just as many of the anti-textbook people have quotations from the Bible in their homes she had a quotation from the Areopagitica in her spare, tiny cubicle behind the high school's library. "Who kills a man kills a reasonable creature, God's image; but who kills a book kills reason itself."

But thousands of people in Kanawha County were willing to die in the war against the blasphemy Nelle Woods believes is freedom. Emmett Thompson, fifty-nine, a riverboat engineer who lives in Nitro, West Virginia, lives quite comfortably in a neat red-brick house larger than Susan Bean's white frame house in South Hills. His oldest son, trim, impeccably dressed, short-haired, had just graduated from the Lynchburg Bible College. Emmett Thompson, whose bushy, cinnamon-colored moustache makes him look a little more dashing than his boy, is what people call a "Wednesday nighter"—so devoted to the Calvary Baptist Church he attends it twice on Sunday and once on Wednesday. He considers the introduction of the books "moral genocide."

"You are making an insidious attempt to replace our periods with your question marks," he says. He thinks the books—and the culture they represent—have to be fought. In a country where coal miners use dynamite on every shift, where every man and boy is a hunter, and every house in every holler has plenty of guns and plenty of ammunition, he longs for a "return to the spirit of the Boston Tea Party," for a "revolution of righteousness."

Skeeter Dodd, the manager of the radio station WKLC, is the sort of person who could help inspire that revolution. A chunky, sturdy man in his mid-forties, Skeeter is an early morning disk jockey, whose taste in Country music, syndicated jokes from the "Funny Wire," and imaginary dialogues with a fictional hillbilly, "Granddad" have made him a favorite with creekers throughout the county. "If they don't wake up to me, they ain't gonna wake up that day," he says in his exaggerated West Virginia accent, laughing heartily.

Though KLC is Charleston's third-largest station, Skeeter spends much of his time worrying about collecting bills from advertisers and finding new sponsors to keep the business afloat. But even while he's absorbed in those detailed, distracting jobs, he talks eagerly about his idea of patriotism. Like Emmett Thompson, he sees the textbook struggle as a salvo in a war "to restore the faith of our fathers. Look at it this way, friend. They tax us for the schools, but the schools don't represent us. Isn't that what them dumb hillbillies and creekers was fighting about two hundred years ago?"

He not only despises the books, he believes they are part of a Communist plot hatched in Dusseldorf, Germany, in 1917 to destroy democracy. He showed me a replica of a document that proposed to "corrupt the people, get them away from religion. Make them superficial. Destroy their ruggedness."

Like thousands of people in Kanawha County, he believes in the existence of an upper-class conspiracy to bring Communism to America. Many of the fundamentalists equate Communism with decadence, and argue that because the wealthy cosmopolitan elite wants to legalize drugs, legitimize premarital sex, pornographic movies, and massage parlors, they are subversive. Skeeter's patriotism has personal roots, too. His dad worked on an assembly line, he says. "Neighbor, you better believe that under a system like socialism this old creeker would be back there."

He'd been in the Navy intelligence in Korea, and now saw himself waging the domestic version of that war against Communism in Kanawha County. He carried a citizens'-band radio in his car so other patriots could alert him if there were trouble. He was "Boots" in a network that included "Kojak," "Blue Flag," and "Money Man." Late on a chilly fall night, wearing his battered black overcoat as he slumped over the mike and exchanged information over his cb, he looked like a weary, dedicated member of a nascent band of freedom fighters, the nucleus of an army that wants to restore America to its paths of righteousness.

Alice Moore, the lone dissenter on the school board, was that army's most popular leader: its Joan of Arc. Her husband, a Church of Christ minister, had had congregations in Tennessee and Meridian, Mississippi, before the couple moved to the lower-middle-class town of St. Alban's. In 1970, two years after her arrival in Kanawha County, Alice Moore decided to run for the board in opposition to sex education in the schools. She was elected.

She is a stunningly beautiful, intelligent woman who adopts a Southern belle's flirtatious style when she argues with the four male school-board members.

When Alice speaks, thousands of people in the hollers listen. Whenever she appeared at board meetings or at public meetings she was greeted with jubilant standing ovations, with cheerful choruses of "We love you Alice, oh yes we do," with clusters of flowers and placards that read ALICE MOORE FOR PRESIDENT. In places like Big Chimney and Kelly's Creek—places most hillers can barely find on their maps, let alone in their cars—her name inspires the same kind of glisteningly popular response as Huey Long's did in the back-country parishes of Louisiana.

When the textbooks came up for adoption in the spring of 1974, she was the only school-board member who read them thoroughly. She was enraged by their emphasis on what she calls "situational ethics"—the heathen creed that teaches kids to believe that any set of actions can be justified by sociological conditions.

We talked for hours one afternoon at the Bonanza Steak House in St. Alban's. When she told me about a teacher-training program she'd recently attended, her tone alternated between Andy Griffith-like wonder and fundamentalist wrath. She talked about an educational expert who sought to prove there was a cultural justification for Eskimo mothers who put their babies outside to freeze. "You know," she said, "I was the only person there who argued she was wrong."

With my longish hair, and my credentials from an urban, liberal newspaper, I must have seemed to represent the enemy. She was courteous, and her southern voice never lost its slight hint of conspiratorial laughter. But: "You just don't understand what you're doing to us," she said. "How can any school board force me to send my kids to a school that teaches that God is a myth, that justifies mothers who kill their young?"

"But how could I send my kids to a school that outlawed the textbooks?" I asked. "I hate censorship as much as you hate blasphemy."

"I don't know," she said. "Maybe there is no school system that can provide for your kids and mine. Maybe we Americans have come to a parting of the ways."

Many teenagers in Kanawha County were as passionate about the holy war as their parents were. I spent one day in South Hills, interviewing the children of the elite, who attend George Washington High, and in Campbell's Creek talking with the working-class kids who attend Du Pont and East Bank. There was no bond of understanding between them—only mutual stereotypes, mutual resentment.

Many students from George Washington were aware that their wealth spawns resentment, that their class position creates an almost insurmountable barrier between them and most other teenagers in the county. Some wish the gap could be bridged. But even though there are many creeker kids at their own high school, not a single one of the hillers I interviewed had ever visited them or invited them home. And, though they're aware that "those kids are angry because they think our parents have money," it never occurred to them that "those kids" had reason to be angry; that the freedom to leave school in the family car, to gather at Gino's Pizza for a pleasant lunch, rankled the kids from the hollers, who had to stay in school all day and eat their meals in the cafeteria.

During an interview, one girl, a lawyer's daughter, asked me, sharply, "why anyone would want to visit people like those coal miners." When I asked some other students to describe the textbook protesters they used terms like "closed-minded and violent"; people "who want to protest corruption, but don't even know how to spell that word"; "Wednesday nighters who carry clubs." Three students gave me an issue of the *George Washington Pride*, the school's underground newspaper, which contained a long satire of the conflict. In it, the protest leader's name is "the Rev. Rodney Necc, but my friends call me Red." He has come to a demonstration sponsored by "the Christian and Righteous Association of Parents . . . to show my deep dedication to upholding CRAP."

That afternoon I drove to a small white Baptist church, off a windy dirt road in Campbell's Creek. I met with about ten teenage children of coal miners, truck drivers, construction workers, ministers. They didn't feel as free with me as the kids from GW had, so their comments were more cramped and constrained. Still, most were scornful of the hillers. In a sense, their caricatured view of the elite was the mirror image of the elite's caricatured view of them.

They talked about wild, dope-filled orgies where maids had to lock themselves in their rooms for fear of being beaten; of rich, reckless parents who were too busy to take care of their kids; of the ease with which the hillers could bribe the police when they got in trouble.

Some kids sounded wounded by the hillers' insensitivity. "I can expect someone who doesn't believe in God not to see anything wrong with the textbooks," said one minister's daughter. "But they can at least respect our rights, since those books do talk about God. And they don't have to insult our faith or our parents by calling us rednecks."

The truck driver's son had a more practical objection. He was afraid the books would hurt his chance of earning a living. He wanted to go to West Virginia Tech, to be an engineer, and he felt he needed "a good basic education."

"They could teach English in school without going to this ghetto language or some of this slang," he said. "If they drop that standard, then society's just going to go down. Until now we've always been taught to make speeches in front of the class, to write letters with correct punctuation. But in these new textbooks they say, whatever sort of speech is common in your area, well, that's all right. But if you move out of state, it will be just like going to a foreign country. How will you know what other people's meaning is? And I know from my father's experience—if you look for a job and can't talk the right English, they won't hire you."

Of course, for many protesters the issues are far more general and ominous than the practical questions of grammar and employment. Many students from Du Pont and East Bank are already into rock music and dope. Their parents are scared that the heretical ideas in the school-sanctioned textbooks will rob them of their last vestiges of control.

At meeting after meeting I heard complaints about kids from Kanawha County who had gone to college and come home acting like aliens. The conclusions? "Don't let them be educated above their rearing."

"I was going to send my boy to college," said the wife of a food salesman from St. Alban's. "But I've changed my mind. It was a difficult decision. In my husband's profession now, you need a college degree. But I'd rather see him become a coal miner or a construction worker than know he was risking his soul."

Of course, religious controversy is nothing new in West Virginia. Nor, for that matter, is religious separatism. The ancestors of the miners and teamsters who live in Cabin Creek and Big Chimney were Anglo-Saxon yeomen who settled there two hundred years ago because they were dissatisfied with Virginia's upper-class Tidewater planters and their moribund Anglican church. They were inspired by the first Great Awakening, the national fit of religious ecstasy which, with its stress on holy fervor and personal salvation, swept westward from New England in the eighteenth century. Even now, in the small Baptist and Pentecostal churches you see in every holler, thousands of fundamentalists scourge themselves by listening to sermons echoing the harsh, terrifying words of Jonathan Edwards' "Sinners in the Hands of an Angry God."

For generations, the fundamentalists were sure that some version of their creed was America's dominant faith. Then, without warning, they found themselves waging a defensive war against the heathen idea of evolution. The Scopes trial was a watershed. Between Clarence Darrow's courtroom tactics and H. L. Mencken's scathing prose, they suddenly ceased to be America's conscience and became its laughingstock. Though they clung to their faith, sometimes defiantly, many of them felt a private, lingering shame. It took decades for that shame to vanish. Now, with the rise of evangelical Christianity, they have confidence that they are part of a church militant once again. They feel as if they're at the dawn of a second Great Awakening.

During the height of the textbook controversy, West Virginia's army of Christian soldiers made life in Kanawha County nearly unbearable. The dynamiting, the firebombing, the shooting, terrified educators from Charleston to Cabin Creek: the fundamentalists' ceaseless attacks on blasphemy made each teacher feel like a potential target. In that setting, English teachers were scared to teach anything but grammar, in case any work of literature, even Shakespeare, seemed atheistic or immoral, and goaded some hothead to bomb the schools.

Late one November night someone threw three sticks of dynamite into a first-grade classroom at the Midway School in Campbell's Creek. What expressions of blasphemy could possibly have been taking place there? The teacher whose room had been bombed had spent a decade collecting books and toys for kids whose families couldn't afford them. Now all that was ruined. That year she'd bought some baby chicks for the children. The chickens' feathers were scattered all over.

The room itself was littered with debris from a waist-high bookshelf that had been destroyed by the blast. Hundreds of books were strewn over the floor. From the outside of the school all you could see were four broken windows, the remains of some tables and chairs, a brightly lettered alphabet attached to the blackboard, and an American flag still perched above the rubble.

The Wet Branch elementary school in Cabin Creek, the most rural part of the sprawling county, was even more vulnerable than Midway. In October, someone tossed some dynamite into that building. Since then, there had been a month-long boycott: People who ignored it usually got phone calls saying that their houses would be burned. The afternoon I visited the school just eight of the three hundred students showed up for classes. "Each day seems like it's two million hours long," said one teacher.

An older woman at the school had taught most of the parents of the boycotting children. The fact that they won't trust her to use the books responsibly troubles her deeply.

"Soon we won't be able to teach them anything," she said. "It's as if the parents and ministers are staring over our shoulders, waiting to get us for anything that sounds immoral. I don't think I'll ever see the children as students again. I'll see them as spies in my classroom."

I have rarely covered a story that left me as emotionally conflicted as this one did. For it seemed to me that some of the pro-textbook people—the northern educators and bureaucrats who devised them, not the local people who adopted them—were involved in a kind of cultural imperialism. But some of the protesters were clearly capable of outright totalitarianism.

I know that the people who designed the textbooks believe that the children of fundamentalists (and, to a lesser extent, of the white working-class in general) have to be freed of the narrow-minded influence of their parents in order to become functioning citizens of twenty-first century America. But is it ethical or prudent to confront them with textbooks they regard as blasphemous, to use their classrooms as "testing grounds," to train their teachers to be "change agents"? To me, that is quite literally a way of telling kids that "We have to destroy your culture in order to save it." I interviewed some curriculum reformers and textbook authors while I was working on this chapter, and it's clear that, from the vantage point of New York or Boston, they saw the creekers in the same derisive terms H. L. Mencken used during the Scopes trial. They regarded the objections of people like Alice Moore as problems to be dealt with, not opinions to be respected.

Their intentions were probably benign, but wasn't their policy a fresh example of the arrogance of power? You can invite a person into your culture. But I don't believe you can impose your culture on another person without risking unforeseeable harm.

If the journey to another culture is voluntary, as Susan Bean's was, then the person is likely to maintain a sense of identity and pride. But if it is an imposed voyage to a totally unknown destination—as it would be for many children in Kanawha County—then it could produce considerable psychological harm. It could set them adrift, with no reliable traditions, no moral compass, in an agnostic, postlinear, multicultural, multi-ethnic Space Age world, with no connection at all to their familiar hollers.

You cannot outlaw school prayer and still pretend that secular humanism—momentarily our national creed—does not carry its own deep assumptions about religion. Why not recognize that both attitudes are dogmas and try to develop an educational system that's flexible enough to furnish federal funds to schools that base their curricula on theism as well as those that base their curricula on relativism?

Still, I couldn't forget Susan Bean's tart remark about "outsiders . . . who can't imagine how much the opportunity to give my kids unlimited freedom means to me." For it described many of the journalists who came to Kanawha County and became fascinated by it. Many of them tended to glorify the protesters a little: not just to say they were victims of a class struggle, but to use that argument to explain their excesses. They were sentimentalizing a potentially dangerous movement.

The last scene I witnessed in Charleston is the one that lingers most painfully in my imagination. It was a rally to protest the textbooks—not in any of the rural churches or parks, where the movement was nurtured, but in the cavernous Civic Center, one of the most modern buildings in Charleston.

The audience of two thousand was in a fervent mood. Most of the textbook protesters wore large stickers that asserted JESUS WOULDN'T HAVE READ THEM. As they sang "Amazing Grace," "We Shall Not Be Moved," and "God Bless America," more than half of them swayed back and forth, waving their right hands in the air to show that they were born-again Christians. On the right side of the podium, a stern, trim youth held the American flag aloft throughout the two-hour program. On the left side, an equally rigid young man bore a Christian flag with a silky white field and a blood purple cross as its emblem.

The main speaker was the Rev. Marvin Horan, a protest leader from Campbell's Creek. As he spoke, the flags, and their martial bearers, framed his body, which was bathed in light for the TV cameras. His voice rolled with righteousness; the audience applauded nearly every sentence. He held a Bible in his right hand, two textbooks in his left, and, shaking both arms angrily, he cried "Which are we going to stand for, the word of the Lord or the filth in these books?" Then he threatened his audience—"the Bible says not to use the Lord's name in vain, or the person who does will not be held guiltless at the seat of justice"—and read several blasphemous sentences from *Catcher in the Rye*, a text he had clearly studied quite carefully. For he told his audience that "out of all this book—almost three hundred pages—there's only twenty pages that doesn't mention the Lord's name in vain." Then, waving *Catcher in the Rye*, he asked, "Do we surrender or do we fight?"

Behind me someone yelled "burn 'em," and hundreds of people began to applaud.

Soon Horan began to talk about the importance of maintaining the school boycott. "The board of education thinks we're yellow, but we're red, white, and blue. If we stand united, we can rid Kanawha County of those filthy books and the people who put them there."

It wasn't just platform rhetoric. In 1975, the Rev. Horan was convicted of conspiring to bomb two elementary schools. (Many protest-supporters claim he was framed.) But, while he was in jail, the creeker parents won control over their children's educations. Except in South Hills, the English textbooks, which had kindled the holy war, are rarely used. In 1975, when the Board of Education had to adopt a new set of social-studies textbooks, it was careful to choose innocuous, obviously patriotic ones—some of which appeared to be updated versions of books that had been written in the 1940s.

When I revisited West Virginia in March 1978, I spent a morning at the Midway School. There—as at many schools in the county—a committee of parents had veto power over the books that would be used in the classroom or the library. For the most part, teachers anticipated their objections and practiced self-censorship. In fact, the parents had only had to use their power once in three years—when they'd banned a book about the conception of babies. Mostly, that book dealt with animals. But it contained one drawing of a pregnant woman pushing a shopping cart, with an oval-shaped object sketched under her coat to show where the fetus would be. That drawing convinced the parents the book was obscene. The committee refused to allow it in their school. Just one copy remained, hidden in a faculty member's drawer.

Maybe the prominence of the Christian flag at the Civic Center rally awakened my own Jewish fears, but that experience left me deeply unsettled. Maybe Alice Moore was right. Maybe some of the tribes of America had come to a parting of the ways.

The thousands of conservative Christians who'd applauded the Rev. Horan that day 1974 are absolutists. My question marks are sacred to me. Both attitudes are dogmas, but the difference between them is vast. I would like to think there is room for the fundamentalists in my America. But I'm not sure there is room for me in theirs.

CHAPTER 5

Jesse Jackson:
A Return to the Fundamentals

For the present, the Negro is a radical on race matters, conservative on others, a forced radical . . . rather than a genuine radical.

That sentence was written fifty years ago by the black scholar Alain Locke. When I first read it, in the late Sixties, it sounded like an intellectual relic—especially in contrast to the Black Panther Party's wholeheartedly revolutionary rhetoric, which pervaded the left back then. But later, when the movement fell apart, it was clear that the mood Alain Locke had articulated so long ago still had deep roots in the black community. And the Rev. Jesse Jackson, a disciple of Martin Luther King's, had emerged as its latter-day spokesman.

I first realized that when I heard Jackson speak at an anti-abortion rally in New York, shortly after I'd covered the textbook controversy in West Virginia. Before that speech all I'd known about Jackson was that he was an economic progressive, a thirty-three-year-old transplanted South Carolinian, whose sleek, sexy good looks and flashy style of dress had prompted his fellow Chicagoan Studs Terkel to dub him "the son of Shaft." I'd assumed that he shared the freewheeling, liberal personal values the creekers attributed to the cosmopolitan elite.

But that night, with the wrath of a Jeremiah, Jackson denounced abortion as "murder"; he insisted that "when prayers
leave the schools, guns come in"; he argued that the disobedience
children show toward their teachers and parents represents moral
decay and implied that spanking is the best remedy for it; he
suggested that, while he supported woman's liberation, his wife, at
least, should stay in her place—his home.

It was a speech that would have pleased Alice Moore and
Skeeter Dodd—and enraged the white liberals and radicals who'd
supported the Rev. Martin Luther King.

Jackson's morality is based on the church-oriented traditions of
the rural South. And hearing him reminded me of conversations
I'd had in the mid-Sixties, when I'd worked in the civil-rights
movement in Mississippi and when I was a graduate student, living on the South Side of Chicago. So I decided to interview him,
and talk with some blacks I knew in Chicago, to see if they
shared the mood he articulated.

Jackson is a highly controversial leader. But most of the people
I spoke to—even those who disagree with him—share his reverence for the spirituality and order of the Black Belt towns where
they were raised. They dislike the materialism, the rootlessness,
the violence of urban life in the North. They were born in the
South and retain a lasting personal conservatism.

I decided to couple my chapter about them with my chapter
about Kanawha County, to let it precede my accounts of racial
battles over a low-income housing project in Forest Hills, and over
busing in Boston. For, as Jesse Jackson, Vernon Jarrett, and Grace
and Arthur Sherman talked to me in their offices or their living
rooms, I saw that they had a great deal in common with people
who seemed to be their enemies in territorial battles. Those interviews reinforced my feeling that, for blacks and whites alike, any
progressive movement in America must combine economic radicalism, an appreciation of tribal differences, and a genuine respect
for ideas about family and personal discipline that sometimes
seem old fashioned from the vantage point of Greenwich Village
or Berkeley or Georgetown or Harvard Square.

In church, Jesse Jackson's power is immense. His sermons—like
Mahalia Jackson's gospels—combine control with frenzy. As he

denounces corporation heads and black criminals, his voice soars, transforming even the stiffest, most bourgeois congregations into thousand-person amen corners. When he punctuates his passage with the traditional Baptist question "Can I get a witness?" the church comes alive with "Preach it, Jesse," and "That's right." As his sermons reach their climax, three or four people—usually women—spend themselves talking in tongues, while solicitous matrons fan them so their rapture doesn't dissolve into uncontrollable fits. When he's finished preaching, Jesse stands behind the alter and announces, in an inviting, lulling voice, that "the church is open now." Dozens of people file toward him to affirm that they've been born again.

As a controversial black leader he is constantly in danger of assassination, and his grace under fire is immense. One Saturday, as he was speaking at his weekly Operation PUSH rally on the South Side of Chicago, a well-dressed black man stood up from a pew in the back of the church, hollering for his attention. I expected a moment of polemics. But when a bodyguard gripped him in a bear hug, a loaded .45 spun out of his pocket. As the potential assassin was hustled out of the room, his gun fell to the floor.

Jackson began to perspire. Still, however nervous he was, he never lost his place in the sermon: His calm soothed the congregation. But I was so shaken by the specter of the gunman that I could barely concentrate on Jackson's words. Afterward I asked him if he'd been frightened. He said he hadn't, that risks were part of his work. Then he tried to calm me.

The episode brought out the best in Jackson. It let him play the traditional minister's role: protector of his congregation. And the role suits him perfectly. In it, he seems at ease with himself, at home.

Paradoxically, outside church, Jackson personifies much of what he denounces. Though he's always talking about the need for the old, rooted ways, where families lived in tiny towns, within the "love triangle" of the home, the church, and the school, he rarely spends a full week with his wife and four kids. Though he constantly denounces materialism, he has a vast wardrobe of elegant clothes. He is a celebrity-businessman-activist who makes deals all over the country, who travels so much that the Chicago news-

paper columnist, Mike Royko once dubbed him "Jet-stream Jesse."
PR releases and advance men usually precede him. He lives in the
media, not the world.

Rachel and I interviewed him in his spacious Chicago office,
where the phone rings constantly with news of some intrigue in
Chicago politics, some business arrangement involving a record
company or food store, with requests for speaking engagements.
That day he insisted that the values of small-town religious life
were at the core of the moral crusade he was launching in the
ghetto.

He was least guarded when we talked about abortion. During
that part of the interview Rachel had stopped taking pictures to
join in the conversation. Instead of including her, though, Jesse
used her as an example—an illustration of his unstated assumption that abortion is a man's decision. Looking at me, waving his
hand toward Rachel, he said, "If you've got to choose between
your wife, who is already alive, and an unborn baby—well, you
shouldn't sacrifice her life.

"But you have to remember you *are* killing a baby. And it's
wrong to take life lightly, to go out and get high and have sexual
relations with your wife, and then say, oops, I made a mistake, I
don't want to have a child. You cannot emphasize your immediate needs and make an ethical principle of inconvenience.

"Anyway, in my tradition we believe that God will make a way.
And we believe that you're not necessarily the children's blessing.
The children may be your blessing. I know that my children have
helped to stabilize my life. If we hadn't had them, my wife and I
wouldn't have survived as a marriage."

He drifted off for a second. Then, when I asked him why his
marriage would have collapsed, he stammered a little. His language was tantalizing but deliberately vague—and somewhat
more cynical than his pulpit rhetoric:

"Well, you know, my life is very dynamic and, variety being the
spice of life, alternatives keep occurring. But no outside woman
could compete with my children for my affection. So my wife has
kept some babies. But she's kept more than that. She kept her
husband and a house and some other things, too."

Of course, Jackson's opposition to abortion is far from his central theme. Still, though he continues to speak out against white racism, continues to focus on the issue of jobs, he devotes an increasing amount of his attention to issues within the black community—to questions of personal conduct which, he hopes, will restore discipline to black culture. He's combating what he calls "freedom without responsibility, though I hate to use that term because our adversaries do." He's waging a rhetorical war on the new materialism, which, he feels, is one cause of the terrible surge of black crime.

Didn't that seem paradoxical, I asked him, since much of the new wealth had been generated by the movement he'd been identified with? "Not really," he said, and indicated that, in his terms, many civil-rights workers had borne decadence to the rural South in much the same way as the creekers feared the textbooks would bear decadence to the Appalachian hollers.

"Remember, I looked at the movement from the perspective of a southern black. A lot of blacks and whites from the North brought degenerate values with them. They didn't share our roots. Stokely Carmichael, for example, came from the West Indies, not from the South. Many of them had a real contempt for our church and our values. It was real chauvinism. And many of our youths down South got carried away with the smooth-talking rhetoric of the easterners and the liberal whites. They were attracted by the wing of the movement that went off into open vulgarity— into experiments with sex and dope that Abbie Hoffman and that crowd were trying. They adopted values that were foreign to us."

"You see, our roots were in something different than being jealous of white people. What we wanted to change were the oppressive laws of segregation. We didn't want men standing up and allowing women to sit down to change. We didn't want children respecting adults to change. We didn't want that ability we had down South to leave our doors open and not worry about crime to change. If someone died in the neighborhood, we didn't have an orphan home. The children went to the neighbors. We didn't want that to change. This tremendous will we had to work—we didn't want that to change. We just wanted to get paid for what we did. And we have to return to those values."

"But how?"

"By raising up the institutions that held them dear. Like the church. Some of our generation left the church, but the church didn't disappear. It's still very much there. As a matter of fact, during this economic depression—which is accompanied by our spiritual depression—many people are going back in that direction. The church is growing. It's falling into its own as the center of activity in our community."

Jackson's feeling that permissive schools contribute to moral decay comes from his own memory of school in South Carolina. "I went to first grade in Greenville. Mrs. Georgia Robinson was the teacher. My mother knew her from the Springfield Baptist Church. So my mother talked to Mrs. Robinson one Sunday and said, 'Teach my boy all you can. Sometimes he gets unruly. If he does, use the strap on him.' And she said, 'I can't make the PTA meetings, but I'll see you in church on Sunday.' So, between Mrs. Robinson, the church, and my mother I was in a love triangle. But it was also a discipline triangle. I think that sort of atmosphere shows the beauty of the opportunity to learn and the moral responsibility to learn.

"I look at my own children, who are four, seven, eight, and ten. Their character is being put together now. I can tell you the one who's inclined to cheat, the one who's honest, the one who's working hardest. All that is developing right now. And you cannot take the sacred elements of discipline and belief in God out of the chemical composition and believe you are going to have a decent end, a decent person. I know that sounds very fundamental to some people—and it is."

Arthur and Grace Sherman are the kind of working-class blacks Jesse would like to reach. Like him, they're transplanted southerners who migrated North twenty years ago. But they're still uncomfortable with Chicago's fast-paced life. They miss Arkansas, their home state, and envy their relatives who were able to find good jobs in the post-segregation South. They agree with Jackson's ideas, admire his energy, but never attend his PUSH rallies or even remember to listen to them on the radio. They don't go to the demonstrations he organizes. He doesn't offer any services that are useful to them. So they feel more intimately connected to their ward captains and the Democratic machine than to Jackson.

I met the Shermans in the Sixties, when we'd lived in the same shabby neighborhood on the edge of Chicago's ghetto. I was a graduate student then, and I'd eat with them once or twice a week, or we'd go roller skating on a Saturday night, or go out for a movie and a few drinks.

Arthur worked most of the time. That year, 1964, he had a job as a janitor in one of the fancy office buildings in the Loop. Then he'd come home for a hurried dinner, and, most nights, moonlight by using his battered 1957 Ford truck to haul furniture all over Chicago. He had an eighth-grade education, and talked too slowly, too ungrammatically, to land an office job. But he was determined to rise to the top of the working class.

In those days, he was an extremely gregarious man who drank and gambled, who loved to sit on the low rails in front of his building and "signify"—talk—with the old men who were always there, guzzling beer. But he put tight limits on his pleasure. He didn't want to get trapped in the ghetto—in his freezing three-room apartment with its peeling walls, its squat third-hand refrigerator, its old gas stove.

Grace, an effusive, devout woman, felt threatened by the street life Arthur enjoyed. It scared her physically—she almost never went out of the building alone at night. And it scared her morally, too, for she could never quite rid herself of the fear that some day Arthur would fall over the precipice and land in the world of booze and dice and fast women that had destroyed so many of their friends from down home. She was so eager to move that she refused to get pregnant until there was enough money in the bank to pay for a larger, warmer apartment in a quieter neighborhood. Arthur was too proud to let her work, but she kept busy. Several times each week she'd make the three-bus trip to a church where preachers and parishioners she'd known from her childhood in Arkansas worshiped. Of course, there were countless churches in our neighborhood, but she insisted on making the long trip because it was one of the few ways she could preserve a bit of her familiar South in this frightening Chicago slum. As she would have done down home, she busied herself with choir practice and Bible study and railed at Arthur because, for all of his hard work, he was a fast-living back-slider.

Neither of them ever doubted that they should give a tithe of their earnings to the church or send a check back South every month so their kinfolk could buy some extra food, extra clothes, so their younger brothers and sisters could afford the education they'd missed. They were the most disciplined, upwardly mobile couple I knew in those years, much more like nineteenth-century American Calvinists than the hipsters Norman Mailer described when he eulogized blacks in "The White Negro," an essay that influenced scores of my friends in the early Sixties.

In 1975 the Shermans were living well. For nine years, Arthur had been employed by a Chicago trucking company, working up to twelve hours a day, six days a week, carrying goods from loading docks and railroad depots to stores all over the state. He'd earned enough money to buy a semi-attached house far from the South Side ghetto. He and Grace both had cars. They had bought a new refrigerator, a washing machine, and a dryer. Their one son, Henry, had his own TV and a game room full of toys. Henry had inherited his parents' self-discipline. On the door of his room there was a chart that listed the hours he had to study and sleep, the hours he could play and watch TV. Each violation of the schedule was marked with a large red X.

In 1965, Grace had sometimes talked about working, but Arthur wouldn't let her. In his traditionalist opinion, a man should earn money, a woman should raise children. But, by 1975, Grace had found a form of labor that involved her more than any job could have. By then, she was more than an ardent churchgoer. She was a born-again Christian whose faith prevented her from drinking or smoking, from wearing makeup or short, provocative skirts. She spent her spare time doing missionary work, bearing witness to her faith in black and white communities all over Chicago.

For years Arthur had refused to accept her religion. They'd quarrel—sometimes jokingly, sometimes angrily—over his desire to spend an evening at a bar.

He thought he needed those moments of relief. He had bought everything he owned on credit and for years he'd tried to escape the tensions of his debts by drinking heavily. He'd terrify Grace with his desperate, raging midnight moods. Finally, in 1972, he'd collapsed on the job. The doctors told him he was suffering from acute hypertension. He was hospitalized for three weeks, forbidden to work for two months. Now he's quit smoking and drinking, he takes his blood-pressure pills, and watches his diet very carefully. And, to Grace's delight, he's become an elder in the Baptist Church—though his roundish face still takes on a dourly teasing expression when she launches into one of her long testimonials to the glory of God.

In the old days, the Shermans and I used to talk politics a lot. For instance, they knew I was planning to do voter-registration work in Mississippi in 1964. Arthur was tempted to come with me, he said, but he couldn't afford to take that much time away from work.

Now, though, they're more worried about black disorder than discrimination. They're eager to support the kind of harsh social measures liberal whites often oppose in their names. For example, since Arthur has spent most of his adult life trying to build a secure economic foundation for his family, he hates the Aid to Dependent Children (ADC) program. He wants the city to hire a squad of detectives to track down absentee fathers.

The Shermans were still living on the South Side in the late 1960s, when the Blackstone Rangers were the darlings of local liberals. They saw the gang terrorize the neighborhood. Arthur says he was delighted when Mayor Daley responded to some small-scale riots in the city by issuing his famous "shoot to kill" order. He wanted to band together with other adult men and fight the Rangers. "I believe if we'd cut down a few of those punks, the South Side would be a safer place right now," he says. He's disappointed with the cops—and with himself—because they never did wage a decisive war.

When I revisited the Shermans in the summer of 1978, those problems seemed like distant ones. A few months earlier, Arthur had been laid off by his trucking company. He'd paid all his debts by then, and he had a year's worth of severance pay coming to him. He was hauling goods on his own truck, as he always had—only now it was a full-time job, which meant that, for a while, he'd earn two salaries. He wanted to buy a 1976 Peterbilt rig, to become an owner-operator, but he didn't know whether his age would allow him to put in enough hours to pay off *that* heavy mortgage. A cousin of his, a twenty-five-year-old native of Gary, had volunteered to be an assistant driver. But the cousin hadn't held a steady job in four years. Unlike Arthur, with his Arkansas-bred Calvinism, the younger man preferred drawing welfare to taking a job that only paid four dollars an hour. Arthur couldn't quite understand that attitude. He wondered whether the younger northerner would serve as the sort of trustworthy partner he needed to realize his dream of rising to the top of the working class.

Maybe his son, Henry, the vessel of the Shermans' hopes, would achieve that. He and Grace—like many of their Kanawha County counterparts—had decided to send the boy to a vocational high school, instead of an academic one, so he'd have the specific skills to compete in Chicago's job market. Grace worried constantly that, despite the wholesome atmosphere she and Arthur tried to create at home, he'd acquire decadent habits from the kids he met at school or on the street. So she did her missionary work in the morning and early afternoon and was always in the house when Henry returned from school. She tried to keep him with her for the rest of the day. If he went out, she set strict curfews. In theory, Arthur agreed with her protective attitude. But it was encouraging Henry to behave in a way that confused his gregarious father. For he couldn't understand why the boy was always inside, watching TV or reading, instead of playing basketball with the other kids—enjoying the street life that had given Arthur so much pleasure. At those times Arthur wished, wistfully, that Henry could roam free in the fields he'd loved so much in Arkansas.

The more I talked to the Shermans, the clearer it became that, in their minds, Arthur's work, Grace's faith, are nothing but fragile shelters from the increasingly violent, disorganized northern world they'd entered as refugees from the strict segregation of the 1950s South. The turmoil they witness daily has made them as conservative, on social issues, as the creekers in West Virginia. They plan to remain in Chicago. But, after twenty years, the city is still their diaspora and, late at night, as talk about it wears thin, they both reveal their deep longing for their homeland: the blood-stained Zion of the rural South.

Vernon Jarrett is a black columnist for the *Chicago Tribune*, whose cluttered office is an integral link in the community's grapevine. He is a hefty, middle-aged man, an avid talker who loves to pick up his phone and listen to some fresh tidbit of gossip.

Jarrett is every bit as troubled by the decay of black society as Jesse Jackson. But, when I interviewed him in 1975, he talked freely of his dislike for the man.

"No one in black history has been able to manipulate the media and the white power structure as skillfully as Jesse," he says. "He's been campaigning for president of black America for years. But he never accomplishes anything. He pulls in money for PUSH that should be distributed to broad-based organizations."

And, Jarrett says, he's brutal to blacks who disagree with him. He complains about dissenting journalists to his friends, the newspaper owners. He denounces reporters at PUSH rallies. "He'd like to get us all fired and staff the media completely with his own PR people. Then he could control black life completely."

Where Jackson's criticisms of black society are primarily religious, and the Shermans' concerns are largely economic, Jarrett's analysis is sociological.

In segregated communities, he recalls, "We had to develop a code of morality for ourselves because the whites didn't give a damn about us. Peer pressure was crucial in those days. We lived for each other because we weren't trying to impress the whites. So, for example, the speakers in our schools would always dramatize the difference between black morality and white morality. White crimes were sick crimes. Whites were the ones who chopped up bodies and burned people up. That kind of thing would have been inconceivable for us. It's only begun since we moved North.

"The essence of the black code said this: You must be moral, no matter how poor you are, how disadvantaged, or how illiterate. That's why, even today, so many of our working-class people refuse to accept the excuses of white liberals and black intellectuals for black crimes. How can we accept poverty as an excuse for hurting each other when so many of us are poor? If we did that, we'd wipe each other out."

It was urbanization that undermined the old morality, Jarrett says. You were anonymous as you moved, gypsylike, from one housing project to another. How could you be influenced by traditionally powerful institutions, like the church?

"And, you know, the crazy thing is that in the wake of the great black revolution—of all the talk about how black is beautiful—there's been an unparalleled diminution of black pride. Those pimp clothes look hideous. I think the reason is that in the mid-Sixties we began to write off everything our people did here in America. In order to find a heritage we could be proud of we made a quantum jump all the way back to past African civilization.

"But it didn't work. All the conventional values were wiped out but we couldn't come up with a new ethic. So now the ethic is, do any damn thing you want.

"And the burden is on the poor. Why, in Inglewood, where I used to live, my neighbor was on ADC, but she reminded me of one of those aristocratic southern sisters who were really unlettered but who used to pull their breeding out of the air. One day I was putting bars on my windows. She began to tell me how much she envied me. I thought she was talking about my salary, or the fact that I could write, or something like that. But she meant that she wished she had bars to protect her TV. She was scared to go out. The TV was one of the few small things that gave her pleasure. But she could only afford small sets—ones that were stolen easily—and she'd already lost four. It had gotten to the point where her family took turns guarding the set.

"I have very few friends—professional people—who go out on the street without a gun now. A few months ago, for the first time in my life, I began to consider buying a pistol and taking target practice. I've spent most of my life fighting white society. But now I feel safer in a white neighborhood than I do in the ghetto. I know I'm not buying a gun to protect myself against the Klan.

I'm doing it because of the probability that I might have to kill another black, a youth. And that makes me sick to my gut."

Once, before the civil-rights movement grew impossibly rancorous, it would have been possible to imagine blacks and whites talking candidly about the problems Jarrett was describing, and forging a strategy to combat them. It was even possible, in 1975, to see the outlines of that strategy. An integrated urban movement could develop a program against crime and unemployment —the twin scourges of every city. It could try to regulate large corporations, which deprived blacks and whites of jobs whenever they decided to leave a unionized area in search of cheaper labor. Moreover, an integrated movement could build trust—the cement of organizations—out of mundane, populist issues, like fights against soaring utility rates and banks that redline, fights for better day care, better programs for the elderly, a national health-insurance program crucial to all middle-class and poor people.

But, during the Seventies, only a few faint signs of that movement had emerged. Instead, throughout the decade, the integrated, populist coalitions that did exist were usually shattered by highly charged issues, like scatter-site housing and busing, which released the tribal hatreds that became so intense in Forest Hills and in Boston.

Besides, there was never, at any point in the Seventies, anything approaching the enthusiasm for political discussion—and for working with people of other cultures—that had swept through the campuses and the media just a few years earlier. The left had suffered a handful of setbacks. Some of them were internal, like the split between the blacks and whites who had worked in the South; some were external, like the wave of conspiracy trials that put the left on the defensive; all of that made many of us wary of the emotional risks that came with political actions. Besides, there was no widespread agreement among the people who'd once fought for civil rights and against the war about more complicated issues like busing and affirmative action.

Those setbacks and complexities seemed to paralyze a generation that had once prided itself on its activism. Suddenly, it was psychologically suspect to worry about other people's oppression. Mental health meant a singleminded effort to realize one's own human potential. To those who possessed the educational background or the economic resources for it, the battle for personal liberation seemed tremendously important. But, from the vantage point of the black ghetto, the ideological and emotional energy that went into the search for better sex, better highs, the ideal form of rural life, the perfect brand of psychotherapy, seemed self-indulgent to say the least. It was a parody of a generational promise—a tribal promise, really, embodied in organizations like SNCC and SDS, the Peace Corps and Vista—to work toward political liberation, toward a society where opportunity would be distributed equally.

So there was a terrible vacuum where a movement might have been.

When I interviewed Jackson, the Shermans, and Jarrett in 1975, I thought a political figure who seemed "radical on race matters" conservative on others, might fill that vacuum. In my *Voice* article, I flirted with the apocalyptic notion that George Wallace—still a power to be reckoned with in those days—could take advantage of that situation. After all, he'd done so in the Deep South, where blacks like Charles Evers supported him strongly. Evers went so far as to speculate that Wallace's soul had been redeemed by an assassin's bullet.

Wallace, like Jesse Jackson, was a born-again Christian. Since Arthur Bremer had tried to kill him, his speeches had been laced with the same reverence for God that Grace Sherman had displayed when she talked about her fundamentalist faith. The Shermans sounded harsher than Wallace when they talked about the role the police should play in black communities. Wallace—like Jackson and the Shermans—enjoyed reminiscing about his southern childhood. With his down-home speaking style, he was able to intimate that most liberal politicians were upper-class hypocrites, while he was an unflinchingly honest man who could always reflect the aspirations of blacks and whites in his own social class.

None of that mattered much, as it turned out. Wallace's health was too weak, and his image as a segregationist too strong, to let him win many votes in the North, particularly in the ghettos. But my hunch was not entirely wrong. For Jimmy Carter, an energetic man with no particular image except that of a rural populist, a born-again Christian, campaigned on the same church-centered, traditionalist themes Jackson and the Shermans had sounded; he managed to project himself as a liberal on race and economic matters, a conservative on others; he was elected on the strength of millions of black votes.

If anything, though, Carter's failure to deliver on his campaign promises left blacks, like all Americans, more hungry for leadership than ever.

Jesse Jackson stuck to his strategy for filling the void that the failure of the movement and of conventional politicians had left. He wanted to establish himself as a latter-day Booker T. Washington, an apostle of self-help. He wanted to become a fulcrum for a new set of alliances between blacks and whites—alliances based on ethnicity, on common tribal needs, not on the older patterns of black complaint and white guilt. That was the line he took when he delivered a rousing keynote address to the Republican National Committee in January, 1978: "Blacks need Republicans to compete for us. . . . The Republicans need black people if they are ever to compete for national office." It was the theme he sounded when he told me how blacks and Poles in Chicago—traditionally bitter enemies—could unite around issues like equal opportunity in city government. "We're the two biggest ethnic groups in Chicago, and we both invest more in the Democratic Party than we receive from it. The two smallest ethnic groups, the Irish and the Jews, get much more than we do. In other words, those who get the most out of city government are those who have the least to put into it. That's the basis of an alliance. It's just a matter of groups coming together and realizing who they are."

By 1978, education for blacks had become Jackson's main focus. He had created a nationwide organization called Project Excell, which embodied his ideas about returning to the fundamentals, about instilling self-discipline in black students. It was a way of transporting the southern "love triangle" Jackson had talked about with such nostalgia to the northern ghettos.

He had a plan. Under it, high school students would sign pledges that they'd stay away from their telephones, their record players, their TVs, and any visitors between the hours of seven and nine each night, while they did their homework. Their parents—prodded by ministers or by trade-union leaders—would monitor their activities at home, and go to school to pick up their report cards and consult with their teachers. Their teachers would give out rigorous homework assignments instead of bowing to the sociological argument that black kids couldn't succeed in school because of their broken homes, poor housing, inadequate diets. And the school itself would be an orderly, quiet place, where kids were forbidden to curse or play radios or pop their fingers or dress sloppily or fight.

In 1977, nine schools in Chicago adopted the plan. In 1978, the Los Angeles Board of Education allocated about $400,000 to PUSH to implement the program in eleven schools. That year, the Department of Health, Education, and Welfare granted Excell about $400,000 to implement the program nationally.

One winter day I watched Jackson describe the program to about five hundred teenagers at the all-black Benjamin Cardozo High School in Washington. It was the tenth anniversary of the Kerner Commission report: the week when pundits all over America were concluding that the economic divisions between black and white society had grown even deeper than they had been before the 1967 urban riots. Now, Jackson was using the assembly hall as a church, as he exhorted the kids to reverse that situation by achieving self-mastery in school.

He was an unabashed moralist, but a hip one, who'd woven comedy routines that seemed to have been borrowed from Bill Cosby, gestures of confidence that resembled Muhammad Ali's, into his sermon. He was far more understanding of the black kids than he had been of my generation of civil-rights workers.

Shortly after he began to speak, he told the captain of Cardozo's championship basketball team to stand up, and he asked the kid a litany of questions designed to illustrate his message.

"How often does your team practice?" Jackson wanted to know. "Every weekday." "How many hours?" "Three hours a day." "Do you ever have the radio or the television on during practice?" "No." Jackson pretended to be surprised. "You mean you don't stop to watch TV?" By now, the other kids were laughing and applauding. "Well, suppose," Jackson asked, "suppose you start running and start sweating and start getting tired. Do you sit down then?" "No." "You mean you even work out when you get tired?" More laughter. "Well, do the kids on the team who come from poor families, do they practice at one end of the court while the others practice on the other end of the court?" "No." "You mean," Jackson continued with mock incredulity, "the coach doesn't tell you that because you come from a poor home you can't jump high and run fast?" "No."

Now the captain sat down and, in swelling tones, Jackson delivered the moral punch. "Contrary to what we read in the newspapers, we're not good at basketball because we have soul. I mean, if we had soul we wouldn't have to practice no fifteen hours a week without the radio and the telephone and the television.

"What that really means is that whatever you do—whatever you *decide* to do—for three hours a day, you can do. Whatever people do much and do often they do well. So I challenge you today: If we practice reading and writing and counting for three hours a day, we will be as good at those things as we are at running and shooting and jumping." The applause rolled down like thunder.

The rest of the half-hour speech was studded with remarks that sounded like an updated version of Poor Richard's Almanac or McGuffy's reader—the kind of material Alice Moore (who'd come to admire Jackson by 1978) wanted to see in the Kanawha County textbooks. Jackson warned kids not to smoke cigarettes ("The first little puff is a puff toward winding up in the hospital with some tubes tied down your throat and trying to figure out if you'll survive"); he urged them not to drink alcohol or use dope; he argued that "self-mastery is a revolutionary concept."

Then, using a variety of down-home accents, slapping the podium to express his glee, he turned the traditional John Wayne cowboy movie into an entertaining cautionary tale. In his version, the hero wasn't the rough, tough frontiersman, but the old, bespectacled doctor. "Doc was the strongest man in town not because he could shoot somebody or rassle cows to the ground, or make a lot of noise when he pulled up to the bar, but because he had strengthened his mind. Everyone had to come to him—the preacher, the teacher, the baddest cowboy. You're a real man because you can heal somebody, not because you can kill somebody."

Then he used the allegory to move into the theme he'd discussed with such passion three years earlier. "You're not a man because you can make a baby. You're a man if you can raise a baby, provide for a baby, direct a baby."

Another cascade of applause.

"And you cannot be a first-class woman if you put more emphasis on your butt than on your brain. You will never be respected that way."

The last part of his remark was drowned out by astonished laughter, and even more applause.

Jackson, the preacher, knew how to use that mood. "Say amen."

"Amen," the students chorused.

"Say amen again," Jackson said.

"Amen."

Then, in a swelling voice: "This is your choice. This is your day." And he bade them make the "fundamental decision"—to "take the pledge"—to study two hours a night.

First, those who made it—most of the kids—stood in their places. Then, he invited them to file toward him—the students who wanted to be doctors first, then those who hoped to be lawyers, journalists, engineers. And they came, by the hundreds, filling the front of the auditorium. It was like the Sunday, three years earlier when he'd finished speaking and, in his throbbing voice, urged everyone to come toward him. "The church is open now."

In Chicago, Vernon Jarrett was still writing columns maintaining his criticisms of Jackson. It was increasingly clear that Operation PUSH existed to further Jackson's career, not necessarily to help people like the Shermans. Moreover, Jackson's attempts to reach out to white ethnics had often foundered on his moralistic language—on a Baptist rhetoric laced with phrases like "The good people have remained silent too long"—which sounded self-righteous and patronizing to the mostly Catholic white people he wanted to embrace.

But at the Cardozo High School, that morning, his flaws and failures didn't seem to matter as much as the fact that he was reaching those kids. The auditorium was open. The pledge was a baptism.

There was a rustle of noise in the balcony—for a second my mind flashed back to the assassination attempt I'd seen at the PUSH rally three years before. But it was just a few youngsters who wanted to attract the attention of some TV cameramen who were filming Jackson's speech. Jackson wheeled toward the kids, and spoke to them with a controlled wrath. Now they were villains in a real-life cautionary tale. The Reverend was preaching and teaching by deed—and showing his unceasing obsession with the media as a larger-than-life textbook as he talked.

"Those cameras are projecting us into the homes of people who live in Washington and Virginia, into the homes of congressmen and senators. You should not embarrass all black people by acting uncivilized. Don't just be standing up there and acting nigger. Just be cool so that when they cut the film people will get the impression that black people are civilized. We *are* civilized. Don't embarrass the race."

Soon the auditorium was silent. The five hundred kids in the front of the room bowed their heads and—as they might have in the South—chanted the PUSH pledge as if it were a revived form of school prayer.

"I will help my school and my community by exercising discipline and becoming a positive thinker. I will sacrifice some of my wants of today so that I can satisfy most of my needs of tomorrow. I will learn the secrets of success and practice them daily.

"I will be motivated to accept reality," they chorused, "because nobody can save us from us for us but us."

As I listened to that last grim phrase I thought of how astonishing the entire scene would have been to the Jews, the Irish,

CHAPTER 6

Housing in Forest Hills: But Not Next Door . . .

In the 1960s, it would have been inconceivable to link the Jews of Forest Hills and the Irish of South Boston in the same sentence. Back then, Forest Hills seemed to be a bastion of support for civil rights, a kind of homeland for liberal Jews, a place that would always produce thousands of votes for politicians like Adlai Stevenson or John Lindsay, thousands of dollars for idealistic, progressive causes like the Mississippi Summer Project, busloads of demonstrators for peace rallies in Washington. Southie, staunchly Catholic, proudly conservative, fiercely pro-Vietnam War, already symbolized northern resistance to desegregation. But in the 1970s both communities launched protest movements to seal themselves off from blacks and Hispanics.

Forest Hills wasn't an ancestral home, like Kanawha County or Southie—not a place where each idle conversation moved to the rich rhythms of shared memories that stretched back generations. Until the 1940s, Forest Hills had been sparsely settled countryside, a pastoral place where sheep and goats grazed, where city kids came to hunt or fish or play hide-and-go-seek. Then, during World War II, the first wave of Jews—immigrants from the Lower East Side—began to settle in that paradise. There, they could forget the noisy, crowded tenements where they'd lived as kids; they could free themselves of the last traces of their parents' greenhorn habits; forget about keeping kosher or observing *Shabbos*. They could create a solid, *American* environment for their own offspring.

The world they created contained traces of the *shtetl*—the small eastern European villages most of their grandparents had been raised in—and signs of the assimilated America their children were about to enter. You could see that on Queens Boulevard, at the huge Reform and Conservative temples that overflowed during the High Holy days, Rosh Hashonah and Yom Kippur. There, old people spoke Yiddish; young adults—doctors, lawyers, business people—dressed in their finest suits and furs—mink prayer shawls, the women called them—their symbols of status in America. In the 1950s, teenagers sat on the synagogue steps, discussing Elvis Presley or Camus.

At a time when memories of anti-semitism were still sharp and painful, Forest Hills seemed a safe haven for Jews. So, in the late Fifties and Sixties, the neighborhood attracted fresh waves of migrants, survivors of Hitler's Europe and refugees from changing neighborhoods, like the South Bronx or Bedford-Stuyvesant, where sudden, incomprehensible bursts of violence had made life a constant strain. These were older people, for the most part, who felt they could only achieve psychological stability if they lived side-by-side with other Jews.

By 1970, Forest Hills had become two subtly different communities. The first, relatively well-to-do settlers, lived near Queens Boulevard, near the elegant West Side tennis club, where the annual U.S. national championships were held. Most of them saw the neighborhood as a way station en route to the American dream: Their kids would live in even more prosperous communities like Great Neck or Scarsdale. Meanwhile, the second group, the somewhat poorer newcomers, regarded the community as a refuge. Many of them lived in the relatively inexpensive six-story apartment buildings—garden apartments—near the Long Island Expressway, about a mile away from the comfortable bustle of Queens Boulevard.

Then, in 1971, the Lindsay administration began to build a low-income housing project consisting of three twenty-four-story buildings on a vacant lot near the expressway. The buildings would dwarf the garden apartments where the newcomers lived.

Later, city officials would explain that New York needed those low-income units in order to conform to the Department of Housing and Urban Development's guidelines for federal funding. They decided to locate them in Forest Hills, they said, because the area seemed so much more liberal than Kew Gardens or Canarsie or the Rockaways—other sites that had been under consideration.

They had made some efforts to consult with local people. But their contacts mostly represented the first wave of settlers, those who lived in relative comfort, blocks away from the proposed project site. The city's first meeting with the community was scheduled for a Friday night, when most of the religiously observant people in the predominantly Jewish neighborhood were either at home or at synagogue. The mayor's representatives weren't directly exposed to the undercurrents of tension that were eddying through the area. For example, few of them realized that busing had already produced some racial tensions in Forest Hills's high schools; that some local people were already worrying about the incidents of crime that were occurring in the large nearby Lefrak City housing development—and that those fears would affect the neighborhood's attitude toward the project.

So the city's representatives didn't see the need to prepare the psychologically embattled people who lived near the project site for something that threatened to reproduce the tensions they had sought to flee. There were no widespread community discussions about how the tenants would be selected or how police protection could be increased. Few city officials described the benefits the project could bring the community. They never stressed the fact that the presence of carefully screened minority families in the neighborhood could mean an end to the more random device of busing as a way to integrate the schools or that the project itself could bring social-service programs—lunch programs for the elderly, day-care facilities, health clinics—that could make the area a more pleasant place to live.

As a result, most of Forest Hills was consumed by a wave of hysteria. The few local people who favored the project had to buttress their case with moral arguments or plans that sounded utopian instead of producing encouraging information about improvements in the neighborhood that might actually occur.

As soon as construction work on the project began, thousands of Forest Hills residents—who had voted for Lindsay just two years before—organized a resistance movement, a sustained protest against City Hall, featuring tactics they'd learned from civil-rights struggles. That brought them a barrage of newspaper and TV coverage. They were determined to keep the intruders out of their American Eden.

Their resistance divided Manhattan liberals into camps that had begun to form during the 1969 teachers' strike. Some, like Ed Koch, then a congressman (and the *Voice*'s favorite politician), now New York's mayor, picketed and spoke out in the resisters' behalf. In those days it took some courage for a Greenwich Village politician to do that. But he didn't distinguish between their legitimate fears and the raw bigotry those fears released.

Others, officials in the Lindsay administration for example, dismissed the Forest Hills residents as "rednecks" without ever trying to understand the feelings that made their protest so fervent. The argument lasted only a few months. It polarized the city for years.

Forest Hills was a tormented community. The project's opponents complained about its size and worried that the 840 families slated to move there would leave the already crowded area hopelessly congested. But, beneath all that, they were profoundly frightened of the potential influx of poor blacks and Hispanics. Many of them spoke about the influx as an invading disease that would infest the entire community. Virtually everyone I interviewed agreed that they wouldn't protest a three-building twenty-four-story luxury-apartment complex on the project site. Many said they'd feel calmer if the city had planned a project whose tenants were mostly low-income whites.

They were afraid of *them*. Of welfare cases. Of projects filled with blacks and Latins. Of urine in the hallways, dope in the schools, muggings, rapes, murders. The litany was the same in every interview I conducted, in apartment buildings and public schools, in stores and on street corners, at demonstrations and community meetings. The fact that 40 per cent of the project's housing would go to senior citizens didn't console the people I met. "They" would take over anyway—"they" always do. "They" had already caused at least half the people I met to flee to Forest Hills from the South Bronx or Brooklyn or the Lower East Side. Now, everyone said, another exodus would occur as soon as the project was built.

I continued to support the project, at least in some modified form. For, to me, *them* was Grace and Arthur Sherman or the Martinez family. But, since I believed that fear of crime is one of the starkest realities of the city, and that fear of black crime was turning thousands of people—including many of my friends—into closet racists, I was determined to explore the comments I heard instead of arguing about them. I saw Forest Hills as a looking glass for New York's future, not as a lightning rod for my own frustration with the new racism.

Anyway, I realized, a reporter covering a tribal battle has to be able to hold two conflicting realities in his mind at the same time. He has to let his opinions, his emotions, be influenced by the opinions and emotions of the people he's interviewing. He has to be open to the possibility that an experience will reshape him.

In Forest Hills that meant I had to reexamine some Manhattan-bred attitudes. After just a few days there it seemed to me priggish to criticize the people I met for feeling that the welfare clients who moved into the project (with conveniences like air conditioning and recreational facilities many middle-class people don't possess) would get something for nothing. And, of course, it was dishonest to dismiss the fear of minority-group crime—which was based on real experience—as undiluted racism.

Despite all that, though, there was something more ugly and violent going on than I had imagined when I decided to write about Forest Hills.

Fear was a plague in Forest Hills. It had obliterated reason and compassion. For many, a few bad experiences with blacks and Hispanics had bred racial stereotypes that very few religious, political, or community leaders dared challenge.

You saw displays of that fear from the moment you arrived at the subway station at 71st and Continental Avenue. When the anti-project protests began, a militantly radical group called Youth Against War and Fascism had plastered the walls with posters saying DOWN WITH RACISM IN FOREST HILLS. Within a few days, the words NIGGER LOVER had been scrawled on a few signs. On another poster, someone had crossed off DOWN WITH RACISM and written UP WITH RACISM.

I first noticed those signs on a cold December Sunday, when I went out to Forest Hills for a large demonstration at the construction site. For a while, I was convinced those words were total aberrations. About fifteen hundred people were there, and their mood, for most of the afternoon, was more jovial than angry. They chuckled at their own turgid slogans ("Down with the project."). Many of them seemed to maintain an ironic detachment from their own new militancy.

I spent much of the afternoon talking with an elderly man and woman, refugees from Romania who'd fled to Russia during World War II, then migrated to Newark, Greenwich Village, and now Forest Hills, where they owned a grocery. They'd been chased and harassed all their lives—first by Hitler, then by the Communists, then by blacks in Newark and Italians in the Village. They were convinced that people are better off among their own kind: Certainly they wanted nothing more than to spend their old age among Jews. When I mentioned that I was Jewish, the old woman asked me, "Do you think we'll all be chased from New York, too?" What gruesome experience echoed in her mind to produce that question? Surely, her longing for security was not a form of bigotry.

But, in a flash, it fused with the angry mood that had produced the scrawled Nigger Lover on the subway wall.

We were still talking when some counterdemonstrators— NAACP and Urban League members, people from the Youth Against War and Fascism—began to march away from the construction site. Until then the two groups had been separated by about thirty policemen and about five hundred feet of space. There was little talk between them. Now, hundreds of protesters, including the couple from Romania, began to taunt them. "Good-bye Commies, good-bye Commies, good-bye Commies, we're glad

to see you go. Good-bye muggers, good-bye muggers, good-bye
muggers, we're glad to see you go."

I asked the couple if the crowd's chant about black people had
awakened memories of chants that had been directed at them because they were Jews. It hadn't.

"You see, we're trying to protect ourselves here," the old man
said. "I wish the Jews had done the same thing in Europe.

Several nights later I was walking to a meeting where the protest leaders planned to reveal their strategy for dealing with John
Lindsay. On the way, I began to eavesdrop on a middle-aged man
who was boasting about his. "If Lindsay ever gets to be president,
I'll kill him. I'll do just what Oswald did to John Kennedy."

A companion interrupted his reverie. "You won't get a chance.
Lindsay is going to get shot right here in New York."

A random, ranting threat that distorts a community's mood as
soon as it's put in print? I didn't think so. The day before, I'd
been talking with a sixth-grade class at P.S. 220, across the street
from the project site, and the kids began to complain about Lindsay's refusal to meet with the community. "If he ever comes here,
I'll beat him up," one of the kids said. "I'll kill him," said another. The tone of the session had been quite friendly and now I
asked them, in a relaxed way, whether they agreed with the sentiment. Many of them said they did. A few even applauded it.

I spent several hours one afternoon, going from door to door in
an apartment building near the project site, talking with anyone
who would open the door. Because of the hour, I met only
women—the wife of an accountant, of a jewelry-store manager, of
a restaurant inspector; a widow, a schoolteacher, a divorcee. They
all opposed the city's plan. They expected to leave Forest Hills if
the project were built.

All of them were resentful of the welfare recipients who, they
thought, would get something for nothing. "My husband had a
stroke six years ago," the wife of the jewelry-store manager said.
"That forced us to move here from Long Island, where we owned
our own house. He could be collecting disability here if he wanted
to. But he's too proud for that. Every day he goes into Manhat-

tan, wheelchair and all, and does his job. Why should someone
who doesn't work live as well as we do? Believe me, I don't care
about color. If Negroes who can afford to want to live in this
building, that's fine with me. Plenty do already. But it's the idea
of those people getting something for nothing that burns me up."

The restaurant inspector's wife used to live in the South Bronx,
she said—"a lovely neighborhood until they moved the project in.
Then the crimes began." She'd held on until just two Jewish
families lived on a predominantly Spanish-speaking block. Finally
she left, and her apartment was rented to a Puerto Rican family.
"Fine Puerto Ricans. But I'll tell you something. I went back to
visit the house a month later, and my own things were so dirty I
couldn't recognize them. My refrigerator. My stove. My house
was a filthy mess. That's the way those people are.

"During the Depression, my family was literally starving. My father worked eighteen hours a day to put us through school. Why
do these people need welfare? Why can't they work, too?"

When I hear comments like that, I feel as if I'm on a tape
recording that spools back to my earliest years of political consciousness. I must have argued about whether welfare recipients
are lazy or unable to find work a thousand times by now. So I decided to pass up that debate and find out whether she felt, as I always had, that our own history of persecution gives Jews a special
responsibility to fight injustice.

I might as well have argued about welfare for all the com-
munication that little remark inspired. It had nothing at all to do
with her fears or her resentments. So I said that maybe, under
pressure, there was nothing so special about Jews at all, maybe
most of us were as greedy as Poles or Italians or WASPs. She not
only agreed. She—and all her neighbors—looked at me as if I
were saying the most obvious thing in the world.

The angriest person I met that day was a twenty-five-year-old
divorcee, the mother of a five-year-old, who complained about
"the human garbage" that would move into the project and
"infest" the neighborhood. It had already happened at P.S. 220,
where her son went to school. "The little punks they bus in here

pick on all the neighborhood kids," she said. Then: "The neighborhood has already changed. It's so bad here by now, maybe it doesn't even matter if the project comes in."

She mentioned several places where the black and white schoolchildren fight: at a Baskin-Robbins and a Woolworth's in the nearby shopping area, and at the public schools. During the next several days, I checked them all out.

The manager of Baskin-Robbins told me that he rarely has any problem with teenagers. "I like the kids and I guess they like me, too. Whenever any of them gives me trouble—which doesn't happen often—I'm firm. And the troublemakers are just as likely to be white as they are black."

When I went into Woolworth's at eleven-thirty on a Wednesday morning, the saleslady I interviewed had a very different reaction. "Of course there's trouble here. Every day. It should be beginning right now, at lunch hour. You'll see. They steal everything. They act just like what they are. Cannibals. You know who I'm talking about. The little dears they bus into P.S. 220, Halsey Junior High, and Forest Hills High. It always happens when they come into a neighborhood. They're filthy. They rob and burn and murder. We can't let them in here."

She walked over to the cash register and a young man, the floor manager, began to talk with me. "I don't agree with her," he said. "There's things to be said for the project and things against it. I'd like to see it work. I know I was raised to be a bigot. Anyone who says he wasn't is lying. But in the last ten years I've tried to change."

Then, musing: "Sometimes it's rough around here, though. I'll tell you, if many more black kids call me a whitey motherfucker, I'll go back to being a bigot. Why shouldn't I? It's all so confusing."

"Oh, it's not confusing at all"—now a middle-aged cosmetics salesman who'd overheard the conversation was talking—"I'll tell you what it is. It's time to declare open season."

"What?" I asked.

"Open season. Don't you know anything? Haven't you ever been in the Army or been hunting?"

"Yeah," I said. "But are you going to do the killing or be killed?"

"I can tell you this. I'll do my fair share of the killing."

The saleslady motioned me over to the cash register. "Watch. You'll see what happens here."

What I saw was a five-and-ten-cent store that suddenly became as tense as an airport after a rash of skyjackings. When the first cluster of students entered, salespeople and clerks on every aisle dropped what they'd been doing to study the kids' movements. "Would you believe that one girl stole twelve dollars' worth of jewelry from me the other day?" the floor manager said. "That's the kind of thing we're looking for." A black kid couldn't pick up a piece of candy, a comic book, or a ball without an employee edging closer. Some of the black kids reacted to the surveillance. They'd tense—then pretend to be cool, to disguise their feelings. For the first time, I wondered whether the project would really be so desirable for them. What if it meant a life of being watched?

Most of the kids exited through the middle aisle. Past the candy counter the employees checked some of them—whites as well as blacks—for thefts. They were usually deferential to the whites, harsh with the blacks.

Anyway, nothing was stolen. When it was all over, the floor manager turned to me and said apologetically, "This was a relatively easy one. I guess some of them stayed at home. You should come here when it's really rough."

I left for lunch a few minutes later but, before I could get to the delicatessen where I'd planned to eat, I ran into the cosmetics salesman again.

"Why don't you just make your story up?" he asked.

"Okay. Tell me what it should say."

"I'll write the headline for you. FOREST HILLS DECLARES OPEN SEASON ON NIGGERS."

"So you really want to fight?"

"I'd love to, my friend. I have two guns oiled and ready."

"Are you Jewish?" I asked him.

"No." I guess he thought I was wondering if he lived in Forest

Hills. He'd been born there, he volunteered, but he'd moved to Nassau County ten years before.

I told him I *was* Jewish, and that I didn't like the idea of an open season on blacks. In the Thirties and Forties Germans must have said the same things about Jews.

It was another arrow from my quiver of clichs, and it misfired.

"*You're* safe here," he reassured me. "We white people can live together okay. It's these black people who are ruining the country. They're the ones I'd love to shoot down on the streets."

"What will happen after that?"

"There will be happy days."

I wondered, before describing that interview in the *Voice*, whether the salesman's words were too marginal to quote—the kind of unvarnished racism that can only increase a community's tensions. But the cosmetic salesman said he was a member of the Nassau County grand jury and described his work in such detail that I figured he wasn't bluffing. He really could bring indictments. Besides, in Forest Hills, 1971, where school kids applauded remarks about killing a mayor, where Jews felt free to stereotype low-income blacks as "garbage" or "cannibals" or "punks," where politicians like Ed Koch defended the resisters uncritically, I had begun to wonder whether the cosmetic salesman's views might be closer to the mainstream of New York politics than I thought.

Only a few people in Forest Hills openly supported the project. Most were so concerned about community sanctions that they perferred to remain silent—or anonymous, if they were quoted.

But one day I was talking with people in the lobby of the comfortable Fairview Towers a block from the project site when a schoolteacher named Chuck Favreau, thirty, decided to break that pattern. "I want your readers to know that there are some people in Forest Hills who favor the project," he said.

"You have to understand. I don't believe that the people here are racists. They really have been ripped off by blacks and Puerto Ricans. Their fear is a real thing. If there's more violence after the project comes, a lot of them will move away."

Nevertheless, he thought that harmony depended on how the

white community conducted itself. "If we're hostile, then you can be sure the project people will be hostile. If they think the store owners and apartment owners despise them, they'll begin to rip us off. I see that in my classroom all the time. When people feel threatened, they fight back."

He felt it was crucial to develop institutions to bridge the gap between the two worlds—sports leagues, or a food cooperative, or a nursery school, service centers that would be located within the project's facilities. "Of course, you can't do much now that the community is scared. But maybe those things will be possible once people get used to the idea that the project really will be built. Maybe then people will see that, in a way, their survival depends on getting to know their new neighbors."

After I was finished talking with Chuck Favreau I noticed that the doorman was hovering near me. At first I thought the tenants might have asked him to keep an eye on me. But, after a while, it occurred to me that he might have something he wanted to say.

So I asked him, in English, what he thought of the project, and he said, in a slow, halting Spanish accent, that he'd like to live in such a place. My Spanish was better than his English, so I decided to switch languages to make it easier for him.

Right now, he said, he and his wife lived in a neighborhood in Brooklyn, a place that terrified him. "People here talk as if we're criminals. I'm not a criminal. I don't like shootings or dirty streets or garbage in my building. Sometimes when I walk down the street I want to throw up. I don't want to raise my children there. Of course I'd like to live in a neighborhood like this one."

I asked if he thought people in Forest Hills were prejudiced against poor blacks and Puerto Ricans. "It's not only the poor," he said. "There are some Negroes who live in this building, doctors and lawyers. You should see how nervous the white people get whenever they come to the door. I don't think they want any of us to live here."

A few weeks later, after I described the interview in the *Voice*, I got a letter from Forest Hills telling me that the doorman had been fired. "The other workmen in the building will not say why. We had seen him often up until the time your article was published and then, after a few days, we never saw him again. He was always a very kind and warm person. It shocks us to think that in this day and age people still cannot speak freely. If this man has lost his job because of the free expression of his beliefs, then he is the first casualty of the Forest Hills housing struggle.

"We are sorry that, because of personal reasons, we have to remain anonymous."

Yet the protest in Forest Hills wasn't only a matter of bigotry and intimidation and name-calling. Thousands of people—liberal Jews—were tormented by the issues behind it. One reader wrote me a letter that expressed their agony more clearly than anyone I'd interviewed.

"I've lived in Forest Hills ever since there was a Forest Hills, and I've always been labeled a liberal. I've been a participant in all the 'right' causes for many years, even before it became fashionable. I've preached the 'right' doctrines to my kids not because they are educationally sound but because I believed them. Blacks are important, worthwhile, good people. I've exposed my kids to black kids when I could and have for years sent them to a semi-integrated camp, while all the other kids here in Forest Hills were going to typical middle-class Jewish camps. My kids have had positive experiences with black kids and my words were beginning to make sense.

"Then my son began to attend high school. He would come home at least three times a week with stories about the violent, truly terrifying episodes that occurred there. And each one involved black kids. Two girls were cut up with a scissors. Black kids did the cutting. Kids were fighting in a gang war and the school was evacuated early. Black kids were either fighting with white kids or with each other. My son couldn't leave his books or coat in school during lunch hour. Why? 'They would be stolen by the time I returned.'

"I told him, 'True, this is the way some black kids act, but let's never forget why they act that way.' Then I went on and on with the whole story of oppression and rage felt by black people.

"But then it hit me very hard—I was giving my son *feeling* and he was giving me *reality!* I really do not know what to say any longer. I know what I believe, but at this point my feelings are so ambivalent I can't think straight."

Her letter prompted me to spend some time at Forest Hills High School. It was clear, after talking to whites there, that many of them felt the same way as her son. But it was also clear that she'd ignored the equally deep uneasiness that ate away at the kids who were bused in there from Jamaica and East Elmhurst.

The bus had clearly created its own subculture. The black kids, many of whom had never before gone to school with whites, got to know each other on the hour-long rides back and forth from Forest Hills. They rarely mixed with their classmates during the day. They couldn't visit them after school since they had to be on the bus as soon as the last bell rang.

When I walked through the cafeteria I saw blacks clustered at one set of tables, whites at another. On the street in front of the school, conversations took place in segregated groups. Very few blacks were involved in extracurricular activities, like Sing or the government organization or the school newspaper. Very few whites understood the reason.

After school I listened to Stanley McBean, the son of a cop, the head of Forest Hills's Afro-American Association, discuss the project with some black kids and some very liberal whites. Everyone else believed that once the buildings were actually constructed— once blacks and whites had to deal with each other on a daily basis—the kind of fear-filled isolation that pervaded the high school would disappear. But Stanley disagreed.

"We come from different cultures, different backgrounds," he said. "That's the reason for the isolation in the school. I think it's a class thing—not a race thing—but it is going to exist when the project comes in here. What will happen if the crime rate goes up? Then it will all be blamed on the 'niggers' and the 'spics.'"

One of the blacks began to argue that heroin causes crime, that maybe blacks and whites could base a lasting coalition on a program that kept the junkies out. But that idea sounded wishful to Stanley. I thought his reaction was an appropriate answer to my letter from the tormented liberal.

"What about all the people who are unemployed and have to eat? They may come in with the project. What happens when a person who comes in here gets laid off his job and sees that welfare isn't enough to feed his family? Those people might commit crimes in order to survive. I think people here are going to blame the project, not poverty.

"You know," he said a little bitterly, "sometimes I think people are going to blame the project for everything that goes wrong here —even traffic jams."

It was a time for healers—for people who could tell complicated, painful truths gently and compassionately. And I met some in Forest Hills. The Favreaus, of course. And Mrs. Rose Schwerner, a teacher at P.S. 220 who favored the project. Her nephew, Mickey Schwerner, had been one of the three civil-rights workers murdered in Mississippi during the 1964 Freedom Summer. She was willing to make a sacrifice to live out her beliefs. She and her husband had already applied to live in the project, in one of the apartments for the elderly, just to prove the place was safe for white people. (But they weren't chosen to live there.)

"Some of my old progressive friends tell me I'm crazy now not to fear blacks," she said. "Others say that since even liberal congressmen, like Ben Rosenthal, oppose the project they do, too. And, in my heart of hearts, I worry there might be something to that. I worry about violence in the other projects, like the Baruch houses on the Lower East Side, and I get scared. I guess it may be more dangerous here if they build a project.

"But I always remember a book I read years ago, *But Not Next Door*. . . . And that's what is happening throughout the city. Frightened people are saying, put them somewhere else, but not here, not next door. So the hostility and fear keep getting worse.

"It's got to start somewhere," she said. "I know it may be difficult, but next door might as well be here."

To me, that was the kind of tone politicians like Ben Rosenthal and Ed Koch—and John Lindsay—could have adopted: a calm one that admitted torments and tensions and stressed the importance of working them out in a human way. So, one of my most disturbing moments in Forest Hills 1971, came when Mrs. Schwerner asked me to disguise her identity if I quoted her, for fear that people in the neighborhood would recognize her family name, recoil at its integrationist connotations, and dismiss her ideas out of hand.

When I revisited Forest Hills, more than six years later, the fever of hysteria had broken. Everyone I interviewed—including Mrs. Schwerner—was willing to be mentioned by name.

For the community had won its battle. It had forced the city to compromise: to reduce the housing development into three twelve-story co-op buildings. There are now 434 housing units—40 per cent for senior citizens—which are divided according to the ethnic ratios of the zip-code areas closest to Forest Hills: 65 per cent for white, 35 per cent for nonwhite. That means about eighty of the young families who have moved into the buildings belong to racial minorities.

All the tenants are very carefully screened. They're asked to produce their bank statements and job records, sometimes to list their reasons for wanting to move into the building, sometimes to disclose the amount of years they've been married. It's like a college interview, where the most obviously stable people are accepted.

As the tenants are quick to point out, they live in a cooperative, not a housing project. They have paid seventy-five dollars for each room; in addition, they pay their monthly maintenance cost. You can see from the lovely lawns, the spotless walls, the ease with which all races mingle, that that part of the compromise was a stroke of genius: The tenants have a stake in the appearance and the mood of their home. "Ever since I moved in here I've felt like I was on my way to the American dream," said Martha Cerro, twenty-nine, a Colombian woman, an accountant's wife, who came to this country eight years ago. It was the kind of remark you might have heard from a Jew who'd moved to Forest Hills from the Lower East Side in the late 1940s.

Now, ironically, the surrounding neighborhood regards the buildings as a source of stability. When I revisited Forest Hills, many of the merchants were worried about a new crime wave.

During a three-day period, a bank, a restaurant, and a gift shop were all burglarized. Stanley McBean's prophecy was wrong—no one blames the "project" (as most people in Forest Hills still call the cooperative). Instead, they blame the "garbage"—by which they mean Hispanics—who moved into the garden apartments the Jews deserted in response to the panic of the early 1970s.

Still, for the moment, American Jews, Israelis, Puerto Ricans, Pakistanis, and refugees from the Soviet Union are all coexisting on the same few blocks. They are serviced by a Community House at the Forest Hills Cooperative, which offers the wide variety of programs that seemed utopian when Chuck Favreau outlined them years ago. As Favreau predicted, people in the neighborhood come to the "project"— the turf that once seemed so threatening—simply to take advantage of that facility. Their youngsters all attend P.S. 220, where a classroom full of kids, infected with the plague of fear, once applauded a boy who boasted he'd kill Mayor Lindsay. Dr. Marcia Knoll, P.S. 220's principal, says she always supported the buildings, even the original Lindsay plan, for she was convinced that the families who moved there would be upwardly mobile, eager to educate their kids. Besides, she adds, the 125 students who cross the street from the "project" to the school have given P.S. 220 enough of an ethnic mix that it can qualify for federal desegregation funds and still phase out busing. Now the parents of minority children can visit the school without making the long, expensive, three-transfer ride from East Elmhurst or Jamaica. Their kids don't have to board the bus when the last bell rings. They can cement their friendships with neighborhood kids through after-school play.

So, the melting pot is perking peacefully in Forest Hills. Still, when you drive back to Manhattan, through Harlem, through the Upper West Side, you can't help but see the compromise as a defeat. Eighty minority families in that small housing development. There should be developments like that all over the city. But after the Forest Hills controversy, only the bravest city administration would risk integrating another neighborhood with a scatter-site housing project. For hundreds of thousands of blacks and Hispanics who still live in New York City's tenements, the peace in Forest Hills is like the peace of the grave.

Still, there is harmony that exists on those few blocks in Forest Hills. But when I revisited the neighborhood, I learned that a new racial confrontation was brewing just a few miles away. In the spring of 1978, a school board representing Jewish and Catholic homeowners in the relatively affluent Bayside-Fresh Meadows section of Queens, had voted, five to four, to reject more than a million dollars' worth of federal funds if the district's teachers and students were required to submit to a government-sponsored ethnic census. At the same time, the board decided to reject fifty federally funded jobs, on the grounds that they were all earmarked for low-income kids—which meant black kids. They were weary, they said, of paying taxes to a government that reserved all its jobs for poor kids.

The average income of homeowners in that district was about twenty thousand dollars. It was a little wealthier than Forest Hills. About 70 per cent of the people who lived there told *New York Times* pollsters that they didn't just object to the ethnic census and the jobs program. They disliked busing, too. But, ironically, the largely middle-aged, middle-class population of white people needed busing in a way that Forest Hills had never needed the housing project. For they had just twelve thousand kids of their own, while New York City law says a school district must have fifteen thousand students. So they bused in three thousand black kids from places like Queens Village. Then, when the federally funded job program was announced, they called those same youths a burden to the middle class.

I went to a community meeting there one night, at P.S. 179 in Fresh Meadows. It was as frenzied as the meetings I'd attended in Forest Hills. Some Jews in the audience talked about how Nazi Germany was the most recent country to require an ethnic census, how the census had been a forerunner to Hitler's Final Solution. There were a handful of blacks, and they claimed the white people sounded like George Wallace and Bull Conner in the worst days of the 1960s. It reminded me of dozens of disputes I'd heard during a decade of covering tribal wars in New York: pitched battles between the oppressed, where the century's most blood-curdling atrocities were used as ammunition in each side's rhetorical fusillade. Sometimes it seemed as if history's most honored martyrs—the slaves and the victims of the holocaust—were rising up to fight their own ghostly wars on the sidewalks of New York.

That week the school board had been suspended by New York City's Board of Education. So, alongside the rhetoric of segregation and the holocaust, there were frequent, impassioned speeches about the impending revolt of the middle-class taxpayer, about the tyranny of the central government, about the new Boston tea party that would begin that month in Queens. I'd heard that language from Kanawha County's Christian soldiers; from the vigilantes of Highway 80; on the picket lines in Forest Hills. I'd heard it throughout my years on the New Left. Everyone seemed eager to threaten a second American revolution: It was a highly stylized rhetorical formula, I knew. Nevertheless, its very persistence made me feel that I was living in a country whose ideas about unity had gone awry, whose political center couldn't hold. That night, in Fresh Meadows, I felt the same forebodings that had filled me when I witnessed the terrible violence that accompanied court-ordered busing in Boston.

CHAPTER 7

Busing in Boston:
The Fire This Time

Turf is sacred in Boston—especially if you're white—and that was true long before the battles over busing began.

You weren't just Irish in that city; you were Irish from Savin Hill or Charlestown or South Boston. And, within your enclave, you were part of an even smaller fiefdom. In South Boston, say, your street corner was your turf. You belonged to a gang—the Aces, the Panthers, the Red Raiders—and you put all your passion into rough games, buck-buck or ringolevio, and the ferocious fights where you tried to prove that your block was the home of the bravest warriors in the neighborhood.

Once or twice a year—certainly after the annual South Boston-East Boston football game—you formed an alliance with all the kids from all the adjacent street corners for a drunken, bloody brawl with the Italian kids from across town. Those encounters produced memories, Homeric epics, that lodged themselves permanently in the neighborhood's soul. "We practice ancestor worship here," a forty-two-year-old man who works at a Gillette factory told me in September 1974, when I was in South Boston, covering the first, violent weeks of the busing crisis. "See that man over there? He's been away from this neighborhood for twenty-seven years, in the Marines. I think he's been decorated five times. But I still see him as Honey McDonnaugh's boy, since Honey made his reputation here, among us, as one of Southie's best golden-gloves fighters."

Some strands of experience and memories have always connected the immigrants' children who inhabit the enclaves—the Italians in the North End, say, to the Lithuanians over by Andrews Square and the Irish at the Old Colony housing project.

They are united by their love of athletes (of Ted Williams and Yaz; of the Cooz; of Rocky Marciano). They are Catholics, and even those who don't attend mass feel a special affection for the social events—the hops, the Bingo games, the annual variety shows—that take place at the parish house. They are lifelong Democrats, who speak of John Kennedy as if he were a sort of secular saint, who love to gossip and boast about the tough, intricate, clannish political system his grandfather Honey Fitz did so much to create.

They are united by an abiding distrust of the Yankee elite—for the most part, Republican Protestants—who dominated Boston's politics until the turn of the century, whose descendants still control much of its economy though they live in remote suburbs like Dover and Beverly Farms, Wellesley and Lincoln, Lexington and Concord. It was the Yankees who forced them (or at least forced the Irish, who were here at the time) to go South in the Civil War, then paid them slave wages in the mill towns they'd built, like Lawrence and Lowell; who supported Judge Webster Thayer when he decided to execute the Italian anarchists, Sacco and Vanzetti; who applauded Senator Henry Cabot Lodge, Brahmin of Brahmins, when he insisted on the genetic inferiority of Southern Europeans as he stumped for the 1925 anti-immigrant laws. Those clashes, once so stark and painful, have faded into flickering impressions, traces of memories, but they produced a residue of hatred for the WASP aristocracy. And that hatred spilled over into the busing crisis: sometimes people talked about the court-ordered integration plan as if it were part of the same ancient, mysterious conspiracy between Brahmins and blacks that produced the Civil War.

In the past, Boston's white tribes have fought each other fiercely. These days, though, anti-black feeling can weld them into a unified fighting force. The irony is that though there has always been a residue of racism in the city, it was a latent, passive emotion until the 1960s since less than 10 per cent of the population was black. Then, suddenly, school segregation became the issue that dominated Boston's political life.

Between 1950 and 1960 about twenty-five thousand blacks moved there. In 1960, fourteen of the city's schools were 50 to 85 per cent black; fifteen more were 90 per cent black. Some of them lacked essential equipment, like textbooks, lightbulbs—even toilet paper. The all-white school system refused even to admit that those problems existed. So, organizations like the NAACP and Freedom House spearheaded marches and school boycotts to demand a better, integrated educational system.

Those organizations were part of the civil-rights movement; many of their leaders came from working-class families or were migrants from the South. But some belonged to a small caste of black aristocrats who had lived in the North for generations. In the early 1900s, W. E. B. Dubois has described them and their southern counterparts as "the Talented Tenth" who bore the special responsibility of helping the other 90 per cent of their race. It had been a more difficult process than Dubois had realized back then. Throughout the twentieth century the black aristocracy had experienced a special pain that was rarely discussed in public.

Many of its members had degrees from prestigious black schools, like Fiske or Howard. Some, like Dubois and William Monroe Trotter and Frank Snowdon (whose son Otto now runs Freedom House) had graduated from Harvard in the 1890s, when John Kennedy's grandfather Honey Fitz was still one of a hundred street-smart Irish kids trying to work his way up in ward politics. Their society—mostly Protestant and Republican, like the WASP elite—included highly esteemed doctors and lawyers, ministers and diplomats, scholars and writers.

But their apparent freedom was a constant sorrow. For in generation after generation they saw immigrant kids (like the Kennedys), less cultivated, no more talented than their own, rise to positions of power in America. They rarely acquired any power outside the boundaries of their own circumscribed world. So, when their descendants became involved in the school-integration movement that historic fact added an extra fillip of complexity to the already tense relations between blacks and whites. For they possessed a degree of refinement and breeding that most of the Irish and Italians from Southie and the North End so plainly and painfully lacked. And they felt the special hurt and anger of an aristocracy whose destiny has been aborted.

Of course, they were not alone in the movement. Many other blacks felt the different hurt and anger of people whose children would never get a chance at a decent education in America. Still, by later standards, the marches and rallies they organized in the early Sixties seem mild indeed.

But from the vantage point of South Boston and the North End even those protests looked like a siege. If you think your turf is sacred, any appeal for integration can sound like a declaration of war. Politicians like Louise Day Hicks, then on the School Committee, rose to citywide prominence by promising that the black intruders would never invade ancestral soil. She and her allies compressed a century's worth of xenophobia into a single, simple vow—that they would protect the neighborhood schools.

The promise was impossible to fulfill—which is one reason Mrs. Hicks, the darling of the enclaves in the pre-busing years, lost her seat on the City Council in 1977, when busing was a fait accompli.

There was a little-noted irony behind the School Committee's rhetoric. From the mid-Sixties to the advent of busing, the quality of education improved slightly in black communities—and deteriorated in the white neighborhoods Mrs. Hicks and her allies were pledged to protect. The young, innovative teachers who might have made the curriculum more exciting had too little seniority— and an ideology that was too liberal—to be assigned to the white schools. As a kind of punishment for their enthusiasm, they were usually sent to black neighborhoods, where they made education more interesting. The School Committee didn't authorize the construction of many new facilities in Boston. But most of those that were built were in neighborhoods that changed from white to black before they were completed.

The truth was that, by 1973, the schools in South Boston and Charlestown were no better than the schools in Roxbury or Co-

lumbia Point. For the most part, Boston's public-education system had become a dumping ground for poor kids of every background imaginable. But it was impossible to shift the terms of the
debate from race to class. For both sides had a vested psychological interest in maintaining that the crucial struggle was between blacks and whites.

In 1972, the NAACP filed a class-action suit against the School
Committee and the state Board of Education that alleged that
Boston's schools had violated the plaintiffs' Fourteenth Amend-
ment rights. On June 21, 1974, Judge W. Arthur Garrity ruled
that "school officials had knowingly carried out a systematic program of segregation." He ordered them to implement integration
—which meant busing—at once. The first phase of the program
would involve ten thousand of the city's ninety-five thousand
black and white children. It would put South Boston on the same
busing route as Columbia Point and Roxbury. (Judge Garrity
deferred busing in East Boston, Charlestown, and the North End-
until a later phase of the plan.) It was scheduled to begin in just
ten weeks.

No one doubted, that frantic summer, that the program would
cause some disorder, but few people foresaw the terror that would
begin that first day of school. To outsiders, it was compressed into
the few minutes of news footage showing children and adults
from South Boston stoning buses full of black kids. But, driving
around the city that nightmarish week, I saw that the terror had
spread everywhere.

There were graffiti all along the bus route to South Boston:
DEATH TO THE NIGGERS, BONEHEADS BEWARE, or, simply, scrawled
in chalk, WELCOME TO THE KKK. And the Klan was there—or at
least a branch of it—some dapper young racists from Louisiana.
Thousands of whites—of Catholics, whom the Klan had once
reviled—welcomed them to South Boston and Hyde Park.

Blacks, who had read the graffiti, who had seen the Klansmen
on TV, who had ridden the besieged buses or fought with white
kids in the school cafeterias, vowed to get them a honky motherfucker before the whole thing was over. They started their share
of fights in the schools. At Columbia Point a few of them, young
men, armed themselves for battle. Every night for a week there

was rifle fire in and out of the project. The blacks claimed that white people, dressed as Klansmen, had provoked it. The cops blamed black snipers.

No one in the white neighborhoods believed the city's newspapers. Most of the media were pro-busing; they were tied into the Yankee establishment; they had entered into a widely publicized agreement to suppress news of violence. So the police, born in Southie or Charlestown or East Boston, acquired a special credibility. After all, they traveled around town more than anyone else. They were allowed into the schools, which had banned all other outsiders. As they drove from enclave to enclave they delivered embellished reports of the scuffles they'd seen, feeding the grapevine of horrifying rumors.

White swore oaths of revenge. Their wrath became part of their children's fantasy life. In South Boston's Old Colony housing project kids who ranged in age from seven to fourteen stuffed rags into old clothes, attached the limp, humanoid form to a Styrofoam head, painted the head black, and yelled, "Lynch the nigger," as they hoisted the effigy onto a tree and set it aflame.

I decided to cover busing as a tale of two enclaves—South Boston and Columbia Point. They weren't typical, of course; no neighborhood was. There wasn't even a typical response to busing. Some communities, like Jamaica Plain, implemented the program with almost no trouble at all. On the other hand, residents of the strategically placed East Boston threatened to blow up the tunnels and bridges that led to their peninsula "if they bring busing in here."

Studs Lonigan might have lived in South Boston. Bigger Thomas, the protagonist of *Native Son*, might had lived in Columbia Point. The neighborhoods are separated by a five-minute drive along the gracious Massachusetts Bay. That geographic coincidence was the reason Judge W. Arthur Garrity of Wellesley and his advisers, from suburbs like Lexington and Concord, put the white neighborhood on the same busing route as the black housing project. In 1975, the average family income in Columbia Point and in South Boston's housing projects, where the angriest antagonists lived, was below eight thousand dollars a year. The

average family income in Wellesley was about twenty-five thousand dollars a year.

The plan conformed religiously to the sacred precepts of the
1954 *Brown* v. *Board of Education* decision. It was mostly devised
by well-to-do people and it mostly affected the poor. Its intent was
to improve Boston's schools. At least one of its results was to
transport gangs of poor white kids and gangs of poor black kids
into battle with each other.

South Boston High School is on a hill, overlooking Massachusetts Bay. That location reinforces one's sense that the shabby
gray building is the temple where ancestral memories are stored.
It helps you understand that, at some level, the antibusing protesters have a romantic image of themselves as crusaders, protect-
ing the holy grail of their youth.

They never got much book learning at Southie. "The kids I
knew were terrific when they trusted you," says one man who
taught there from 1965 to 1973. "They were loyal and very generous. But they didn't care about academic subjects. The absentee
rate was the highest in the city. When they went to high school it
was to learn social lessons—to find out where they could score
good dope, who they wanted to drink with, where they could get
the best lay. And, of course, they went there for the sports.

"There were about four hundred seniors most years I was there.
Only about fifteen of them would graduate from college. Even
the good students were scared to succeed in the academic world.
The lure of Southie was greater than the lure of the university.
That was what the school wanted, I guess—to reinforce their passivity, to make them obedient workers. But it encouraged them to
idolize tough guys and outlaws—ball players, dope dealers, street
hustlers."

Sports, at Southie, were as important to girls as they were to
boys. "All my life I dreamed of being a cheerleader for Southie," a
thirty-one-year-old woman I'll call Sharon O'Keefe told me one
hot September afternoon after she'd joined thousands of whites in
a march against busing. "You know what? I made it three times."
After her junior year, she said, she'd been one of a handful of kids
who'd had their way paid to New York for a weekend course in

cheerleading. It was the only time she'd ever been out of Massachusetts, the only time in her life she'd been able to mingle with girls from all over the Northeast. The next November, after her squad of cheerleaders had shouted and somersaulted on the sidelines, Southie had beaten Eastie on the field. It was the climax of her senior year—and the happiest day of her life.

Now she was the mother of six children. Her husband, a sanitation worker, earned about twelve thousand dollars a year, and her sparsely furnished five-room apartment was too small for her family. But her slightly worn face took on a happier look when she described how her successful career as a cheerleader had let her flit from clique to clique and date the most eligible jocks on Southie's winning teams.

There was a way in which busing had robbed Sharon O'Keefe of her only savings, her memories—the most precious legacy she could pass on to her kids. That year, for the first time since she was nine, she and the rest of the family would stay away from the Southie–Eastie game. Some of Southie's best players had been assigned to Roxbury High—kids from Roxbury would be on Southie's starting eleven. Even if the integrated team won the city championship that year, victory would be meaningless: Many of the players would be aliens.

Sharon's senior prom was another happy memory. What would it be like for the high school couples who had been separated by busing? What would it be like for her own kids? Those traditions had been shattered, almost overnight, by outsiders who regarded them as trivial if they knew about them at all.

Sharon was afraid that her kids—who were slated to go to Columbia Point—would be mugged. She couldn't, for the life of her, understand why the court had ordered them to ride on a bus when there was a perfectly good school just two blocks away. She was particularly worried that her seven-year-old son, an asthmatic, would have an attack in a place that seemed alien and hostile to her, among teachers and administrators who were indifferent to his health. There were no rational arguments that could convince her those fears were unfounded.

Nor was there any way to quench her fury at the wealthy suburbanites who supported busing—or at Judge Garrity; at Senator

Edward Kennedy and Mayor Kevin White; at the editors of the *Boston Globe*. Those people didn't have kids who attended Boston's public schools. They dismissed Sharon and her friends as bigots while they hid from the city's tensions behind the powerful reserves of their own wealth. She was angriest at Judge Garrity, once a minor functionary in the Kennedy machine, now, by some process she couldn't understand, an official with more power than anyone she'd ever voted for. And this judge, of all people—an Irishman who lived in the Yankee haven of Wellesley. He was a dictator: That was bad enough. He was a traitor: That was unforgivable.

She saw the anti-busing demonstrations as an act of fealty to an imperiled memory. As her private act of defiance she planned to wear the maroon-and-gold cheerleader's sweater as often as she could. "Judge Garrity will never take that away from me," she said.

In a way, though, he did. When I visited her three years later her mood of defiance had evaporated. Nowadays her life was a rushed haze of financial worries, of sheer exhaustion. She had made a separate peace with the school system, though not with busing, but the cost was the stability of her life. Her three younger kids were in public school ("Niggerville," they called it) since she and her husband didn't have enough money for them to join the three older ones in parochial school. Their tuition there was five hundred dollars a year, a big bite out of her husband's salary. There wasn't enough money to pay the phone bill the month I visited them. All the bulbs on their landing had burned out. Sharon wasn't home much anymore; she'd found a job as a cashier to supplement her husband's income. Between that and her housework and a mother who was sick in a Quincy hospital, the ex-cheerleader felt too tired to cope—too tired, she feared, to pay much attention to the kids, whose need for her was greater than ever now that they spent so much time away from home.

The O'Keefes would have had many of their problems with or without busing. Still, it was clear that the program had upset their lives—and that it had changed many lives in Boston. In the three years since it had been inaugurated, enrollment in the city's public-school system had declined by more than 25 per cent—from ninety-five thousand to seventy thousand, according to the School Committee's figures; from about eighty thousand to fifty-seven thousand, according to other sources, who thought the committee had inflated those figures in order to qualify for more federal funds.

Many of the kids who'd left—like the O'Keefes—are in parochial schools; many either find or invent relatives in suburbs like Quincy or Brockton and go to school there. But a substantial number of them are lost to the system entirely. They lead the kind of violent, desperate lives that can, quite literally, lead to death at an early age.

The girl I'll call Barbara Quinlon, sixteen, had a great deal in common with Sharon O'Keefe—except that she belonged to a generation in Southie where bouncy young girls were more likely to become high school drop-outs than cheerleaders. Three years after the busing program began, I spent most of a school day afternoon talking with her in a sub shop near the high school. Her friend Maureen, another drop-out, kept darting from our table to a telephone, where she was telling her friends about the "time"— the party—that was scheduled for that night. Debby, more composed, a grade-school friend who'd decided to stay out of their gang, listened to their wild talk with sadness on her face. She was in parochial school now. Someday, she believed, she would become a lawyer.

When Barbara Quinlon was a little girl her father, a postal clerk, and her mother, a waitress, loved to tell her their glorious Southie sagas. They'd describe the snowball fights and the egg fights between the boys and the girls, the times they fooled their music teacher by rolling a piano down the stairs, the annual Class Day, where kids would make lasting impressions by imitating Elvis or Bill Haley and the Comets.

Barbara's first day at Southie was the first day of busing. She wanted to go up there anyway, but the boycott was on and her parents told her to stay home. Like most of her friends, she observed the boycott until the Thanksgiving recess.

It was hard for her to make up all that lost classwork when she returned. She seethed inwardly every day, for, she believed, the teachers gave the black kids all the breaks. She spent much of her time fighting the invaders. She had to, she said, for the pride of Southie. But those battles terrified her. She couldn't concentrate in school, or see any point in studying when she got home. Her fear and confusion turned into outright pain when she was left back that spring.

She returned to Southie the next September, but it was a world she'd never imagined—no one went to the football games; cops were swarming all over the school building; outside, you weren't even allowed to pick up a snowball for fear that a fight that began innocently would trigger a race riot. "It was like being in a cage," she says. Depressed, she started playing hooky. She and Maureen would hang out at the sub shop for days at a time, flirting with the customers and countermen, arranging "times" that would prove their corner had kids who knew how to party better than any other kids in South Boston. That spring Barbara was left behind again. Maureen had already quit school. Barbara decided to drop out, too.

Barbara says that dozens of her classmates quit with her—kids who might have been on the football or hockey teams or in the band before the advent of busing. Some of the boys found jobs at the American Brush Company or Gillette. Some are still looking for work.

At first she figured she'd get hired as a secretary with no trouble at all. But, soon, "I realized I couldn't type or file the way they wanted. When they asked me where I'd been employed before, I had to tell them the truth . . . nowhere."

She still goes downtown to look for work once or twice a week, but without much hope. "I feel like a flunky, a bum," she says.

Whenever she spends time with someone like Debby, who has prospects, or with someone who actually has a job, she's reminded of her plight. "I never have any money. When my friends go out and do something at night, I can't afford it." So, more and more, she hangs around in a subculture of kids like Maureen who know how to snatch quick, cheap thrills.

"My parents are upset. They tell me to look for work, but they know I'm not qualified for anything. Sometimes I think they'd like to punish me for quitting school. But they can't—they know what's going on there. They think something is wrong with them because they didn't send me to parochial school. I guess they blame themselves for this mess I'm in."

Sometimes the unspoken family pressures get so intense that "I just want to go outside and smoke a few joints or have a few drinks." Then, the next thing she knows, it's three or four in the morning and she's stoned or drunk in someone's apartment on Dorchester Avenue or riding around in someone's car, looking for a fight. "I don't like doing that, but the other kids would get mad at me if I hung back. *She* would," Barbara said, pointing at Maureen, who was away from the table, making another phone call. There was admiration, not anger, in her voice.

"I always feel terrible about it the next day. I promise myself I won't get drunk again. But then someone calls and invites me to a 'time,' and I get scared I'll miss something. So I stay out until five or six in the morning, sleep till noon, come down to the sub shop, and hang out till dinner. Then I go home, shower, change my clothes, and start all over again. I don't know what else to do."

As I listened to her pouring out her problems I realized that there must be very few adults she could speak to. She'd quit school—there were no teachers or guidance counselors to advise her. Since she'd dropped out, her parents had lost whatever shred of authority they might have possessed. I thought about Jesse Jackson's "love triangle." It had been shattered for her, just as surely as it had for the black kids in northern ghettos.

Did she ever go to church? I asked.

"No. I started hooking out [playing hooky] from there four or five years ago. It was too boring for me."

"But we still go to mass when one of our friends dies," Maureen said.

"It seems like they're all dropping like flies around here," Barbara added. "They're all young kids, too—eighteen, nineteen, twenty." In the past two months, she said, two of her friends had been in car wrecks; one boy had died of an overdose; another had bet a friend he could chug-a-lug a fifth of vodka—the attempt had killed him; a girl who Barbara and Maureen used to fight with had been raped and killed. "I was glad when that happened," Maureen said. "I wouldn't go to her wake." Barbara giggled, then looked at her friend disapprovingly.

"It seems like this is the only corner in South Boston that hasn't been hit," Barbara said. "I'm scared it will happen to someone I know."

Debby had been quiet through most of the conversation. Now she looked at me and said, quite softly, "I'm scared it will happen to me. Maybe that's why I don't go out drinking with the other kids. I'm trying to plan for the future. I know it takes work to get into law school."

Barbara glanced at her with the first trace of anger I'd seen on her round, passive face. "Yeah, but you have a future to look forward to. We don't. I just have to live day by day.

"I don't want to talk about this anymore," she said. "It makes me too depressed." Then, to Maureen: "Hey, did you see my honey? He was just walking down the street. I hope he comes to the time tonight."

The black parents and kids I interviewed at Columbia Point had a great deal in common with Sharon O'Keefe and Barbara Quinlon.

Columbia Point is an exceptionally difficult place to live. Built in the late 1950s, the project is on a spit of land that juts into Boston Harbor. For three years, in the late Sixties, there had been a shopping mall across from the concrete maze of pavement and houses, but the stores soon moved out because there were so many episodes of vandalism. Now the mall looks like a huge, deserted dune. Any project dweller who wants to do a week's worth of grocery shopping, or see a movie, or go to a nightclub, has to walk about a half mile to the Columbia Street subway station or take the half-hour bus ride to Dudley Square—to make a long, complicated journey out of isolation.

From the vantage point of South Boston, the Columbia Point project might look like a monolith. In fact, it is barely a community at all—and it is certainly not an ancestral home. Most of the people who live there have come to Boston from Fairfax, Alabama; or Kinston, North Carolina; or Easton, Maryland—or from the West Indies or Cape Verde or Puerto Rico. The adults' Honey McDonnaughs—the golden-gloves champions, the poets, the clowns whose legends evoke their pasts—are still linked with those remote places, not with Boston. Some of the families who settled at the Point stayed there for more than a decade—long enough to make it a community for their kids—but, especially in the Seventies, after crime became a plague, after the mall closed down, as the buildings began to decay, the more ambitious ones moved away.

Still, like the people in Southie, they were fiercely proud of their neighborhood schools—particularly the John J. McCormick middle school. It had been built in the mid-Sixties, right across the street from the project, and it was Columbia Point's single treasure. The school served as a kind of community center, offering night courses, sports programs to people who often felt more secure in that modern, attractive building than they did in their own apartments. During the years when the chain stores at the mall were being vandalized, nothing was stolen from the McCormick school—a sure sign that blacks in the area regarded it as "their" place.

In 1974, Judge Garrity ruled that the middle-school students had to be bused away from there, to South Boston's Gavin School, built in 1897. Now, mostly white kids attend the McCormick.

That fall I spent several afternoons with a ninth-grade girl I'll call Tammy Lee Russell, who lived with her mother and six brothers and sisters in a crowded four-room apartment that looked very much like the O'Keefes'—except that, outside, Columbia Point is a desert of littered pavement and broken glass while the yards on the O'Keefe's block are somewhat cleaner and grassier. Tammy Lee, an honors student, had graduated from the McCormick School in 1973. Roger O'Keefe, Sharon's oldest son, an honors student, too, was scheduled to go there that September. Tammy Lee, who wanted to be a legal secretary, had applied to go to the predominantly black Jeremiah Burke Junior High School ("the Jerry"), which specialized in business skills. She was assigned to the Hart Dean Annex of South Boston High School, whose specialty was mechanics.

She was one of a handful of black kids who volunteered to ride the bus on the first day of school in September 1974. She was hit on the neck with a rock as the vehicle passed the L Street baths, a hangout for some of Southie's toughest young men. Her older sister, a monitor on the bus, got four bruised ribs and glass in her eye on that day. After that, Tammy Lee's mother kept her home for more than a week.

When she returned to school, she found it a puzzling, disappointing place. Little details bothered her. The Hart Dean's cafeteria was smaller and more crowded than the McCormick's had been. Tammy Lee wasn't used to strict discipline; she couldn't figure out why the teachers yelled at her for chewing gum, for sitting on the bathroom sink, for misplacing her class schedule. She figured the teachers didn't like her, and that was particularly unsettling since she was usually one of just five or six students who were present at that time.

History was her last class of the day. She'd watch the clock from the moment the first bell rang and, by one-thirty—twenty minutes before the buses were scheduled to arrive—"my heart would feel like it was falling. I couldn't think of anything except the ride home after that."

For weeks, whites—including Sharon O'Keefe and Barbara Quinlon—would line the hilly streets outside school, jeering at the buses. From Tammy Lee's point of view "those people were really uncivilized. There was this one old lady, she kept jumping up and down and giving me the finger. Now, why would anyone want to do a thing like that?"

Every afternoon her mother joined dozens of other women from the project to walk up to the deserted mall and wait for the bus to drop off the kids. The week Tammy Lee returned to the Hart Dean her bus was delayed twice because the drivers decided to take longer, less dangerous routes back to the Point. What a terrifying time that was! There was no way those women could be sure that their children were safe.

After a few days, Tammy Lee decided not to go back to the Hart Dean for a while. Her school year was becoming as tentative and sporadic as Barbara Quinlon's. Then the Klansmen showed up in town. Tammy Lee's mother, who was born in rural Georgia, told her tales of their past brutality. She and her neighbors were convinced that a squadron full of robed white racists was prepared to commandeer boats, journey across Boston Harbor, and attack their project.

The child got sick. The stoning incident, the strangeness of school, her mother's stories about the Klan, the sniper fire she heard every night when she went to bed: All of that gave her terrible headaches and insomnia. First she was in bed with a cold, then with asthma. For a while, she considered giving up school for the year.

She didn't, though. When I visited her three years later she talked so freely I felt our conversation had barely been interrupted.

In 1974, she'd seemed disappointed that the Hart Dean didn't place the same emphasis on skills like typing that she'd wanted when she'd applied to the "Jerry." I didn't pay much attention to that then. The stoning episode, the rumors about the Klan seemed far more dramatic—and more in keeping with my image of her as a latter-day version of the black kids who'd integrated Little Rock high school twenty years before. Three years later, I saw that complaint was the most important one she'd made. For now, as we talked, she dismissed her dream of being a legal secretary as something she'd wanted in some barely remembered past. Busing, I realized, had brought her a subtle, devastating message about the relative unimportance of her personal career plans. It had encouraged her to believe—as Barbara Quinlon did—that she might as well enjoy herself however she could. For Tammy Lee, that meant fighting.

She relished combat—something I hadn't understood in 1974, when I wanted to perceive her as a passive victim. At the age of six she'd had to learn how to be tough, to keep up with the kids she met when she moved from the South to Roxbury. (Her mother had migrated North, she said, because it was easier to collect welfare checks than work in the cotton fields.) At Columbia Point, where her family moved three years later, the cliques hassled any stranger. She had to be fierce to survive. By eighth grade, she boasted, she was one of the rulers of the McCormick school; so tough that any girl would give her a precious lunchroom trophy—a piece of cake or a hot dog—whenever she demanded it.

She was a bright kid with a real dream, but she needed the kind of orderly classroom atmosphere Jesse Jackson had talked about to realize it. She needed teachers who were willing to discipline her because they believed in her. She didn't find them in Southie. Many people who observed the school that year said that most faculty members had no idea of how to deal with black kids—they were frightened by their size and strength, by their loud, bewildering culture. They simply wanted to survive a very hazardous time. So, despite occasional outbursts about details like gum-chewing, they'd be lax for hours on end—far more permissive when Tammy Lee used foul-mouthed speech or tussled noisily with her friends than they'd ever be with white kids whom they could discipline with ease. The double standard, which existed all over the city, was enormously destructive. Kids like Barbara Quinlon seethed because "the niggers get all the breaks." Kids like Tammy Lee saw school as a place of whims and rages, not rules. Often she fought simply to see how much she could get away with in that white world, where few people cared if she learned anything or not.

Sometimes she got hurt in the rumbles with the white kids. Once she tumbled down a flight of stairs while she was running from a boy in her class, and had to be rushed to the hospital. She never did tell her mother about that episode. But she reminisces about her victories with a war veteran's proud relish: about the afternoon when she and some friends seized field-hockey sticks and beat away at "those honkey girls until their shins were red." It was a wide-open, frontier environment where she could do almost anything she pleased. She still boasts that "Southie was *my* school."

In the spring of 1975, after a year at the Hart Dean Annex, she got a letter in the mail reassigning her to the Boston English High School. That was happening all over the city. Each new phase of busing meant a redrawing of district lines, a reshuffling of thousands of students. So, in September 1975, for the third time in three years, Tammy Lee had to get used to a new school, a new set of teachers and students, a new travel route. Very few of the kids in her class lived at the Point. The few friendships she formed were very frail. She felt bored and lonely and—for the first time in her life—very apathetic. No one outside the Point, and, certainly, no one in the outside world, seemed to care about her enough to help.

In August 1976 she got pregnant. Her morning sickness made the prospect of rising at 6 A.M. each day to take the long bus ride to the unfamiliar part of the city where Boston English was located seem even more burdensome than it had the year before. When she arrived, she knew, she'd be put in a class with other pregnant girls, a form of segregation she dreaded. That August, two of her closest friends, who live next door to her at the Point, discovered they were pregnant, too. So, at sixteen, the same age as Barbara Quinlon, she decided to drop out of school before the next term began—to hang out with them while she waited for her baby to be born. Someday, she hopes, its father will come back from the Marines and marry her.

She says that Columbia Point is the only place she feels at home. She makes its littered streets and alleyways come alive with her friendly greetings to everyone she meets. But she doubts her shred of a community will remain intact much longer. Near Columbia Point, the University of Massachusetts is expanding and the new Kennedy Library is under construction. Soon this area, near the lovely Boston Harbor, will become an attractive academic community. Columbia Point will no longer be a housing project for poor people. The city plans to transform it into a mixed-income development. Many of the apartment buildings are already boarded up for renovation. The city has promised that families like the Russells can stay there, but Tammy Lee doesn't believe that. "Those houses won't be for niggers like us," she says.

She is very matter-of-fact about the last three years—not at all regretful or bitter. She does think, though, that if she had gone to the "Jerry" with all her friends, she might have managed to make it through high school.

There are, of course, people who still saw some value in busing three years after the program began. But most had deep reservations about it, which often stemmed from stories like Tammy Lee Russell's and Barbara Quinlon's.

Jane Margolis, forty-three, comes from a family that has lived in Savin Hill for three generations. It is a predominantly Irish neigh-

borhood bordering on South Boston. Her father, second-genera-
tion Irish, an accountant at Gillette, was perfectly at home there.
But her mother, a seamstress from the Azores, had a Mediter-
ranean temperament that made her seem a little different from
the other women Jane knew. She had slightly heretical ideas, too.
For example, she didn't want the family to give money to the
Catholic church's mission fund since she believed missionaries
should mind their own business, not meddle in other people's
religions.

Jane had a darker complexion than most of her neighbors. As a
kid she was called a "jigaboo," and that made her feel like something of an outcast. She married a Jew, the owner of a TV store
in Savin Hill, and that match was considered somewhat unusual.

Still, she'd shared much with the people who lived in that small
enclave. Once, as a teenager, she was a black-widow spider—the
villain—in a play at the parish house. It was a major role and the
audience of five hundred had been so impressed with her performance they applauded each time she came onstage. They made her
take several encores. That ranks with the birth of her child as one
of the two happiest days of her life. Every month or so she runs
into someone who remembers it. The praise still thrills her.

When she first heard about busing she was as ardently opposed
to it as Sharon O'Keefe. She had a son and a daughter who would
be affected. But, after a great deal of talk, she and her husband
decided that the best way to protect them was to influence the
way it was carried out. So she joined the Citywide Educational
Coalition, an organization that was trying to preserve peace instead of demonstrating against Judge Garrity's order. She spent
most of her time, in September 1974, mingling with crowds in
Southie, trying to prevent violence. That moderate position made
her a militant in the eyes of much of the community. People
called her a "nigger fucker" on the streets and over the phone,
hurled rocks in her window, slashed her car tires week after week.

I met her late one afternoon in 1974, when she was sitting in
the coalition office on the verge of tears. She had just learned that
her thirteen-year-old daughter had been beaten up by some black
kids earlier that week. "I was feeling very guilty," she told me
later. "I'd been spending so much time watching the blacks get on

the bus at South Boston that I didn't even know what was going on in my own house. I just wanted them to repeal the whole thing."

Three years later there was still part of her that wished the program had never been launched. It had certainly affected her family. Before busing, she'd had a very traditional marriage. She'd kept house and helped her husband at the store. Suddenly, the coalition was taking all her time. "I dropped out of my husband's life completely," she says ruefully. "He'd open up the *Boston Globe* and there I was." They separated in 1976.

Her son was a junior in high school when busing began. He frequently complained to her about the special privileges he thought blacks were getting.

Her daughter, an eighth grader in 1974, has attended three schools in three years. Like Tammy Lee Russell, she was rattled by the constant disruptions in her life. But she did stay in school. Jane is convinced that busing has helped her develop far healthier relations with black people than she would have if—like her ancestors—she'd always gone to school in Savin Hill. That is the basis of Jane's feeling that the program has some merit despite all the anguish it's caused. "Some of the kids, at least the younger ones, will never experience the hatreds and fears we've seen over the past three years," she says.

The black woman I'll call Sonia Beach—a social worker, a member of the elite that originally pushed for desegregation—spends most of her professional life with blacks who have been on the receiving end of all the hatred and fear. She still doesn't believe that there would have been a fair distribution of Boston's educational resources if it hadn't been for the threat of busing—and the plan itself. And she sees some bright spots. She's impressed with some of the programs that Boston's universities have launched in the high schools. She's optimistic about the growing magnet-school program, which takes black and white kids out of their neighborhoods and puts them in schools with good academic programs.

She's pleased that Louise Day Hicks lost the 1977 City Council election, that "Pixie" Pallidino, an anti-busing leader, lost her seat on the School Committee, and that John O'Bryant, a black man, won a place on the five-person board. When I interviewed her, in December, 1977, she was sure that election could bring important innovations in educational policy.

But, when I told her Tammy Lee Russell's story, she shook her head in sad recognition. "We just don't know what price those kids are paying," she said. As we continued to talk, I realized that, though she is personally very comfortable with white people, busing has made her perceptibly more pessimistic about wide-scale school integration in Boston than she'd been a decade earlier.

As a child in the 1940s, she was one of a handful of blacks who attended Roxbury's public schools. Her father, the son of a slave, a deeply religious man, who ran a very successful business, told her she had to work twice as hard as white kids. If she did, she'd succeed. In a way, that was true. She and her husband, a prominant professional, have prospered beyond her father's dreams. She has a large house in the city and spends summers on Cape Cod. Her children went to private schools and then to Ivy League colleges. Still, speaking sadly, she said that the events of the past three years had convinced her that her father's message was largely an illusion.

Her own life is full of stark, disturbing paradoxes. She has the status and the means to travel wherever she wants in America. The day after our interview she and her husband were flying to a conference at a resort in Colorado—Sharon O'Keefe and Barbara Quinlon would probably never board an airplane in their lives. But she can never travel where she wants to in her home town. The anger that Sharon O'Keefe and Barbara Quinlon feel, refracted through Boston's white enclaves, makes freedom of movement impossible. It used to be, for example, that on hot summer nights she and her family would drive over to Kelly's Landing in Southie and have some clams. "We could be killed if we did that now," she says.

"Sometimes this city seems like a war zone. Just yesterday my niece took a subway to Harvard Square. When she got on at Shawmut, three white kids spit at her. She looked at them and asked, 'Why did you do that?' They told her, 'We're prejudiced.'

"That sort of thing frightens my niece, but it doesn't damage her self-confidence. She has a strong, secure family behind her.

But think of what it does to that kid [Tammy Lee] you met at Columbia Point. She might believe it when she tells you how much she likes fighting. But think of the pain she feels when she realizes she'll never be accepted by whites.

"I see those kids when they come home. Day after day, they're exposed to white teachers and administrators who don't really understand them or like them. What can I say to them? How can I tell them they'll succeed in a world whose prejudices run so deep? But I can't say anything that will encourage them to give up. So I'm always straddling, always saying things I only half-believe."

She and her friends discuss those issues frequently. Sometimes, when they're most depressed, they find themselves suprisingly attracted to the idea of high-quality segregated education. Perhaps Washington D.C.'s Lawrence Dunbar High School, which produced black leaders like federal-court judge William Hastie and Senator Edward Brooke in the 1930s and '40s, furnishes a suitable model.

"At least the teachers there understood the kids, pushed them hard, told them where they came from and who they could be. By the time a student graduated he knew who he was. It's possible that in the next few years you're going to see a whole reexamination of integration from that point of view."

I don't see how busing in Boston helped the first wave of students it affected. It may have made some kids, like Jane Margolis's daughter, more open-minded. But it emboldened thousands of others to use prejudice as Sharon O'Keefe had once used her cheerleader's sweater: as a symbol of resistance against a system of authority they can flaunt with impunity because their parents have defined it as tyrannical.

It has robbed Tammy Lee Russell and Barbara Quinlon of the fabric of security and order that was already tattered in their lives. The human ecology of their neighborhoods has been destroyed. To the authorities who decide what schools they'll attend, the girls are statistics, a black and a white figurine who must be shipped from one school to another in order to achieve something called racial balance. Their lives don't really matter.

Still, though, over time, Tammy Lee and Barbara may seem

like casualties of social change, not like harbingers of a citywide disaster. By the summer of 1978, it seemed possible that busing might prove to have been the catalyst for some improvements in the Boston educational system. By then, the schools were in such desperate shape that parents who still had kids in them became a strong pressure group for quality education. The 1977 School Committee elections reflected that mood, as Sonia Beach had indicated. The politicians were sensitive to it, too.

In the winter and spring of 1978, a task force of parents and educators devised a plan for transferring much of the power to hire and fire administrators from the School Committee to the superintendent of schools. Surprisingly, it was adopted. Jane Margolis, who was on the task force, says that one reason for the reorganization was to rid the School Committee of the patronage power that had traditionally made it a launching pad for aspiring politicians. If that happened, then the people who ran for the committee would be interested in education itself, not in accumulating the credits and debts they'd need when they ran for higher office. Furthermore, in theory, the officials the superintendent of schools appointed would be educators, not political hacks.

Then, in August 1978, the School Committee unanimously decided that the new superintendent of schools would be Robert Wood, president of the University of Massachusetts, a former secretary of the Department of Housing and Urban Development. Wood made it clear, from the start, that he'd insist on the autonomy that the reorganization plan gave him—and that he'd use his finely honed bureaucratic skills to fight for quality education.

Wood could never have been selected—nor could any school superintendent have possessed so much potential power—in Louise Day Hicks's heyday.

No one saw his appointment as a panacea. After all, the twenty-five thousand children—the 25 per cent of the student population —who had left the public schools after the advent of busing weren't likely to come back. Some of them were drop-outs, like Tammy Lee and Barbara Quinlon, but others came from middle-class families who had left the city altogether and would no longer provide Boston's educational system with much of a tax base. Within many schools, faculty morale was very low. According to Jane Margolis, many parents, seeing those problems, had grown depressed about the schools' future. "Without the reorganization and Wood's appointment there would have been disaster," she says. "Now we have a second chance."

Most of Boston is segregated by habit—and, in some neighborhoods, by fear. It's hard to see how School Committee appointments can erase the deep-seated resentments that caused those white kids to spit at Sonia Beach's niece—or that caused Tammy Lee Russell to warn me that, for my own safety, I should leave Columbia Point by nightfall. It will take the most creative kind of educational and political diplomacy to carve out a truce among tribes in Boston.

INTERLUDE

Through Their Eyes

When I was in the civil-rights movement and the Peace Corps I
became convinced that it was impossible to bring about political
change without understanding local cultures. In the Peace Corps,
I'd known scores of Americans who'd wanted to bring about a
"bloodless revolution." They'd failed, of course—cultures aren't
clay you can sculpt to your liking. Often, they'd come to despise
the Latins who'd refused to heed their prescriptions for change.

You had to accept other people on their terms—not decide
they were ignorant because they wouldn't accept your terms. I
wanted to incorporate that lesson, which I'd learned as an activist,
into my journalism—into my writing about causes I supported as
well as conflicts that troubled me. That was why, in the chapters
that follow, I decided to focus on individuals—on Hartman Turnbow, in the Mississippi Delta, and Jerry Johnson, in Harlan
County. I wanted to see those epic battles—for the right to vote
and the right to form a union—through the eyes of the people
who waged them.

CHAPTER 8

The Mississippi Delta:
Let Us Now Praise a Famous Man

When Rachel and I worked in the 1964 Mississippi Summer Project, the town of Tchula, population 1,700 was already a legend. It was in Holmes County, the gateway to the Mississippi Delta—America's Rhodesia. It was filled with black farmer-warriors willing to risk their lives for the right to vote.

Hartman Turnbow, then fifty-seven, was their leader. One night in 1963 he'd performed an act of defiance that had been unthinkable since Reconstruction. He'd shot back at the white men who'd opened fire on his house, then firebombed it, the night after he registered to vote. Turnbow's audacity had emboldened his neighbors. His ability to describe his rooted life as a farmer in a series of eloquent speeches inspired thousands of people as he moved across the country, bringing the truth of rural black Mississippi to the cities of the North.

We heard him speak in New York in 1964. That experience clinched our commitment to help people like him fight to change their state. We never did meet him that year—Rachel was stationed in Jackson and I worked in the nearby city of Vicksburg, a two-hour drive from the Delta. Then, a year later, the Student Non-Violent Coordinating Committee, the organization we had worked with, embraced the phrase "black power" and asked

whites to go home. At that time their argument—that our presence was stunting black growth—seemed to make sense. Besides,
they were the major political force in our lives in the mid-Sixties.
So we heeded their request.

In the summer of 1977, we finally returned to the state that had
once meant so much to us. Mr. Turnbow was the person we were
most eager to see.

Tchula, his town, had just elected a black mayor—something
that had seemed impossible when we were last in Mississippi. The
mayor is a twenty-seven-year old college graduate named Eddie
James Carthan, who told everyone, black and white, that Mr.
Turnbow was his mentor. So the seventy-two-year-old farmer-war-
rior was a link between the oppression that had lasted for nearly a
century, the civil-rights struggles of the Sixties, and the victories
of the Seventies. He was also, in a curious way, a living repository
of our own idealism. It had been so difficult to see progress during
the battles of South Boston and Forest Hills. . . . Although we
didn't quite admit it to each other, we wanted to learn whether
he thought the movement in Mississippi, at least, had been of
value.

When we telephoned him he was enthusiastic about talking
with us. He invited us over to his house the next afternoon; we
could talk while he took a break from working his cotton fields.
Actually, the next day was rainy, so he had plenty of time on his
hands.

Mr. Turnbow is a short, stocky man, muscular and fit, but so
gentle in his manner that it was hard, at times, to connect the
courtly person we were talking to with his courageous legend. But,
standing in his screened-in porch, or sitting in his modest living
room, we could see the bullet holes that still scarred the walls.
They furnished a visual intensity to the stories of his childhood,
his early years in the movement, his ideas about the present.

As he talked, his eyes shone and he laughed frequently. He
leaned forward from the brown vinyl couch where he sat. He is a
born storyteller, whose enthusiasm couples with the almost biblical rhythms and cadences of his voice to draw you into his tales
at once. Like all skilled tribal bards, he tells his stories by accumulating details, by winding his way into a point at a more leisurely

pace than most members of my hurried, post-television generation do. His speech is part of an oral tradition spanning cultures and centuries. His language itself, like his courage, is rooted in a very special part of America.

After serving us coffee, Mr. Turnbow began his narrative by recalling his grandfather, who'd been born a slave in Lexington, Mississippi, a town in the foothills just past the Delta. "His old master was his daddy. And, after the Civil War, his old master sold him the place where he slaved him. He never did leave it. Now I owns the place where my grandfather was slaved by his father. It was 118 acres, and I've got fifty.

"I was born in those hills, on my grandfather's place. Then my daddy got drowned when I was eight years old. I didn't know much about him, but after he passed, well, my momma came to the Delta and we growed up in the Delta, first on one plantation, then on another one. But I didn't like plantation life. When I got big enough I ran away and came back to the hills."

Though Mr. Turnbow lives in the Delta now, he is as proud of his hill-country heritage as the whites who live in Boston's enclaves are of their particular street corner. It has made him more independent than blacks who were born on the flatlands, he thinks. As he sipped his coffee, he described the differences between the two cultures.

"The hill Negro always got more education than the Delta Negro. You take the biggest majority of Negroes in the hills, they own where they stay. If it wasn't anything but an acre with a house on it, the hill Negro owned that. And they'd send their children to school and the children would get a pretty good education.

"But in the Delta it was different. You had to work another man's land. The little school they had didn't go on for more than three months, then it was time to let out. If a family had boys of any size they had to be cutting cotton stalks or ripping land open with a big yellow-jacket mule buster for most of the year. Down in the Delta in mule days, they didn't have no Negroes with educations."

Like the schools, the church played a different role in the hills than in the Delta. "You take the hill Negro preachers, they would carry a little political along with their preaching. They'd get up and tell for you to do well and always try to be your own boss and have your own home."

But, in the Delta, "the preacher just come and preach and he's gone. He couldn't come there and preach no kind of political to the labor. If he did, the plantation bosses would give him some of that strap. On a plantation everything black was the same with the bosses. I natural born got tired of plantation life. There wasn't no future in it."

It was a muggy afternoon. Sometimes Mr. Turnbow would pick up a paper fan from the coffee table and wave a few strokes through the thick air. We asked him to tell us more about plantation life—what it had been like for those six years before he ran away. There was disgust in his voice when he answered.

"Them plantations was all the same. All the days were the same. They had a big bell. They rang it every morning before dawn. The boss hisself, he'd be out there. And if you be late, he just jumped up and grabbed you and got his strap, and gave you a stropping and turned you loose. From then on, you'd be on time.

"Breaking-up time, you'd be breaking up land, getting it ready to plant. Then all the Negroes would start planting. And right after that you'd start plowing. They had a single plow back then. It would take you three days to plow fifteen acres. A man and his wife had fifteen acres. A big family, they'd have thirty, forty, fifty. You'd make a big crop year in and year out, and you'd never clear more than one hundred dollars—sometimes just fifty or sixty. The boss told you you'd be making a sharecrop. But you'd just be working for him, that's the truth of it.

"They had a little joke they'd always say on the plantation among the colored folks. They'd say, 'an ought is an ought and a figger's a figger. All for the white man and none for the nigger.'" Mr. Turnbow laughed as he recalled the rhyme. "And that is about as true a joke as I ever heard.

"And those sharecroppers' houses was terrible. Wasn't nothing but old shacks throwed up there. Some of them wasn't even sealed. You could lay in bed and look up through the top of the house, through the cracks. And everything was built out of old rough-sawed lumber, from those little old groundhog saw mills, out of those gum logs and oak logs."

Mr. Turnbow's voice deepened with anger when he talked about law and order on the plantation. It was totally up to the whim of the white man.

"Negroes, they'd go to those Saturday-night juke joints and juke all night. And then they'd get drunk and kill somebody every Saturday night. That was wrong to kill folks for nothing, but there is many a thousand Negroes that has been killed and butchered by one another, for nothing. And the boss man, he'd go to court and say, 'That's my nigger, he's a big shot,' and that's all there was to it.

"They ain't but one time the white folks in those days would have a big lynching. That was when the Negroes bulled up or wanted to do something to the white man. If you hurt a white man, they'd kill you then. But for killing one another, it was as if you hadn't done nothing."

Had Turnbow known of any rebellions on the plantation? "No, Lord. They wasn't going to talk about fighting back. Because in them days plantation owners whip you like you whip chillens."

Blacks did have one informal means of exercising power, though. "Come Christmas time, the fall of the year, the Negroes would move from one plantation to another. If a man's name got out that he didn't whup his labor, why he was overcrowded. He couldn't use all the people that was trying to work for him. So that's what kind of changed them from beating Negroes up. They wanted a good name so they could keep a big piece of the labor."

In a way, the abrupt, unexpected end of the sharecropper system was as bad as plantation life itself. In those days, Mr. Turnbow was earning his living by hauling pulpwood—he'd established his own small business. But he saw the white plantation owners mechanize their farms, turning away thousands of sharecroppers, ending "mule days" with as little thought to their workers' futures as they'd once given to their daily lives.

"Now you take a plantation that's got a lot of shacks," Mr. Turnbow said, as if he was recalling something he'd seen yesterday. "Well, the boss gets ready to change over so he gets him as many tractors as it takes to work his place. Then he huddles that

many houses together for his tractor drivers. And he just tells the
rest of the Negroes they can go where they want. He can't use
them. Then he begins tearing the Negroes' shacks down and burning them and hauling them off and selling them. And then the
people get to leaving."

At first most of them headed for the nearest towns, little settlements like Tchula. "They just overloaded those little towns. The
Negroes just huddled up and piled up and got with one another.
They'd go from one little town to another one. And they'd get
these little jobs in those towns, mowing lawns for the white folks
and working gardens. The ladies would nurse babies, they'd clean
up the house and cook. In the morning, well, you'd get up to
Greenwood and get up at that river bridge and see folks crossing
over the bridge. You'd think they was going to a show. But it
wasn't nothing but cooks, going to cook for them white folks.
These here rich white folks all through Mississippi, they'd have a
chauffeur, they'd have a cook, they'd have a housemaid.

"But all of that's gone now. Now, you see a whole lot of white
ladies mowing themselves. But, of course, they don't have the old
push mowers the way they used to. They got a gas mower, and it
looks like they're happy over it. Folks would wonder, though.
They'd think the world was coming to an end when they saw a
white lady mowing."

When the sharecroppers were displaced from the land, Mr.
Turnbow recalls, there wasn't any welfare. "But since they com-
menced to turning folks away, off dry-handed, giving them nothing while folks were getting hungry, well then the federal government fixed the welfare. If it hadn't been for the welfare, well, folks
would have starved to death. They were all poor people. They
didn't have nothing. All this land over the Mississippi Delta
belonged to white people. You could go from Memphis, Tennessee, to New Orleans, Louisiana, and you couldn't find a hundred
acres of land owned by the Negroes in this Delta.

"And they didn't have no cows. You couldn't have cows on a
plantation because the pasture belonged to the boss, and he'd
have a hundred head of mules on it, and he didn't want no cows.
So there was nothing between them and hunger except the welfare."

Most of the refugees from the plantations soon left the small Delta towns. "The white people tore down all the shacks and the Negroes left the Mississippi Valley," Mr. Turnbow says. "A Mississippi Negro would go to Chicago. Why, that was just like heaven to him. There's many thousands of letters been wrote back here telling about the wonders of Chicago."

But, as far as Mr. Turnbow is concerned, there is just one difference between a Chicago white man and a Mississippi white man. "The Mississippi white does all the dirty work on the Negro himself. He doesn't ask nobody else to do it. But in Chicago, in Detroit, they got a police force to make sure you don't deal with them big-shot white folks. If you do, you'd as soon be in Tchula. The big shot ain't going to get you himself. But the police will do it."

The rain had stopped. Rachel and I wondered if we were keeping him from farming. But he was eager to keep talking, to reminisce about leaving the plantation. When he was fourteen he'd been beaten by a white man for failing to perform a trivial task. He decided, then and there, that he could never live in a setting where another human being had the right and power to beat him.

It was his hill heritage, he thinks, that gave him the courage to escape. "If I hadn't been raised up there, I'd have just thought I couldn't live if I didn't eat out of that commissary store."

It was the hills he went back to—to Lexington, Mississippi— where he began to work for white folks. "Mowing the lawn, raking up leaves, weeding the garden, and sometimes cleaning up the house. They liked it and they said I was a good little nigger." He laughed as he recalled the epithet.

"So I fared pretty good. I liked it much better than plantation life. I got all the clothes I wanted, all the food I wanted, and then I got five dollars a week. You take right now, I wouldn't work that way anymore, on those terms. No way. I just wouldn't do it. But it sure run a ring around what the rest of my brothers and sisters was doing on the plantation.

"When I got to be a grown man I bought me an old piece of truck and I went to hauling the pulpwood. And I hauled pulpwood for fourteen years. Then I bought the hill place with my

pulpwood money. And my wife, well, she had another husband
before me, and they done worked and got this piece of land near
Tchula. We got sixty-seven acres here and we got fifty in the hills.
That is plenty. I don't want no more. That is enough for me to
make my living, and what do I want with a whole lot more to be
worrying about? A man don't need more than he can work."

The painted wall behind the Turnbows' sofa is decorated with
framed pictures of their three children—students in their gradua-
tion caps and gowns. All three are now living in Chicago. "I
didn't want them to fare like I fared. I suffered for them to get a
high school learning and go to college. This one," he said, pointing to the nearest gilt-edged photo, "is a secretary for Mont-
gomery Ward, and this one, she's a case worker for the Chicago
welfare department. I got a boy up there who's a mechanic for the
railroad company. They'd rather be here at home than up there.
They just went there because there was nothing to do down here.
My boy would come back in the morning if he had a job."

By now the sun was out, and Mrs. Turnbow had returned from
fishing in a nearby bayou with a basket of small catfish. We admired them for a moment, then she took them to the kitchen to
cook for supper. By now, Mr. Turnbow was completely engrossed
in his memories of the civil-rights days.

"It took many years to work up to a black mayor. I didn't think
it would ever be, but it came. It must have been a plan of God's
for under the conditions we lived in, there just wasn't any way for
a Negro to come and say he was going to run against a white man.
They'd have him in the bottom of the lake before you could look
around. Didn't nobody rebel against the white man—not in them
days. Not and live."

The movement in Holmes County began, he recalls, when a
black SNCC organizer named John Ball came to Tchula in 1963.
"The first time he came in here, talking about civil rights, and we
met and heard him talk, I said 'Fellah, what's ailing you? You
want to get all the Mississippi Negroes killed?' I said, 'You know
Mississippi. This is Mississippi. I mean, Tchula, Mississippi. And
you can't come in here talking about some sort of registering and
voting. When did you ever hear of a Negro registering and voting? It just ain't never been. Not in Mississippi.'

"He say, 'Why, it can be, Mr. Turnbow.' I said, 'What do you have to do for it to be?' He said, 'The first thing you have to do is study citizenship.'

"When he first came, we told him to come back. Then we met some more, and studied over what he said. And he made several trips back to Tchula before we would accept it. We talked it over, then we surveyed the county—near about the biggest portion of Holmes County—before we decided to start. We wanted to know if anybody else in the county wanted it. 'Cause if we had come up with something like it, and it wasn't any place but here that was for it, them white folks would have ganged up on us and killed all of us, and that would have been the end of it.

"I went to an all-Negro settlement in the hills, Mt. Olive. There was a great big church there, and well-educated people. When I made my first talk they told me, 'Why, Mr. Turnbow, that sounds good.' They said, 'Why, Mr. Turnbow, every word you say is right. Sir, you didn't say nary a word out of its place. But we don't know whether it's time for that or not. We ain't going to accept it today, but you come back again, and we're going to study it, and pray over it. And if we accept it, we'll let you know."

"And I went back another Sunday. They said, 'Well, Mr. Turnbow, we done prayed over it, and studied over it, and everybody says yes.' They said, 'We'll shed blood over it. We'll sell our cows for it. We'll spend our money for it.'"

Soon, Mr. Turnbow says, there were citizenship classes all over the county, mostly conducted in churches. "We always had six or seven watchmen on the outside. The white men couldn't get up to the church because there were plenty of guns there.

"Everybody got a little taste of that citizenship class. We had some funny little old books telling you about law. What was law and what wasn't law, and how you was supposed to reddish [register to vote]. It just opened my eyes and astonished us all to death. We just didn't know. We were just dumb and ignorant. Our heads had been under a cover, all them hundreds of years.

"And then I asked a question I never will forget. I asked the teacher, 'Sir, do you think we can become first-class citizens and then still live in Tchula, Mississippi, be living folks?' He said,

'Yeah, yeah.' I said, 'No, man! These white folks will kill all of us.'
He said, 'The federal government can help you.' I said, 'Well, how
come it ain't never helped us before?' He said, 'Simply because
you-all ain't tried to do nothing.' I said, 'Yeah, that's right, because we ain't knowed what to do.' He said, 'But, see, you know
what to do now. And all you got to do is start doing it, and if they
start to killing you, we'll call the federal government in here.'

"So, when we set a day to reddish out at Mt. Olive, why the
people poured in there. They just poured in. And when they
couldn't get reddished in the courthouse, the way they're supposed to, the federal government sent a federal registrar down
here. And he set up his office in the post-office building. And then
everyone went and got reddished. No trouble."

But it hadn't been that simple for Mr. Turnbow. Months before that outpouring at Mt. Olive, he had been one of six blacks
to register in the town of Tchula. They were the first blacks who
had even tried to do that in decades. That night a carload full of
white men stopped near his house.

"That was because they had me branded as a leader, and they
wanted to kill all leaders. They wasn't playing when they came in.
They firebombed this room. They firebombed the back bedroom.
They shot holes in each room."

He got up and walked across the living room to point out a bullet hole that was clearly visible in the pink wall, just beneath a
decorative wreath. He beckoned us to come on a tour of the house
and pointed to the bullet holes in the kitchen, the hall, the back-
bedroom walls. Then he described the night it had all happened.

"My wife woke me and said, 'They're bombing the house. It's
burning up.' When I woke up, the living room was burning. And
if I hadn't of had the nerve to chase the white men away, the
whole house would have burned up. I got my rifle and went out
the back door. They were still shooting and I started shooting.
And it wasn't long before they were all gone."

We followed him out the back door to a large yard where hens
pecked for food and a cow grazed on her tether rope. We passed
the well from which his wife and daughter had drawn the water
to put the fire out. Then Mr. Turnbow walked over to the spot

where he'd stood that night, and aimed an imaginary gun at the place where the white men's guns had blazed.

As soon as the fire was out, he recalled the lesson he'd learned in the citizenship class and called the Justice Department. "The next day we had the FBI from Washington sitting in this living room, writing the story. And the sheriff came, and they told him they didn't need him, and he went back.

"But late that evening, after the FBI men had gone, the sheriff came back and arrested me. He arrested me for arson. Said I had done the whole thing, that I was telling a lie. Said ain't nobody been here and shot in here. Said I shot them holes myself. Said I set fire to the house myself. He arrested me and I spent two nights in jail. Then they tried me and convicted me for arson. That fall, when we got to Jackson to have the court, they done dropped the charges. They knowed that stuff like that wouldn't stay up in federal court."

We walked back around the house to the screened-in porch in front. Mrs. Turnbow was sitting with a basin full of butterbeans she'd just picked and was deftly scooping the beans out of the pods into a yellow bowl. Her husband sat down next to her on the wooden bench and resumed the narrative. She looked up occasionally, to nod in agreement or add a comment.

"All of us what used to meet here was neighbors. The same folks still lives in Holmes County. Sometimes now we laugh about how scared we was, and how we had that citizenship class, and about what it costed. You know that thing cost lots of lives and lots of money. Hadn't of been for stuff like that, why John F. Kennedy wouldn't have died, Robert Kennedy would have been living, Martin Luther King would have been living."

For him, the movement had strengthened a resolve he'd never even known he possessed. "Five years earlier, the white men would have shot in my house and I'd have run off. I'd have just run gaddap off. I got the nerve to shoot back out of the lessons that fellah taught us in citizenship class. He said everybody has a right to live. And he said they have a right to own as much as they can, just so long as they don't take nothing from nobody, but work for it. And he said it was wrong to live on those plantations all those years and make big crops and don't clear no money. And here's another thing he told us in the citizenship classes. He said that the United States don't have one Constitution for Negroes and another for the white men. He said they got one Constitution and it answers for both. It answers for everybody. He said, 'You're an American, but they call you a nigger. They look at you with eyes of scorn, not like you're an intelligent human being.' I found all that to be true. And it makes me mad to see how many years Negroes have been cheated out of their rights."

Now Mr. Turnbow straddles two worlds. When he drives into Tchula to visit his protege, Mayor Carthan, he remembers the past that created him, and sees the present he helped create but can't quite accept.

"It used to be they'd kill you if you bumped up against a white woman," he recalls. "It was their street. When you saw them coming, you gave them plenty of room. Of course, there ain't nothing to that now, but when I see a white man or a white woman coming I just give them plenty of room.

"I got too old before I got that lesson, but these young'uns, it's a different life with them. They act and treat white people in Mississippi just like they is Negroes. I never did believe that would happen. They say 'yes' and 'no,' instead of yessah and nossah. They just ain't got all that respect we old Negroes had. And it ain't going to be like the old days and the old Negro.

"Mayor Carthan is going to treat Negroes and whites just the same. In other words, he's kind and friendly, and he knows what's right and wrong, and he ain't scared. And that's what it takes to deal with white people in days like these. 'Cause a heap of them is going to come to him and kind of want him to push the Negro back for them. But he ain't going to do it. He's just going to hew the line and let the chips fall where they may. And that is something that ain't never happened in Tchula. Never."

We wanted to know how he felt about the 1964 Summer Project and the outside volunteers—and he welcomed that question in a hearty, enthusiastic voice.

"Those white kids from all over the world came to Mississippi just to help us. The good that those students did, the praise ain't never been expressed enough. They came in and did their job and was gone, and they didn't know how much help they was, how they saved Mississippi.

"A whole lot of them students, their parents was rich people, and knew other rich people in the North, and they were well-prepared and knew the law. So they got folks back North to help us, to protect us. If it hadn't have been for the white students, we might have made it, but too many people would have been killed for nothing.

"I loved them. This house was their headquarters. We'd have sleeping bags and pallets all over this room. We'd go to a church and get places for them in different parts of the county, but this was where they stayed first. This was their home."

Mr. Turnbow has no idea of why the civil-rights workers left. "I didn't know when they was coming and I didn't know when it was all called off." And he didn't know what became of them. "I got letters from a few of them after they left, but not very many. It wasn't more than one or two."

Traveling through Mississippi in 1977 we saw plenty of signs of desegregation, but not enough to warrant the euphoric descriptions of the egalitarian New South. Everywhere we went, we saw signs of deep, widespread poverty. In Delta towns and cities, the white neighborhoods still looked prosperous. But, in most black neighborhoods there were still, mostly, wood shacks—some of which had been hauled from the plantations when mechanization set in—and rutted, unpaved streets, where groups of unemployed kids still gathered in the middle of the afternoon. So we were curious to know what Mr. Turnbow thought about the New South.

"I ain't learned nothing about that," he said with just a trace of irony in his slow, gentle voice. "I heard them talking about it, but I ain't never thought enough about it to dig into it. The changes didn't get far enough. They still want the Negro to stay where he is."

Mr. Turnbow is a man who loves to weave tales. He often laughs at memories that are bitter. But his anger shows when he talks about the injustices that confront Mississippi Negroes today. Holmes County is still one of the nation's poorest places. Blacks today own even less land than they did twenty years ago, since many farmers sold their few acres to white people when they decided to move North.

As a farmer, Mr. Turnbow has a dream. He lives on land that his wife's ex-husband bought from the government back in the thirties. During the New Deal the Roosevelt administration acquired a few failing plantations, broke them into smaller lots, and sold them, with no down payment, to local farmers or sharecroppers, black or white. Mr. Turnbow wishes the civil-rights movement would return to Tchula. He wishes that, this time, it would fight to see that the land was parceled out fairly.

"Whoo! That would make it better all over the United States if enough poor white folks and enough Negroes could get homesteaded down here in the South. A lot of them would leave the North, and that would mean more work for them folks what ain't never going to leave.

"They'd be putting up help-wanted signs all over Chicago, Detroit, everywhere. You'd be surprised how many folks would leave New York and come home. They'd come right back to Tchula."

CHAPTER 9

Harlan County:
The Power and the Shame

Introduction: The Lost Tribe of the Working Class

I first went to Harlan County, Kentucky, in April 1974, to cover a coal miners' strike against the Brookside Coal Company and its giant North Carolina–based parent organization, the Duke Power Company. At the time, the battle to form a 180-man United Mine Workers chapter at Brookside—which would cost the UMW about one million dollars—seemed like an opening skirmish between Arnold Miller's reformed union and the region's coal operators. It seemed to be the beginning of a long struggle for control over eastern Kentucky's rich coalfields, which, in 1974, were producing about one third of all the nonunion coal in America.

For years I had been entranced by the legends of "Bloody Harlan," the center of some of the fiercest labor battles in the 1930s. In fact, a song those struggles produced, "Which Side Are You On," had formed a vivid, enduring link between the labor movement and the Mississippi civil-rights movement. Some of the journalists I admired most—Theodore Dreiser, Sherwood Anderson, and John Dos Passos—had been part of a committee that investigated working conditions in Harlan in 1931. *Harlan Miners*

Speak, the Dreiser committee's book, symbolized the journalistic tradition I wanted to emulate. It was also an invaluable account of the legacy of injustice which the Brookside miners were trying to challenge.

It described the hardships Harlan's people had faced in the early days of the Depression, when most of the sixty-five thousand people who lived in the county earned so little they were in perpetual debt to the company store. In some places, like the Cary Coal Camp, the poverty bred illnesses, like pellagra, a form of dysentery that caused seven children a week to die in the summer of 1931.

That year, hundreds of men—organized by the left-wing National Miners Union—decided to fight back. One May morning eleven miners and law-enforcement officials were killed at the battle of Evarts—an episode local people still describe in the slightly reverent tones American historians reserve for the battles of Gettysburg or Bunker Hill.

The battles of Bloody Harlan were over free speech as well as the right to higher wages. For the operators controlled the legal system, and they were ruthless with their power. The National Miners Union distributed copies of the *Daily Worker* to each of its recruits. In Harlan, anyone who had the newspaper in his house could be arrested on charges of criminal syndicalism. Often, the miners were taken across Pine Mountain, to jails in remote hamlets, towns that had no roads, which could only be reached on mule back. Sometimes the isolation broke their spirits: Many swore they wouldn't have anything to do with the union again. Then the charges were dropped and they'd be released to go back to search for work again.

When Theodore Dreiser came to Harlan he attacked the concept of criminal syndicalism by reminding Harlan's Prosecuting Attorney, William Brock, that free speech was a constitutional right in America, that the *Worker* had a circulation of forty thousand, and that it was admitted to the U.S. mails without interference. "There are things that go into the mail that aren't legal," Brock replied. "This is one of them."

Such episodes—the legends of "Bloody Harlan"—had helped form my political and journalistic consciousness. But, in 1974, when I read about the strike at Brookside, I realized I had no idea of what had happened in the county itself in the past forty years. My knowledge ended with the glamorous writers' departure. What, for example, had become of the miners who had fought in battles like the shoot-out at Evarts? They had attained a union— John L. Lewis's UMW, which had been more moderate and con- ciliatory than the National Miners Union. But what good had it done them, especially since the union had been debased by Lewis's corrupt successor, Tony Boyle? Why did their offspring have to or- ganize the same territory all over again?

I figured I could find the clearest answers to that question by experiencing the real life behind the political legends. So I de- cided to see the Brookside strike from the vantage point of a coal camp—a miner's home—in the 1970s, to learn about the culture that had produced the labor battles; to focus on the human de- tails I found in Harlan.

It turned out that my journalist's instincts jibed with the un- ion's organizing strategy. Some of the young reformers who had become part of the UMW bureaucracy when Arnold Miller had been elected president had received their political baptisms in the civil rights and peace movements. They realized that the public relations methods that had been so important in those causes could be introduced into the battle for the coalfields. That was particularly true in the Brookside strike because the Duke Power Company, an absentee landlord with no strong supporters in Harlan's local oligarchy, was trying to create a liberal image of it- self across the country. It would be particularly vulnerable to bad publicity. So the union tried to encourage as much newspaper and television coverage as possible. Its officials in Washington were glad to arrange for me to spend ten days with a strike leader— Jerry Johnson, twenty-eight; his wife, Dorothy, twenty-eight; and their three children—in the Kildav coal camp, where Jerry's par- ents also lived. The union and the Johnsons were delighted that Rachel planned to arrive later on, to photograph the miners and the town.

Jerry and Dorothy, who'd spent nearly a decade in Chicago, adjusted to our presence easily. Within a day or two I felt very close to them. In fact, as Jerry and I talked endlessly, with mutual fascination, about our very different backgrounds or drove around Harlan, planning half-serious, half-surrealistic confrontations with the local oligarchy, I began to fantasize that we were a latter-day version of Butch Cassidy and the Sundance Kid, pledged to cleanse the mining town of its heritage of corruption.

The Johnsons, like most of the people I met in Harlan, came from families that had been sealed off from the rest of America until the early twentieth century, when giant corporations owned by the Morgan family, the Mellon family, the Rockefeller family, came into eastern Kentucky and carved roads and railroad tracks into the hilly, rocky timberland that happened to have rich seams of coal beneath it. For a short time the mines were a symbol of unbridled prosperity. Between 1916 and 1921, the population of Harlan increased from thirty-five thousand to sixty-five thousand. But they were part of a thoroughly unplanned economic system, which sent thousands of families scurrying across America in search of work each time the nation's demand for coal slackened and the mines shut down.

The mines played the same role in eastern Kentucky as the mechanization of the plantations had in the Mississippi Delta. They destroyed the ecology of a culture that had existed for centuries. They made economic refugees of people who might have banded together in a sustained battle for power. They made proud, independent people, like Jerry Johnson's parents, thoroughly dependent on forces they couldn't understand or control.

Once, they'd been mountain folk—part of the rich American tradition symbolized by Daniel Boone. Now they had to earn their living working underground, like moles. Most of the old people wheezed with black lung and hobbled from the injuries they'd sustained in the mines. The younger people lived with the knowledge that they were never more than a rock slide away from death. As a result, their labor battles—especially in the Seventies —were not simply over wages but over demands for health and safety as well: over issues of human survival.

They were very friendly people. But, as I came to know them, I realized that they felt a smoldering resentment toward outsiders— those who promised to help as well as those who owned the mines. For, except for brief, well-publicized confrontations like the Brookside strike, they were isolated and abandoned in their coal camps and hollers. I began to think of them as the lost tribe of the working class.

Part I: April 1974: Ten Days in a Coal Camp

It was a pleasant April afternoon when I arrived in Harlan. At about four-thirty, just after the second shift at the mines had ended, Jerry Johnson and I were driving through the mountainous Kildav coal camp in Jerry's old Ford. Everywhere we saw sooty-faced men returning home from work. Jerry, a lanky, well-muscled man with an easy, rueful smile, knew almost all of them. He kept honking his horn and shouting out pleasantries as we drove up the winding dirt road, with its hairpin turns, toward his home.

As we approached Jerry's four-room cabin, his neighbor, Estil Phillips, thirty-five, a red-haired miner, stepped out on the cluttered front porch of his unpainted cabin and signaled us to stop.

He had some bad news. Three men had been killed in Harlan mines that afternoon—on the second shift, in roof cave-ins at the Dixie Fuel Company and the Glenbrook Mines. The deaths seemed particularly ominous since the Dixie mine—where Stanley Hill, thirty-seven, was crushed—was owned by the same person who owned the V & C mine, where Estil worked as a machinist.

Fatalities are not abnormal in Harlan—or anywhere else in America's coalfields, where an average of 120 miners are killed each year. As Estil talked, his face, still streaked with coal dust, looked completely composed. Three of his four red-haired children were shooting baskets into a low net at the right of the house. A mammoth turkey was scurrying and squawking around the back yard. The sawmill, located at the base of the Kildav camp, made a constant almost hypnotic thud. The atmosphere seemed so tranquil, so normal, to me that I did a double take, realizing that the man standing beside the car was chatting about death.

When Jerry said, wryly, that the fatalities might prod some men at V & C to sign union cards, Estil's honest, depressed answer was, "That won't never happen, buddy. Not until you'uns

has won your strike. Those boys aren't like you. They're scared
they won't never find themselves no work again."

Jerry just nodded and drove on up to his house, where his wife,
Dorothy, was waiting with dinner.

Jerry had been raised in Black Bottom, a remote holler outside
of town, where his family had lived in the 1950s. His father,
George Johnson, seventy-nine, descendant of farmers, a retired
miner, had only left the county once in his life. When he was
seventeen years old he had walked all the way to North Carolina,
in search of any work he could find. Since then, he'd lived in Harlan, raised a large family, and dug coal—when the mines were operating. He still feels some nostalgia for the old days, when men
were paid by the amount of coal they mined, not by the number
of hours they put in. "They've got machines to do everything
now," he told me once, with more than a trace of bitterness in his
voice. "Jerry and his friends just ride those old trolley cars into the
mines and never strike a lick of work. Buddy, when I was in the
mines, if you didn't shovel nothing, you didn't earn nothing."

The elder Johnson had worked a twelve-hour day. When he got
home, no matter how tired he was, he'd bathe in the tub of water
his wife heated for him, change into his farming clothes, then
walk to the small patch of muddy soil outside his coal-camp shack
and spend another several hours working on the vegetable garden
that helped his family keep down its debt to the company store.
Farming came natural to him. He'd learned how to do it from his
daddy's generation.

In the 1930s, when the Depression began, it seemed like a man
couldn't get by on hard work alone. In those days, it didn't seem
to matter how much a miner shoveled. No one was earning anything.

Soon George Johnson became a dedicated union man.

Even today he prefers the confrontational tactics he recalls
from that period to the slower, sleeker public relations methods
Jerry and his friends were using in the 1970s.

He would reminisce about the dangerous times when "The
company had machine guns trained on us. The UMW organizers

would peck at our door at two in the morning, tell us to get our weapons and leave our houses without being seen. We'd take our guns to the ridges across from the mines and open fire. We didn't want to hurt nobody, just to shoot so close to their feet that dust kicked up around their ankles. Of course, some scabs was killed. Buddy, let me tell you, that didn't hurt none. It scared the rest of those boys so badly they wouldn't work until their bosses signed the contract.

"This Brookside strike would be over if they'd just shoot a few scabs. That's what I told Jerry and them from the start. But those boys' idea of action is to break a few commissary windows. Now I don't hold with the destruction of property. It don't do you a bit of good. I believe in doing the right thing as it comes along."

During the Thirties, the ideological battles between the United Mine Workers Union and the National Miners Union seemed immensely important to writers like Dreiser, Dos Passos, and Anderson. George Johnson barely remembers them. For him, the whole period is symbolized by John L. Lewis, the single outsider who, he believes, served as his steadfast protector. After all, for about twenty years it was the UMW who guaranteed him steady work at decent wages under bosses who had to treat him with some respect.

But then, in the Fifties, when America's demand for coal tailed off so swiftly and unexpectedly, Lewis became convinced that he could only preserve the union by making decisions that would soon change George Johnson's life. Lewis decided to concentrate the UMW's waning resources on the large, stable mines in West Virginia and western Pennsylvania, where giant companies, like U. S. Steel and Bethlehem Steel still had "captive mines" that would continue to produce fuel for their mills.

The union abandoned eastern Kentucky, urging operators to cut labor costs—and save a few jobs—by mechanizing, enabling some of them to shut down their mines altogether, signing sweetheart contracts with the few bosses whose successful businesses would sweeten the union's pension and welfare fund. No one ever explained those decisions to George Johnson—or to the approximately 350,000 Appalachian coal miners who, like him, lost their jobs during those years. He never understood the forces that left him unemployed, without prospects, in his middle age.

When the mines were still open he had farmed as an avocation. Now that he couldn't find steady work he tried to transform that ancestral tradition into a source of livelihood. But he barely grew enough to feed his large family. The Johnsons had no money for amenities. Jerry couldn't afford the pencils and paper he needed for school; when he went to the grocery store with slightly more well-to-do friends, he didn't even know the brand names of the candies and soda pops they bought. Later, he couldn't afford to court girls in his grade-school classes by buying them Cokes.

George Johnson, like many miners, had contracted black lung during his years underground. He can barely finish a sentence without fighting off a cough or a wheeze. By 1974 though, that physical ailment was something of an economic blessing. Five years earlier, militant miners had forced Congress to provide black-lung benefits, and now he survives on the money the government pays him for his disability.

He spends his days in his cabin in Kildav, watching old Western movies on TV while his wife grows peas and beans in the small garden outside their house. They are on the periphery of a fundamentalist Christian sect whose members experience blissful seizures of the holy spirit, which, they believe, enable them to handle poisonous snakes or thrust their arms into fire without being singed.

That religion troubles Jerry. For one thing, the Pentecostal creed seems hypocritical: Growing up, he would hear his parents and their friends gossiping, even though that act is supposed to be taboo. More important, the frenzied faith reminded Jerry of the superstition-bound culture in which he was raised, just as his father's support of picket-line violence reminded him that most miners felt too small, too powerless, to devise long-range political tactics that might achieve their goals. Jerry longed to transcend the passivity and fatalism that dominated Harlan County's culture.

In seventh grade he began his break. He quit school and went to work, gathering coal around the mine face. He tried picking cotton over in Lexington, Kentucky, hauling moonshine from

Cumberland to Harlan, working in a sawmill. He wanted to become a truck driver so he tried to enlist in the Army, where he could learn mechanics. But Harlan's schools had been so bad he had trouble with the literacy tests and was rejected.

Then, in 1962, Jerry's friend Estil—who had found a job in the mines and was earning about ten dollars a shift—moved to Chicago in search of more lucrative work. He was one of 3.3 million people who left Appalachia in the vast, barely visible migration northward. A year later Jerry joined him. He was seventeen years old at the time.

Despite his lack of education—something that still embarrasses him—he was able to adapt to Chicago's ways more quickly than did most of his friends. The first time he went to a factory, asked to be "ha'rd," and was turned away with a blank stare, he decided to change his accent. Most of his friends still retain the harsh, slightly nasal Elizabethan mountain twang, in which a thin road is "na'r"; where water "burls"; where an hour is an "ar"; where you "peck at doors," "cut off lights," "trade at stores," describe "nones" as "narys" and groups of people as "you'uns." But Jerry acquired a softer, more comprehensible southern drawl. Sometimes he had to translate for his friends. Soon he was in a position to hire them, too. His skill with machines and his uncanny ability to recall the details of a blueprint or the layout of a cluttered storeroom made him a foreman in the body shops and the carpentry and ball-bearing factories, where most of the migrants found assembly-line jobs.

At nineteen, he married Dorothy—a woman from Jellicoe, Tennessee, who was working in the mail room of a greeting-card printer's—and the couple had three girls.

Still, Jerry—like many of his friends—felt cramped in Chicago. He knew that his body was going slack. He missed the mountains.

Sometimes, out of sheer devilment, he would go into restaurants in the Loop and shock customers by putting on his thickest mountain accent and asking for a plate of possum. At least, pranks like that helped relieve his restless boredom.

But mostly his lonely community of refugees from Appalachia huddled together in their tiny apartments on North Lincoln Avenue. They found each other jobs and mates. They organized wild, drunken Saturday-night parties where banjo players like John Shepherd, who now works in a sawmill near Kildav, picked blue-grass tunes like "Nine Pound Hammer" and "Wildwood Flower," which made their nostalgia almost unbearable.

Then, suddenly, there was no reason they had to bear it. In the early 1970s America's energy problems began to crystallize.

Suddenly, oil was an expensive fuel. The "energy crisis" was a blessing for Jerry and his friends. The outside forces that had controlled their father's lives—and driven them to Chicago—now dictated a set of terms that enabled them to end their urban exile.

Once he was back in Harlan, Jerry could grow a garden, as his father and grandfather had. Still a mountain man, he would climb a slope above his house in Kildav and pick poke (a sprout that yields a delicious dish), ramps (a garlic-like vegetable), elder-berry (which supposedly stops kids from peeing in their beds), and rabbit tobacco (a bitter weed men chew in the mines). He'd blasted a small mine near his house, with safety conditions he considered ideal. He got most of the coal he and his family needed from it.

Now he had work he liked. Even at its best, under decent conditions, mining was risky, but that made it more interesting than the assembly line. Besides that, working underground, he felt a sense of comradeship he'd never found in the factory. Lives were so interdependent in the mines that even the bitterest enemies would forget their feuds and holler life-saving warnings over the booming machinery to help each other avert the danger that was always lurking.

Jerry was proud of the fact that at Brookside, before the strike, he'd had the riskiest job of all—operating the roof-bolting ma-chine. Like the other men, he rode the flat, motorized cars through the low, damp, mile-long tunnels to the area where the coal was mined. Then, he and a partner crept beyond the frontier where the men were digging to scout out new, dangerous territory. They wheeled the heavy roof-bolting machine along with them, and used it to secure the treacherous ceiling for the people who would follow.

During his eight hours underground, Jerry had to hunker in the clammy tunnels (many of Harlan's mines are just thirty inches high), concentrating all his sharp senses on the roof. Amid the blasting of the dynamite, the rasping, clattering of the digging machine, his ears had to be alert for the faintest hint of a dangerous rumble overhead. The nerves in his fingertips had to be attuned to every ominous vibration from the heavy drills. His eyes studied each clump of dust for signs of the discoloration that might signal a roof cave-in. He had to be aware of the changing odors, be prepared for the first hint of the methane gas, which causes explosions.

In eastern Kentucky's nonunion mines, safety violations are often treated casually. The dangers are the result of a vicious circle. Mine inspectors often tell coal operators when they are coming—and the operators, in turn, order the miners to make sure the work area meets minimum safety requirements on that crucial day. A worker who complains is often targeted as a troublemaker and blacklisted.

Jerry, like most miners, saw past the cover-up. He knew about safety violations that occurred every day. For example, some Harlan operators dig their coal in tunnels whose width is closer to a hundred feet than the prescribed twenty-five. That attenuates support for the all-important ceiling. Furthermore, the operators were often sloppy about propping up the roof with timber, Jerry said. Such carelessness was one reason so many men were killed in rock falls. He knew that many operators were unwilling to invest money in the new machinery—motorized dollies with decent brake shoes, or methane detectors that flash if the level of gas is too high—that would make the mines safer places to work. But, during his first years back in Harlan, Jerry didn't see any way of changing that. It never occurred to him to begin organizing a UMW chapter, for he was still very cynical about the union that had betrayed his father's generation.

So he transformed his pent-up rage at the operators into a deep pride in his own work, his own self-worth. He told people, "I'm Jerry Johnson. I can do anything." He never doubted the truth of that Paul Bunyan-like boast.

He was making good money in the mines—forty-two dollars a day, as opposed to the ten dollars Estil had earned a decade earlier, or the twenty cents George Johnson had been paid for every ton of coal he could shovel before the UMW first came to Harlan. With that salary, Jerry bought himself some of the amenities he had never imagined himself owning as a child in Black Bottom: a refrigerator, a television set, a secondhand freezer, a car, a Honda. Nevertheless, it was hard for him and Dorothy to transform their community into a place they could be proud of. For Kildav—like most coal camps—was still at the mercy of the oligarchy that has controlled Harlan for most of the twentieth century.

Once, in timbering times, the coal camp had been a lovely forest of white oaks and hickories, maple trees and poplars. The relative handful of people who lived there owned three or four acres of land and tended their plots fastidiously. Then, when the large corporations moved in, they bought most of the land and herded the mountain folk into coal camps that were really workers' barracks, not family homes. The shacks were intended to serve as places where men could sleep when they weren't underground, not as places where parents could raise kids. Many operators didn't even bother to provide the cluttered settlements they'd created with paved roads or sewage systems or garbage-disposal services. They forced the miners' families to buy all their goods at company stores, and the debts they incurred meant that the people—who'd once been so proud and hardy—were really indentured servants. Over the decades, a gray attitude of dependency and despair came to pervade their lives.

The situation had changed slightly by the 1970s. Though most of Harlan's dwelling places are still in coal camps, miners didn't have to live in company-owned housing—they could choose any settlement they pleased. But Kildav, like most of its counterparts in the county, remained a rural slum. Near the Johnsons' house, the ground was littered with car bodies, beer cans, the remains of a month's meals. In other coal camps, outhouses jut over the mountain streams, dumping human waste into the water. On rainy nights the rivers swell, draping used toilet paper, scraps of plastic, old rags, on the willows and sycamores that line the riverbanks.

Kildav is a violent place, too—another reflection of Harlan's history. In the nineteenth century the folk who moved there were among the most restless people on the continent. They had left the certainties of settled America to carve out new, free lives for themselves. They were never a very peaceful tribe. During the Civil War, hollers—and even families—split over the issue of union. Those feuds lasted for decades. Sometimes the Appalachian battles became legendary: The Hatfields and the McCoys waged their war between fiefdoms just a hundred miles from Harlan County.

After the corporations came in, the mountain folk had to bear the frustrated knowledge that their precious independence was gone forever. That fact intensified the violence that had flared up so often. Since the coal companies—the captors, the enemy—were so remote, the workers turned on each other. Sometimes they did so for political reasons. Union families still remember—and despise—those who were scabs in the 1930s. Sometimes the quarrels had to do with sex or money. They were physical fights, though, not just heated verbal arguments—and the mines provided one strong psychological argument for that. Why stop yourself from defending your honor tonight when you might die for the company in the morning?

In the evenings, when I was at Kildav, the Johnsons' neighbors would shoot .38s off their back porches. On picket lines, over by the railroad tracks near the Brookside main office, strikers idled away their leisure time shooting .45s at beer cans. One night a close friend of Jerry's came over to the house and talked freely about the afternoon his father—whose fear of going into the mines had turned him into an alcoholic—got drunk, lay down on the couch, and was shot—by his wife, who had been beaten once too often.

Jerry and Dorothy often talked about moving away from Kildav —or at least improving their own living conditions. But both things were hard to do. They couldn't even obtain the conveniences they'd taken for granted in Chicago. They couldn't afford an indoor toilet since it was very expensive to dig a cesspool into Kildav's hills. So Jerry and Dorothy and their three children used the slatted wooden privy outside their house. When they wanted to bathe they had to pour water Dorothy had heated on the stove into a tub that was about two feet deep and three feet in diameter. That was particularly inconvenient for Jerry, since in those days Brookside didn't provide the showers for workers that are common in most American coalfields. When he came home from work, he had to hunch his six-foot frame into the tub and scrub off all the coal dust and grime he'd accumulated during the day underground.

Jerry and Dorothy wanted to find a home in a cleaner, more peaceful community. But Harlan's banks, run by the same families that owned the mines, were reluctant to loan workers' money for a down payment on a decent house.

There was no construction industry in town—only one company, which took advantage of its monopoly position to charge outrageous prices. Besides, even if a family somehow got the money to build a house, it would have been almost impossible to find flat land to put it on. The few open acres that had once existed were now obliterated by new state roads. Some of the Johnsons' friends had decided to settle in the town of Harlan, but the aristocracy—the local "hillers"—owned the acreage on the highlands. The miners' houses were at the basin of the Cloverfork River, which floods every year or two. So, for the few workers who could afford them, mobile homes were palaces, or at least a higher rung on the ladder of upward mobility. Maybe, some day, Jerry and Dorothy would buy one.

Still, there was never a time, after Jerry returned from Chicago, that he'd regarded the conditions he encountered back in Harlan as acceptable or inevitable. After all, he had succeeded in a world that his parents, and many of his contemporaries, could barely imagine. He'd bossed more people in Chicago's factories than did most of his supervisors in Harlan's mines. Someday, Jerry Johnson would show *them* that he could do anything.

In July 1973, he got his chance. Wary as the Brookside miners were of the UMW, they still reasoned that a union-elected safety committee and a union-sponsored pension plan would give them more protection than the company-approved Southern Labor Union ever could. So they voted, 113 to 55, to affiliate with the UMW.

Duke Power, the operator, refused to sign a contract. For three months the miners waged a lonely fight. Then, unexpectedly, the Miller administration decided to use the strike as proof that the union was once again willing to embrace the workers in eastern Kentucky. It used all the outside resources at its command to launch a nationally publicized organizing campaign.

Over the next year, powerful forces poured into Harlan to help the miners—forces that represented a world that seemed omnipotent and wonderfully glamorous from the vantage point of Kildav. One weekend a panel of prominent citizens—including then Senator Fred Harris and former Secretary of Labor Willard Wirtz—came to town to investigate the miners' grievances. Senator Edward Kennedy made a radio commercial on behalf of the UMW. Reporters from *The New York Times* and the *Washington Post*, from CBS and NBC, from *Ms.*, the *Voice* and *New Times*, all provided the strikers with favorable coverage. Students at the University of North Carolina—in Chapel Hill, where Duke Power was located—gave the strike a great deal of attention, linking it to their fight against higher utility rates. Dozens joined the miners when they picketed the power company's headquarters. Some came to Harlan County.

In the heady spring of 1974, all the changes Jerry had ever dreamed of seemed within reach. Furthermore, simply by staying in Harlan, he could display his talents on a national stage. He was the subject of many of the articles about the strike. He was lionized by the college students. He was helping Barbara Koeppel shoot the footage that would become the Academy Award-winning *Harlan County, U.S.A.* The UMW organizers seemed to be paying him special attention.

He was convinced that if he and his friends won the Brookside strike, thousands of men like Estil Phillips, who were slowly gaining courage, would feel secure enough to fight for unions all over the county. Sometimes he imagined himself traveling to Washington and spending hours with Arnold Miller, talking, miner to miner, about the next steps in the struggle to control eastern Kentucky's nonunion coalfields.

In those days, Jerry believed he would grow with the union.

In Harlan, where coal miners—though fairly well paid—were disposable instruments of production, the Brookside strike was primarily a battle over safety and health care—over the means of survival. I began to see funeral homes and hospitals as crucial settings for my story. In the coal camps I listened for the occasional moment when the proud people I lived with let down their carefully constructed defenses and revealed their stark, bottomless fear of death.

My second day in the camp, the day after Stanley Hill had been smothered at the Dixie Fuel Company, Jerry and I went over to the funeral parlor to see his waxy body, which had already been placed in the smooth satin of his black coffin. Soon his friends and kinfolk would "view" the corpse. The mortician had done a fine job of preparing it. Stanley Hill was dressed in a neatly pressed gray suit and an expensive blue tie. His thin brown hair was parted in the middle. His closed eyelids seemed about to flutter awake.

One of the morticians—a skinny twenty-one-year old from over in Muhlenberg County—came out to greet us and offer us some coffee. When he reached to shake our hands, Jerry flinched. But, then, impressed with the mortician's craftsmanship, he asked how a face that had been half-crushed by rocks could be restored. "Well," the boy said, "one side is intact. It's easy when you have that much idea of what they looked like. Besides, I've been fooling around with corpses ever since I was four or five. I'm pretty good at it."

After we left the funeral home Jerry and I needed a drink. But Harlan is dry. Whenever there is a referendum on prohibition, the bootleggers bribe the preachers to scare their congregations with jeremiads about how legalized liquor would make Harlan a latter-day Sodom. The law helps operators, too. It means that there's no place in the county where miners can sit around over a few beers, sharing the complaints that can sometimes become the emotional underpinnings of a union.

So you buy your beer and liquor from bootleggers. I'd done that earlier in the day, when I'd driven my rented Malibu down a dirt road—which, older people say, is inhabited by a "hain't"—the ghost of an old woman who walks it at midnight. I'd been told to look for a small trailer at the back of an abandoned lot filled with the carcasses of old cars. The bootlegger was there when I arrived.

His place was furnished with one bare light, a rumpled bed, and a refrigerator that contained nothing but a box full of sixteen-ounce beer cans. I'd bought a six pack and left.

Now, sitting in the car, Jerry and I downed two cans, very quickly, and headed for home.

Dorothy was waiting for us, half-concentrating on a Martin and Lewis movie on TV. Angie, eight, was asleep in the baby's crib while Brenda, three, lay next to her on the pink tufted quilt the Johnsons used as a couch cover. It seemed as if Dorothy was always waiting for Jerry.

Since the strike began he had become acquainted with feminists who came to Harlan. He had glimpsed what seemed to be freewheeling, easygoing relationships between the men and women who hosted him when he spoke on college campuses. He'd been very impressed by those relationships and spoke about them often. But they had no connection to his own Harlan-style marriage, in which sexual roles were strictly defined, where men's conduct was based on the assumption that the risks they took in the mines entitled them to be treated like lords at home.

When Jerry was working, Dorothy would wake up to the blurry sound of a clock radio that was never quite set to any station. While he slept, she'd fix him a huge breakfast of fried eggs, biscuits, and gravy made of sausage fat, flour, milk, and pepper. She would prepare five thick sandwiches and two thermoses full of coffee for his lunch pail. Then she'd wake him up and, hollering all the while, get the girls off to school by seven-fifteen. Since she couldn't drive she stayed in Kildav all day, gossiping with Jerry's sister, his parents, other miners' wives.

Her world was so circumscribed that a trip into Harlan—to shop at the A&P instead of the small grocery store near Kildav— seemed like an adventure. But Jerry rarely took her there.

He rarely took her anywhere. When he came back home from work or from the picket line he usually ate dinner in front of the TV while Dorothy fed the kids in the kitchen. Then he changed clothes, polished his boots, combed his hair, and rode his Honda down to the Jiffy Cafe or Ackley's Diner to catch up on the latest gossip. When he got home he'd mumble responses to Dorothy's comments about the weather, the kids, his parents. Then he'd go to bed.

But tonight he wanted to talk, to confide his fears in Dorothy. It was the only time I ever heard him mention those feelings during the ten days I lived in his house.

He was haunted by the image of Stanley Hill's mutilated face—and by his own brief encounter with the mortician. "When that boy shook my hand, all I could think of was that he'd just had it in a miner's blood," he told his wife. "Paul was just sitting there, drinking coffee, but, buddy, I went right into the washroom and washed my hands about ten times. I don't reckon they're clean yet."

Then he described his own ever-present terror that a mine roof would collapse on him. "I'd say that in a way a cave-in like that is good for you. It scares you all over again. I know I'd never go into a mine if I wasn't a little bit scared. Buddy, you get killed if you're too calm."

As he talked, Dorothy's eyes widened with fear. She punctuated each mention of a hazard with an awed, frightened, "Gosh, Jerry," and finally with a plea to "stop talking that way, buddy, or you'll have me so scared I'll be wanting us to move back to Chicago." Then, with her haggard face under tight control, she turned to me and said, "I never think about what might happen to him. Whenever his shift is ending I just put the bathwater on, cook dinner for him, and wait for him to come back home"—as if that wifely ritual would somehow provide a talisman against the mine's dangers.

In *Road to Wigan Pier*, George Orwell's account of British coal mining, there are two extraordinary chapters where Orwell visits a mine and makes you feel what it must be like to work there. I'd hoped to do something similar in Harlan County, but none of the owners would let me go below ground. Then I began to notice how often Harlan's Appalachian Regional Hospital came up in conversation. In a world where serious injuries are commonplace occurrences, the hospital is an extension of the mines. I decided that a day spent there might be as valuable as a day underground.

The Harlan hospital was another symbol of the UMW's betrayal of its members. Originally, it had been part of a chain built with union funds—hospitals that were, in effect, owned by the miners themselves. In the 1940s and 1950s, the union had provided extraordinary medical care. It had recruited top-flight doctors from all over the country. But, when the union withdrew from eastern Kentucky, it sold off the hospital. According to everyone I interviewed, the nonprofit corporation that runs it now provides more expensive, less efficient health care than the union did.

I was told that the best way to get a firsthand look at the hospital was to ride with an ambulance driver. That meant that I had to make another visit to a funeral home, since all but a few of the ambulances in town are owned by the morticians.

They compete fiercely with one another for the bodies. One driver even told me how he'd stolen a corpse from another, who'd been called to the scene of an accident but arrived five minutes late. Still, competitive as they are, the morticians resent the hospital for the way it treats patients. The undertakers hate the long waits in the emergency rooms and the garbled conversations with the Hispanic, Filipino, or Indian doctors who can't understand the mountaineers' English or make their own English understood. They think the nurses are careless and incompetent, and that many of the doctors are undertrained and can't diagnose the miners' special illnesses. So, one funeral director let me ride with an ambulance driver who had just had an emergency call.

The patient was an old black man named Beauford Lawrence, who had worked in a UMW mine but who'd been housebound with black lung for the past three years. He lived in a four-room apartment, four steep flights of stairs above the railroad tracks.

When we arrived he was coughing and gagging. An old friend —a woman—was with him, trying to calm him as he gasped desperately for breath. She went along with us to the hospital. In many parts of the country, the law requires two people with some medical training to ride in an ambulance, but that was not the case in Harlan, 1974. If I hadn't been along, the driver, who'd had no medical training, would have had to scour the neighborhood for help, or load Lawrence's two-hundred-pound body onto the stretcher and drag him down the four flights of stairs by himself.

It was early afternoon, and Lawrence was admitted to the hospital quickly. Within fifteen minutes the nurse, a woman in her mid-fifties, had moved another patient from the oxygen room and told the driver and me to wheel Lawrence in there. There was no doctor on the ward. The nurse handed the driver a respirator—a piece of equipment he'd never used before—and, without showing him how to administer the oxygen, hurried away to find help. Lawrence stayed alive (the driver had been worried about overdosing him), but his gasps grew shorter and louder, and the bottom of his face filmed hideously with spittle and phlegm.

The nurse returned with good news: The doctor was on his way. Now she instructed the driver to hold the respirator over Lawrence's mouth while she stuck a rubber catheter into his nose to suck out the mucus. Then she drew blood from his arm. While she was doing that she joked about how, maybe, Lawrence had been "bending his elbow" (drinking) that morning, about the thick layer of mucus, which made his black face look almost white.

Presently, the doctor arrived and ordered the lab to check Lawrence's blood-sugar level. While he was doing that an ambulance driver from another funeral home came in. He began to tease the driver with me about how his boss ran the fastest mortuary in Harlan. "We're going to drive you out of business and buy all your fancy equipment at your last auction." As he joked, the nurse treating his client—a teenager who had totaled his car on one of Harlan's narrow mountain roads—called him over to the cubicle where she was working. She was short-handed, too, and needed him to swab the cuts that covered the boy's face.

There were no orderlies in the Appalachian Regional Hospital. The doctor decided Lawrence should be taken to the Intensive Care Unit on the third floor. As he was filling out the chart, the nurse said she wasn't going to wheel any stretcher to the elevator with two such strong men around. So we took him there, very slowly, since I was guiding the stretcher and didn't know my way around the winding corridors. Finally, we got to the elevator and, after a long wait, to the third floor. For a moment the elevator door jammed. "This thing *will* do that," the nurse chuckled. "It's gotten pretty cranky, now that it's eighteen years old." She told me to pry it open.

Inside the Intensive Care Unit the nurse put Lawrence's charts and papers onto his bed. She told a second nurse, the driver, and me to lift him off the stretcher while she gave him some oxygen and put the catheter back into his nose. The move required some skill. If one of us had jerked the patient, or bobbled him, the catheter or the respirator might have come loose. As we transferred him his rasping breath seemed to fade to a faintly murmuring rumble. But once on the bed he began to choke and gasp loudly again.

Before we moved him from the stretcher, we'd put a sheet belonging to the funeral home onto the hospital bed. When the driver said we had to leave, the nurse insisted that we take the sheet with us. For fully five minutes she and the driver argued about who should keep it. Finally, her contention that the sheet would cause a long bureaucratic hassle between the hospital and the funeral home prevailed. We lifted Lawrence as gently as possible and retrieved the sheet.

The old woman, his friend, had brought his union medical card with her. When we got downstairs we realized that no one had bothered to tell her where Lawrence was. She was still standing at the front desk, looking very frightened. She'd been told to hand over Lawrence's card—that without it the miner couldn't be admitted to the hospital. She couldn't find it.

It turned out she'd given it to the nurse. The nurse had placed the card in the sheaf of papers she'd put on Lawrence's bed. Now we had to go back upstairs and search around his panting, writhing body for the card that would permit him treatment.

We had a cup of coffee and drove back to the funeral home. At seven o'clock that night Beauford Lawrence died.

In the spring of 1974 few journalists focused on the issues of health care and safety. Many of them stressed the unusual militance of the miners' wives, who had formed an organization called the Brookside Women's Club. Its activities are the centerpiece of

Harlan County, U.S.A. The club represented a very important departure from Harlan's male-dominated culture—and from the region's traditional labor history. For, since the strike began, it had been Harlan's women—not its men—who reenacted the legendary battles of the 1930s and confronted the scabs.

The Brookside Women's Club prevented the strike from becoming a bloodbath since everyone—striker, owner, or scab—agreed it was a sin to hit a woman in public. So the women kept the mine closed. Harlan's chivalry let them drive off strikebreakers with switches and broomsticks—acts that would have been fatal if Jerry and his friends had performed them.

Bessie Lou Cornett, twenty-seven, was the treasurer of the women's club, one of its most fiery members, one of its most effective ambassadors to the outside world. One afternoon she came to Kildav to talk with Jerry and Dorothy about some nurses who were picketing the hospital for higher wages. She and some of the Brookside women planned to join them in a couple of hours. Then she mentioned some waitresses at Ackley's Cafe who were thinking of organizing a walkout. Harlan—at least *her* Harlan— seemed to be in the throes of strike fever. And that thrilled Bessie.

For she felt an enduring rage at the coal operators. During the Fifties, when work was scarce in Harlan, her parents were drifting through Illinois and Indiana, working at a restaurant in one town, a gas station in the next. She'd been raised by a grandfather in the county, a retired miner who would tell her long stories about the 1930s whenever his memory was jogged by some fresh battle in the coalfields. "He was a real fighter. And he was so generous. It was like he felt guilty if he had more than anyone else. I grew up worshiping him."

When she was eleven her grandfather died of black lung. "In the end it got so bad he breathed like he was running a race. Real fast, you know. It was like he was running constantly. And he perspired all the time. He never slept, night or day. It was like he lived to get his next breath. He never stopped until he went into a coma.

"First I prayed selfishly for God not to let him die, but when I saw his pain, I prayed for him to die." Then, in a flat, determined voice: "The coal operators killed him. The night he died I promised myself that if I ever had a chance to get back at them I would."

For a few minutes she and Dorothy, who also belonged to the Brookside Women's Club, reminisced about their confrontations with the strikebreakers. Bessie talked about chasing a scab up the hill, beating him with a broom handle, and knocking him to the ground—a precious moment that must have given her a measure of revenge for her grandfather's awful death.

She kept looking at the clock. Her husband, Gerald, worked at the Glenbrook mine, and his shift was just beginning. Now she was no longer the firebrand, fighting because her grandfather's memory was so alive, because the strike allowed her to engage in *her* form of ancestor worship. She was transformed into an ordinary miner's wife, consumed by a mood of helplessness verging on fatalism.

"You know," she said wearily, "he was on the shift just before those men were killed, in exactly the place where the rock caved in. He doesn't even know how scared he is. But at night, when he's asleep, he grinds his teeth and yells out that the roof is collapsing."

What if her husband had an accident and lived? I flashed back to my hours with Beauford Lawrence, and thought of an ambulance creeping up a mountain road, the driver trying to lift a battered body onto a stretcher, the nurses joking over him, telling the driver to do some crucial medical task he couldn't perform, the elevator jamming on the way to the operating table. If the mine didn't kill him, the hospital might.

After Bessie left I described that gruesome fantasy to Jerry.

He said he was sure the union would take over the hospital after the Brookside contract was signed; the UMW Vice President, Mike Trbovich, had promised as much at a Harlan rally in support of the strikers. Why, there was a rumor that Arnold Miller was meeting with some people in New York that very Saturday to discuss the possibility of the union buying the hospital back.

He was convinced that, in a few months, the Appalachian Regional Hospital would be the miners' friend again.

I had asked Rachel to bring a bottle of tequila down to Harlan, and Jerry wanted her to bring a recipe book for the homemade bread he'd tasted when he'd spoken on campuses in North Carolina and Boston. Those were the staples of a party we organized one Saturday night.

We spent most of that afternoon in the kitchen, while Rachel used the *Tassajara Cookbook* to show Dorothy how to bake banana bread, and showed her how to make chili from hamburger meat, peppers, onion, and pinto beans. Then, when John Shepherd, the banjo player, his son, an electric guitarist, and some filmmakers from North Carolina came over, we served up plates full of those exotic foods.

John Shepherd, who usually needed a few tastes of moonshine to start him singing, learned to drink tequila and salt, Mexican fashion, that night. After a few shots, he began to pick and sing ballads, hymns, and mining songs for three uninterrupted hours. At one point, using a tenor, which kept breaking into gleeful yodels, he sang a country version of "I'm Sitting on Top of the World."

"That's the way I feel," said Jerry, who was washing down a second dish of chili with a glass of tequila. "I'm sitting on top of the world. And I'll tell you what. Those rich people don't have any more fun than we do. Right now, the mine owners are probably sitting around, worrying about some unionist shooting them. I don't have to worry about that." Then he banished all political thoughts with his inviting, boyish chuckle, and asked John Shepherd to sing an old song about breaking in a new pair of shoes.

Jerry had picket duty the next morning. There was no reason for Rachel and me to accompany him. Instead, he suggested we spend some time in the town of Harlan, in a community called Fairview, a slum that was far worse than Kildav.

Two blocks of particularly rundown houses were owned by Roscoe Petrey, who had been Harlan's mayor in the Sixties. In fact, the neighborhood was often called Petreytown.

It was inhabited by disabled miners and by the enormous impoverished families of welfare recipients like Sue Ellen Jenkins. There were twelve children in the Jenkins family. Sue Ellen's youngest boy was younger than her oldest daughter's third child. None of the kids had any toys. When Rachel and I visited their cabin all the intermingled generations were entertaining themselves by watching two boys blow up balloons that whistled as they let out air. All their clothes were hand-me-downs. Their teeth —the most visible sign of their physical condition—were either decayed or missing completely.

The ground around their house was bare mud, covered with coal dust. There was no greenery at all. Their small wood shack was riddled with cracks and leaks. They had no windows, just pieces of plastic or old newspapers to keep the rain out. Since the shanty was so small, and the family so large, the Jenkinses kept their appliances outside. The front porch was littered with fifth-hand sofas and washing machines and coal stoves they'd managed to accumulate in Harlan's junkyards. So the kids played in the muck, amid worn-out merchandise.

They had an indoor toilet, but it didn't work. Since there were no faucets inside the house—and no outdoor spigots nearby—the Jenkins family, like their neighbors, had to walk half a block to fetch the water they needed to flush their toilets. Baths were out of the question. The odor in the house was terrible.

We went to see the County Attorney James Brock, to ask whether there were any way to force landlords like Petrey to make the houses they owned more habitable. Our interview was a quick trip through the looking glass of Harlan's history.

The Brock family has been a pillar of the county's oligarchy for more than a decade. Hiram Brock, James's father, had been State Senator during the 1930s. His uncle, William Brock, had been the Prosecuting Attorney who told the Dreiser committee that a miner who possessed the *Daily Worker* was guilty of criminal syndicalism.

Now, as I walked toward James Brock's office, I saw a picture of President Eisenhower hanging in a nearby cubicle. My sense of time suddenly seemed hazy.

Brock, a courtly, gray-haired man, was totally mystified by my question about Petrey. It was not an issue anyone had raised before. He didn't know how a landlord in Harlan could be made to do anything. Anyway, he said, "I don't think the people you're talking about would want to challenge Mr. Petrey. They've never known anything better than what they have now. It's a sad commentary on the present condition of the human race, but it's true."

The town's mayor, Beecher Rowlett, was standing outside the courthouse when we left. I introduced myself, described our visit to Fairview, and asked if he had a program to improve slum housing in Harlan. The mayor didn't want to answer that question. In fact, he didn't want to talk to me at all unless James Brock's brother, Hiram Brock Jr., was there to witness the conversation. *That* Mr. Brock was out of town for the day, Mayor Rowlett said. Then he walked away.

Harlan has one newspaper, *The Daily Enterprise*. When Rachel and I went over to its office, to find out how its reporters handled issues like slum housing or the fatalities in the mines, we quickly found ourselves in an argument with Ewell Balltrip, twenty-three, who had been covering the Brookside strike. Balltrip was furious at an article in the *Chicago Tribune*, which talked about "bloody Harlan." The piece featured a picture of a shack in a coal camp with the snide caption: "This is one of the finest houses in Harlan." It was the kind of remark that big-city papers often print about rural people and their problems, and Balltrip took it personally. "Why, my house is fifty times better than that," he said. "I wear $150 suits, have a graduate degree at Baylor, and my house cost me twenty-five thousand dollars. Why don't you outside reporters ever ask about people like me?"

Rachel asked if she could photograph him outside his house and use the picture to contrast with the ones she'd taken of the cabins and shanties. He refused.

We wanted to know his attitude toward the mines and the town's slums. But he saw no reason to talk about those things—or to write about them in the *Enterprise*.

From my journalist's perspective they seemed pretty shocking, I said.

"Well, what's shocking to you is old hat to us," he answered.

Besides, he continued, it was emotionally difficult for reporters to dig up dirt about Harlan "because we have to live with people here. We see them socially all the time." From his vantage point the paper's role was to show the positive aspect of the community's life.

It was nearly lunchtime when Rachel and I returned to Kildav. While we got ready to leave, Dorothy hung some laundry on the line and Jerry sat on the front porch, tinkering with his Honda. Then we went in the kitchen for some chili and banana bread, fresh poke salad, and sauerkraut. Dorothy told Rachel how much Estil had loved her cooking. She showed us some drawings her daughter Angie had made in school, Jerry shared an old Johnson family recipe for curing a hangover by eating a pound of cheese and a raw onion.

I realize now that he must have been very eager for us to stay. When I described our encounter with Balltrip at the *Enterprise*, I said I'd love to edit an alternative newspaper that regarded Harlan's miners, not its oligarchs, as "the people we have to live with." At that moment, the fantasy seemed like a real possibility. It must have merged with some plan of Jerry's. Within a few minutes, he was listing story ideas and some very sophisticated plans for distribution. "You'd be the most powerful man in Harlan County if you ran a newspaper like that," he said. "Or you'd be dead."

We started talking about the prospects of a strike settlement. All week long there had been rumors that it would come within a few weeks. (UMW officials had told me that an agreement was imminent before I'd left for Harlan.) That morning Jerry had been talking with some organizers, and they thought the rumors were true.

When he said that, Dorothy's thin, sad face broke into one of its rare smiles. After nearly a year, they'd have decent money again, not the hundred dollars a week the union had been paying in strike benefits. She had been terrified that Harlan's powerful Coal Operators Association would place Jerry on a permanent blacklist if the strikers lost. Now, at last, it sounded as if their future would be protected.

Laughing happily, she said that when she heard the strike had definitely ended, she would jump for joy so long her living-room floor would break. Jerry talked about the drinking and dancing he would do at the gleeful victory celebration.

It was time for Rachel and me to leave. The four of us stood by my rented car, chatting; then we all embraced each other. We were sure the separation would be brief—that Rachel and I would be back in Kildav soon, so we could be with Jerry and Dorothy and Bessie when the contract was signed, when Harlan's miners won their first major victory in more than thirty years.

Several days later I realized I'd been so absorbed in Harlan I'd lost my perspective on the outside world.

When I called officials at the UMW's Washington headquarters they said they doubted the strike would be over in a few weeks. It might last for months, they said. They cautioned me not to take Mike Trbovich's remark about the Appalachian Regional Hospital too seriously. He'd made it in the midst of an emotionally charged rally of Harlan miners. In reality, the union had never planned to buy the facility back.

When I talked with them I wondered whether history would repeat itself, whether the reformed UMW would betray Jerry and Dorothy and Bessie just as the aging John L. Lewis and the corrupt Tony Boyle had betrayed their parents. I concluded my first article on that brooding note.

Part II: Some Clashes and a Settlement

I sent the *Voice* articles to Jerry as soon as they were published.

Several weeks later a reporter who'd just returned from Harlan told me he had been disappointed with them. I called him that night. In a painful conversation he told me that he and some people involved with *Harlan County, U.S.A.* felt I should have ignored customs like the snake-handling religion; that I shouldn't have dwelt on the random violence so prevalent in the coal camps, or talked about his traditional Harlan-stye marriage. They thought I had patronized people who had trusted me, extracting bits of local color, snatches of personal drama, in order to titillate Greenwich Village readers. Instead, they argued, I should have focused on the purely political aspects of the strike.

Those criticisms hurt me deeply. But I have come to agree with some of them. I did try to interest readers by including minor—but, to New Yorkers, exotic—details, that seemed inconsequential to me, but that embarrassed the Johnsons. I have omitted those details here. And, as I read up on Harlan County, in preparation for this chapter, I realized that I'd neglected to show the historic and economic reasons behind the fatalism, the fights, the messiness I'd encountered in Kildav. I have tried to remedy that in this book.

More importantly, I realized that when I'd fantasized about starting a newspaper, I was as guilty of insensitivity as Mike Trbovich had been when he'd talked about buying the Harlan Regional Hospital. In the heat of my strong feelings about the fatalities in the mines, the squalor of the shanties, I had half-proposed a project that seemed unfeasible when I thought about it later. I had failed to realize that, when I lived in the Johnsons' house, I wasn't simply Paul Cowan, Jerry and Dorothy's friendly, well-intentioned contemporary; I was a representative of the outside forces that had promised so much, who seemed to possess a degree of mobility and access to power that seemed almost magical in eastern Kentucky. So, through the looking glass of culture, my hastily chosen words must have indicated a set of commitments—and an unquestioning acceptance of Jerry's view of the strike—that my articles didn't really reflect.

So, I had lost a good friend. And that hurt. Still, I didn't really recognize myself in the general criticisms of the articles. Instead, the disagreement helped me distill the argument that was the genesis of the book: It blends into the pessimism I feel about busing in Boston, my ambivalence about the textbook controversy in West Virginia. I don't believe that political ideas—or even tactics—can be imported, intact, from one situation to another. I am convinced that they are always shaped by the particular details of a local culture.

Harlan *was* an isolated, violent, superstition-ridden feudal society. That was why change there was so crucial. It was also the reason that the groundwork for change had to be laid with the greatest care. For the place could not be altered by grandiose schemes and idle promises—but only by disciplined, long-term work with the people who lived there. It has been done—by Tom

Gish, for example, who abandoned a promising career as a national reporter and settled in the small eastern Kentucky town of Whitesburg to edit a local paper called the *Mountain Eagle*. Gish, raised near Whitesburg, has paid some heavy dues. His life was threatened when he tried to establish the simple right to cover city-council meetings objectively. His office was bombed after he'd exposed corruption in the sheriff's office. He is a populist—a harsh critic of the mine owners and the UMW's bureaucracy—but his political views don't keep his paper in business. His circulation depends on the more mundane—and important—fact that he prints reliable, chatty news from the hamlets outside Whitesburg that everyone else ignores. That makes his political opinions palatable. But few other voices of changes have tried to adopt his necessarily slow-paced approach as their model.

The Brookside settlement, when it finally occurred, did not produce the exuberant victory celebration Jerry and Dorothy had dreamed of that day in April. For the strike ended as the result of a tragedy.

On August 26, 1974, a Brookside miner named Lawrence Jones, twenty-four, was shot and killed by Billy Brumer, a foreman at Highsplint, the second mine Duke Power owned in Harlan. Until then, the strikers had shied away from violence. Suddenly, bloodshed seemed almost certain. Under that pressure, the power company agreed to recognize a UMW chapter at Brookside.

There was no party when the contract was ratified. Instead, the three top UMW executives, Arnold Miller, Mike Trbovitch, and Harry Patrick, accompanied strikers to Lawrence Jones's funeral.

But the union wanted the strike—despite its grisly climax—to be recognized as an unblemished success. So the next issue of the *United Mineworkers Journal* was filled with optimistic interpretations and promises.

In the *Journal*, Arnold Miller prophesied that "When the history of the great organizing battles are written, the Brookside strike will be seen as the turning point for all coal-mining families, and the beginning of the end for nonunion coal in this country." It cited his assurance that "We've shown we're in eastern Kentucky to stay." It featured a buoyant prediction that Huston Elmore, the chief UMW organizer in Harlan, had made a week after the contract was signed. "This Brookside victory is breaking everything wide open," he said. Soon, he forecast, two more mines in the County—Highsplint and Pathfork Harlan Number 4—would elect UMW chapters.

The *Journal* portrayed Jerry as the miners' spokesman. He'd attended Lawrence Jones's funeral, of course, and accompanied the cortege to the cemetery. There, he pointed to the casket and promised, "We'll make them pay for this by signing up every mine in eastern Kentucky."

In that issue, there was a photograph of Jerry and Dorothy and their daughters, Angie and Brenda, looking very sad and very determined. Jerry had his left arm around Dorothy. He and Angie raised their right arms in triumphant Vs.

"This strike has brought us all together," Jerry said at the end of the page-long interview. "It has taught us who the real enemy is, and showed us we can fight back if we're organized. We'll never forget that."

Part III: Harlan, December 1977: Tattered Dreams

When I returned to Harlan during the nationwide coal strike of 1977–78 all those hopes were remote memories.

Jerry and Dorothy had gotten divorced a few months after the settlement. The picture in *The United Mineworkers Journal* must have been one of their last appearances as a couple.

Jerry had married Ann Lewis, the assistant producer of *Harlan County, U.S.A.*, and moved away. The couple had spent several years, working in coal towns in West Virginia and Ohio. Then, in 1977, Jerry and Ann bought a farm in the hill country of Virginia —one of three houses in a large holler. Estil Phillips, who still lived in Kildav, visited them often—to sell Jerry a pig or help him clear a road through the wilderness. He said his old friend seemed quite happy, farming his remote, unspoiled frontier.

After the divorce, Dorothy had taken the children back to Jellicoe, Tennessee, her home town. She'd return to Harlan once or twice a year so the girls could visit their grandparents, who still lived in Kildav. Those visits were her only connection to the town. She never used them as occasions to call on her old friends.

In April 1974, Estil Phillips had seemed to typify the thousands of Harlan miners who were still intimidated by the operators but who might gain enough courage to fight back if the Brookside strike were successful.

Even before the settlement he tried to organize the V & C mine, where he worked. Most of the men assured him that they wanted a union chapter. But when he passed out UMW cards they voted, 39 to 11, to keep the union out. He guessed that was because V & C's operator had decided to offer the miners higher wages than they could earn at the UMW mines.

Soon afterward, Estil quit working at the V & C—before the bosses could fire him for organizing, he said. For a few months he'd received feelers—requests to return to his job—but he'd been too proud to heed them. Since then, he said, he had been unable to find work at any other mine in the county. He reckoned he'd been blacklisted. So, for three years, his family had lived on food stamps while he had picked up spare money by hiring out as a welder, a construction worker, a timberer. By 1977, though, the old animosities had subsided. He thought he could get his old job at V & C back—and he wanted it. Someday, though, he hoped to leave Kildav, which grew dirtier every month, and push on to the frontier, where Jerry Johnson had settled.

In 1974, the Brookside Women's Club was usually portrayed as the most resilient, militant branch of the Harlan County labor movement. That impression was reinforced in 1976, when Barbara Koeppel released *Harlan County, U.S.A.*, with two Brookside Women—Bessie Cornett and her mother, Lois Scott—as the protagonists.

But in Harlan, the club had already dissolved into rancorous factions. Bessie and Lois were brave, outspoken women—others felt threatened by them. There were quarrels over money. Should the funds the women's club raised all be channeled into the strike, or should they be used to make the club into an independent political force, with a program of its own? During the strike, the existence of a common goal had enabled the club to remain unified despite those disagreements. But when the settle-

ment was reached—when the enemy had been defeated—the
women's club fell apart. By 1977, its members—even those who
had remained allies—rarely saw one another.

Bessie Cornett's marriage had collapsed at the same time as the
Brookside Women's Club splintered—in fact, her private life had
become a public issue. For she'd had to go to court to fight for
custody of her thirteen-year-old son, and some of her old friends in
the club had taken sides against her. She'd lost that battle. And
she'd become so controversial that she'd begun to have trouble
earning a living in town.

Finally, broke and exhausted, she'd gone to Chicago and gotten
a job in a candy factory. In time, though, she could probably
have parlayed the reputation she'd acquired from the strike—and
from *Harlan County, U.S.A.*—into a comfortable berth with a
progressive organization that wanted a hillbilly on its staff. (That
would have been particularly easy in Chicago, where scores of
thousands of impoverished Appalachians still live.) Instead, she
met and married Charles Parker, the son of a metal-ore miner
from Telluride, Colorado, whose father, like her grandfather, had
been afflicted with a lung disease. They moved back to Harlan,
where they both became involved in union politics.

Bessie regarded herself as part of a nationwide movement of
people who shared the ideas passed on by her grandfather and
amplified by the outsiders she met in 1974. But she wasn't a wan-
derer like Jerry Johnson. She wanted to use what she had learned
to help the people she had been raised with.

Carefully at first, and then with more confidence, she resumed
her relationships with the Brookside women who had distrusted
her just a year or two earlier. She attended weddings and funerals,
sent gifts when babies were born, asked for advice about her own
infant son. Most of the people I talked to praised her now, sometimes grudgingly, sometimes effusively. As I listened to them I realized that her transgressions—her divorce, her period of strident
radicalism—would be forgiven. She *had* come home again. She
had remained faithful to her tribe. In the end, that overrode everything.

Bessie was the most optimistic person I met in Harlan. In 1978,
she was sure that the grass-roots movement that had seemed so

strong a few years before could be revived. But, for the most part, pessimism once again dominated the coal camps.

In 1974, when Arnold Miller had termed the Brookside strike "a turning point," Huston Elmore had been certain that High-splint—Duke Power's second mine in eastern Kentucky—would vote in a UMW chapter. It would be a second domino in the war against the coal operators. So the union scheduled an election for October 1974, two months after Lawrence Jones was shot, to take advantage of the momentum the settlement had provided. The union was trounced.

There was an economic reason for the union's defeat. Before the vote, Highsplint's operators promised miners an average of seventy dollars a day—ten dollars more than most Brookside workers got under their contract. Management adopted a health plan that provided the men with Blue Cross and Blue Shield. They figured, correctly, that many miners—particularly the younger ones, who now formed the majority of men working un-derground—cared more about cash out front than they did about a union-elected safety committee or a guaranteed pension plan.

The initial investment in higher wages and a private medical plan saved money for the operators in the end. They didn't have to worry about pouring their earnings back into the UMW health and pension fund or about spending money on the new equip-ment a UMW safety committee would demand. They didn't have to worry that production would falter during strikes and slow-downs. Many eastern Kentucky mines, including Highsplint, kept working during the 108-day coal strike of 1978—and the operators made huge profits.

Management's victory at Highsplint more than compensated for its defeat at Brookside. Suddenly, unexpectedly, the UMW had to make a crucial decision: whether to concentrate its re-sources on eastern Kentucky and risk more setbacks or close off the region from organizers once again.

In the autumn of 1974 the union faced problems that made Harlan County's look small. Miller and his aides were confronted by that year's round of coal negotiations. They had to devise strat-egies that would allow them to control the convention of the divided union the next summer. Strip mines in the western states would soon be producing nearly one-half of the nation's coal, and that created difficulties that few people foresaw when Miller took office in 1972. Westerners had none of the traditions that one found in Appalachia and western Pennsylvania. What could the UMW offer them? How could it remain a national union instead of shriveling into a regional one?

In the midst of all those difficulties, the union became a hotbed of factionalism. The right-wingers—who'd supported Miller's predecessor, Tony Boyle—were sniping at the new union leadership, claiming that some of the Washington-based reformers were really Communists. The old-timers had their base in the coalfields and in union locals—Miller couldn't get rid of them. Increasingly, he bent his policies in their direction.

When he did that the reformers and their allies in the union leadership protested loudly. They were the people whose technical expertise had bolstered Miller during the 1974 contract talks. By 1975, the UMW president was convinced that they were conspiring to depose him. He fired some. The rest drifted away. For the next year Miller, increasingly isolated, increasingly desperate, devoted most of his energy to the union's 1977 presidential election. He didn't have the time or resources to prepare for the 1978 contract talks, let alone think about eastern Kentucky.

In January 1978, there was only one organizing team in the region: at the Blue Diamond Coal Company's Justus Mine in Stearns, Kentucky. Under different circumstances, that UMW campaign could have been a symbol of the need for safety that was such an important part of the long nationwide strike. For the Blue Diamond Coal Company also owned eastern Kentucky's Scotia Mine, where twenty-six men were killed in two successive explosions in June 1976. The miners at Stearns were concerned that the conditions under which they worked were equally hazardous. Their strike had lasted twenty-two grueling months. They'd been subjected to a degree of violence that had never existed during the Brookside strike. When Blue Diamond decided to use scabs at Stearns the union picketed the mine face. They were billy-clubbed and tear-gassed in a confrontation with Kentucky's state police.

The Stearns strike had received meager coverage in the media, largely because the UMW's public relations experts had quit two years before.

Since 1974, every other organizing effort in eastern Kentucky had failed. Ironically, in 1975, the year after the Brookside settlement, there were twice as many fatalities in the area's mines as there had been in 1974, when the Harlan County strike had seemed the very beginning of the UMW's drive to make eastern Kentucky a safer place to mine.

Brookside had not been "the beginning of the end of nonunion coal in America." If anything, it had been the beginning *and* the end of the UMW's renewed commitment to the lost tribe of the working class."

Part IV: December 1977: On the Trail of Broken Promises

The day before I returned to Harlan in late December 1977, there had been a fatality at the Highsplint mine.

Estil told me about it, talking as calmly as ever against the thudding background of Kildav's sawmill. There was snow outside, so his four red-haired kids sat in the living room, watching television. His wife was cooking biscuits and red-eye gravy for lunch. The atmosphere in the Phillips house seemed as jarringly tranquil as it had three years earlier, when Estil told a similar bit of bad news. When I said I wanted to learn more about the fatality he nodded obligingly. A friend of his, whom I'll call Ronnie, had worked at Highsplint until the previous October, when he'd been injured in a rock fall. Ronnie could probably tell me about working conditions inside the mine. He gave me directions to the man's house.

I drove over there, introduced myself, and said I wanted to know what had happened—just as I'd wanted to know what had happened to Stanley Hill and Beauford Lawrence in 1974. It was freezing outside, but Ronnie insisted on walking out to his front yard instead of letting me come in. He didn't want to be interviewed.

"What good would it do me? I saw what happened in 1974. You all came in here and wrote articles and made movies about us. Then you left. I've heard that some of you made a lot of money by telling the world about our problems. The miners never saw a penny of it. Why, somebody told me that Estil got blacklisted because he hung around with too many union organizers and talked to too many reporters. Did any of them ever protect him?

"They treat me real good at the mine. I'm making a nice living, and they've been paying my hospital bills since I got hurt. Hell, the injury was my fault anyway. My wife and I just made a down payment on a trailer. The company would cut me off all that if I talked to you. Why should I risk that, just to give you a story?"

There were plenty of journalist's tricks that might help me convince Ronnie to talk. But I wasn't sure I wanted to try them. Instead, I gazed at him, trying to figure out what to do next.

I'd spent the morning with Jimmy Lunceford, a retired miner who'd lost his UMW hospital card the previous April because the union was short of money. Because of the contract strike, he—and all the other pensioners in Harlan—wouldn't get their checks the next month. His wife, Minnie Lunceford, had been the oldest member of the Brookside Women's Club, a stalwart in the fight against the scabs. The switch she had used was hung like a trophy on her wall. Now, though, the couple were furious at the UMW.

In Washington, I knew, an enfeebled Arnold Miller was trying to negotiate with the coal operators. He'd bargained away pension increases for the older, retired miners like Jimmy Lunceford. He was letting the companies develop their own health plans—as Highsplint had—instead of forcing them to contribute to the more stable UMW-supported one. He was supporting limitations on wildcat strikes—which often meant strikes for better safety conditions. In other words, he was bargaining away most of the tools of human survival that the Brookside miners had struck for.

Now, standing outside Ronnie's house, I thought back to those ten days in April 1974, when Jerry and his friends had been so eager to talk, so sure that their words and our films and articles and the union's deeds would change their lives forever. Those few hours with Jimmy Lunceford were a painful, terrible reminder that we'd all shared in—and contributed to—an illusion.

I couldn't, honestly, tell Ronnie that it would do any good for him to talk to me. From his perspective, I must have looked like another circuit rider on the trail of broken promises. So I remained silent, hoping that he would find his own reasons to volunteer some information.

He didn't. He must have gotten tired of staring at me. At last he ended our motionless moment by sticking out his hand and saying, "You might be a very nice fellow, but I really don't want to talk." Then he turned around and hobbled the few snowy feet to his house.

INTERLUDE

Coming Home

When I was a teenager I used to imagine myself as an intellectual's version of the Vagabond John Dos Passos wrote about in *U.S.A.*, as a journalist who would never tire of roaming through America. During the past seven years, experiences like my ten days in Kildav have allowed me to feel I'm living out that dream. I've had the sardonic sense of being a jet-age frontiersman, using my credit card and journalist's credentials to explore any outpost that interested me. Furthermore, in my imagination, I was whatever I covered—a truck driver one month, a Mexican in Juarez the next, a coal miner the third. Back home, I'd talk obsessively about whatever I had observed. But I always had to remember that my fantasies were other people's realities, and that, as a journalist, my primary, all-absorbing job was to be faithful to their experience.

Anyway, Rachel and I have our own rooted lives. We've been married for thirteen years and have lived on the same block for ten—ever since Lisa, our first child, was born. Our community of friends on the Upper West Side of New York has become very important to us—so important that I can't imagine myself as a drifter anymore. In fact, I am increasingly reluctant to leave home.

P.S. 75, where Lisa and our son, Mamu, go to school, is six blocks away from our building. When Lisa was five I used to hoist

her on my shoulders and join the parade of parents and children
walking down the hilly streets on West End Avenue. Back then,
I'd kiss her very lightly on the lips when I left her off at school.
That was 1973, the year I wrote "Still the Promised Land" and
"The Lower Depths of American Labor." I remember, that fall,
we all went up to a house Rachel's mother had rented in Maine.
Sitting over a hard-wood table, Rachel's sister Connie taught Lisa
how to read her first words. I wrote about the experience in the
Voice: "I can't imagine myself as the father of a girl who reads,
of a first or second grader who goes to school by herself and stays
overnight at friends' houses. A child like that needs guidance, not
simple tending. It makes me realize that the boy-man I still am
will have to find the resources to help guide a daughter who's
growing up into the dense world of words and books and conflicting ideas."

Now, Lisa is ten and Mamu is eight. I still walk down the hill
to school with them. When we part these days, Lisa makes sure I
kiss her on the forehead, not the lips. Mamu gets embarrassed if I
kiss him at all. Those street-corner scenes remind me of how embarrassed I was when my father kissed me.

Now the kids do talk about the books they're read, about
sleepover parties, about TV shows. There is a new wave of children's literature that tries to expose kids to adult subjects, like
abortion or what happens when a divorced parent lives with a
new lover. Lisa gets exasperated with such books; she says she
doesn't want to deal with those problems yet. Sometimes she says
that when she grows up she wants to make carefree movies like
the Gene Kelly films she loves. Mamu is able to make a pun or a
joke out of everything he reads. He is a walking baseball en-
cyclopedia—as I was at his age. I listen to both of them with wonder. And I rejoice, during that ten-minute walk, in the fact—
which once seemed so terrifying—that I am an adult, maturing as
the kids mature, growing with them. Those experiences make me
feel linked, as no interview ever can, with most of the people I've
written about in this book.

They also help me understand why the experiences in the chapters that follow—about the Jews on the Lower East Side and the
fair-minded, no-nonsense Americans I met in the heartland city of

Harrisburg, Pennsylvania—were so very important to me. Some of what I discovered about old age and Jewish poverty troubled me deeply. Nevertheless, my involvement with those communities, like my increasing wonder at my own children, made me feel as if I'd come home.

CHAPTER 10

Jews Without Money, Revisited, 1972

The poverty among the poor Jews who live on New York City's Lower East Side compares with the poverty I've seen anywhere in America—in Harlan County, in the Mississippi Delta, in the Columbia Point housing project. Most people think of the Jewish immigration as the most spectacularly successful one in American history, but the long journey from the *shtetl* to the Space Age left many casualties in its wake. According to Ann Wolfe, a social-welfare consultant for the American Jewish Committee, an estimated 250,000 Jews in New York City live below the 1970 poverty level of $3,500; an estimated 150,000 more earn less than $4,500 a year. About two-thirds of those 400,000 people are over sixty-five; many are Orthodox, but there are young people among them, too, and Jews with all shades of religious belief. They live all over New York City: in Far Rockaway, in Coney Island, in Borough Park, in Williamsburg, on the Upper West Side. In 1972, I came to know scores of the ten thousand Jews without money who still live on the Lower East Side.

Traces of the earlier era remain. Delancey, Rivington, and Orchard streets are still noisy, open-air markets, where Yiddish-speaking, yarmulke-wearing Jews peddle their cut-rate shoes or pants, their briny pickles or strong-smelling fish. Only now most of their customers come from the *barrios* of San Juan or Santo Domingo, not the *shtetls* of Eastern Europe. Besides, most of the Jews who own the small stores lining the quieter streets near East Broadway have earned enough money to move outside the neighborhood. So the market is no longer an old-world bazaar, where landsman haggled with landsman in terms familiar to everybody. And, though the relationships between the shopkeepers and their customers are usually friendly, there are occasional unsettling signs of conflict. At lunchtime one day a drunken black man walked down the street yelling, "Jew bastard" at merchant after merchant. It was an unusual exception to the rule of civility. But it echoed menacingly in the memories of Jews who once endured pogroms or concentration camps.

Walk into the courtyard of the city-owned Vladeck Houses, near the Henry Street Settlement just a few blocks from the corner of East Broadway and Essex, which the Daily Forward building, the Garden Cafeteria, and Seward Park once made the hub of immigrant life. When the project was built, over thirty years ago, most of the tenants were Jewish. Many of those people are dead or have moved away. Now the Vladeck houses mostly blacks and Hispanics. But on a hot summer day you can still see plenty of old Jews sunning themselves on the benches of the noisy courtyard. For them, the immigrant days are faint, haunting memories. Most would rather grieve than reminisce.

Many receive Social Security checks and small pensions, often living on less than two hundred dollars a month. One reason they stay in the projects is that the rents are so low—about thirty-five dollars a month. They are too proud to supplement their incomes by applying for welfare. And they are afflicted with the diseases of the aged—diabetes, arthritis, Parkinson's disease. Many are widows or widowers, obsessed with memories of dead relatives.

They feel as if they've been abandoned by the uptown liberal Jewish intellectuals, politicians, and philanthropists who, they think, care more about blacks and Hispanics than the nagging problems of the Jewish slums. And, worse than that, they feel abandoned by their children. Many successful young people who have escaped the neighborhood haven't sent their parents money —or even mail—in years. And many of those who still help out do so with visible annoyance. It is impossible to know the inner history of each family situation—whether a particular parent was unforgivably cruel to his offspring or whether a particular child is now unforgivably insensitive to his parent. But it's clear that many old people on the Lower East Side feel a lasting bitterness toward assimilated, middle-class Jews. When I talked about the feelings I'd had covering the housing controversy in Forest Hills, some of the old people seemed secretly happy about the problems afflicting that Americanized neighborhood. "They've never helped us out," one man in the projects told me. "Why should we care about them? They got what they deserved."

During my weeks on the Lower East Side I began to feel some tribal loyalties I never knew I possessed. Yet I also realized that I represented many of the things the people I met there were complaining about. I have always lived in an assimilated environment. I married a gentile and felt no trace of emotional conflict. I knew very little about my own religious heritage. During the Sixties, when their resentment of well-to-do radical Jews crested, I'd been working with blacks in the civil-rights movement and Latin Americans in the Peace Corps. But, except for a six-month stay in Israel, I had never worked with or written about dispossessed Jews —or even realized they existed in America.

I've always seen my politics as the outgrowth of the Jewish tradition that obliged one to work with the oppressed both because it was morally right and because the oppression of any ethnic or racial group could spread quickly to include Jews. Those are still my deep commitments, of course, but as I grew to care about people on the Lower East Side, I became aware that many of them would regard my ideas and activities as a form of betrayal. And the more I learned about their problems, the more unsettling the contradictions within myself became.

One morning I went to the Vladeck project to visit Moishe Kimmel, an eighty-seven-year-old former watchmaker—"Moishe the cleanly," as he calls himself proudly. He'd come over from Warsaw sixty years ago, after a series of episodes in which Polish soldiers beat him up because he happened to be out, walking after a curfew.

Moishe found a job in a Lower East Side jewelry store and learned English quickly enough to rush through the "greenhorn" phase every immigrant dreaded. Now he speaks with only a pleasing trace of an accent. During the Depression his wife died and the small store he was working in went bankrupt. He had a nervous breakdown and was hospitalized for several years. When he got out, the Henry Street Settlement House gave him a job greeting visitors. He kept a very careful guest book, and told everyone that celebrities like Mrs. Roosevelt and Herbert Lehman, who met him on brief visits, were his very close friends.

Now he is too old to stray far from his three-room apartment. But he's still eager for company; he urged me to visit him moments after we met in the Vladeck courtyard. When I appeared at his door, several days later, he kissed my cheeks with joy. He had to stand on his tiptoes to reach my face with his lips.

Proudly, he showed me around his immaculate apartment. He'd built a tiny brown frame house with windows and green shutters out of popsicle sticks and cellophane. He'd built a shrine around a routine letter from Herbert Lehman thanking him for some shred of political advice. He still had the police whistle and toy badge a friendly cop at the Seventh Precinct station had once given him. Clean ties and perfectly pressed suits filled about one-third of his small closet. His refrigerator was spotless—and empty. He'd polished his galoshes in March to make sure they'd stay in shape for the next winter. "This is the cleanest of all the 3,071 apartments here," Moishe told me joyfully.

Until a few years ago he used to go out at night, to sit in a small park on Water Street where his compulsive gregariousness found an outlet in conversations with old friends. Then, about eighteen months before we met, he was mugged in the lobby of his building. The muggers got eighty cents. It had happened again, a few weeks before my visit, when he was walking to Gouverneur Clinic for a check-up. Two black men darted out of a cluster of bushes, shoved him hard enough to push him to the ground, and ripped the pocket from his shirt. They found a dollar. Moishe rarely goes out anymore.

After the first mugging, Moishe's daughter, the wife of a doctor, offered to rent him a small apartment a few blocks away from her house in Yonkers. But she never repeated the invitation. "It's all right," he said. "I never wanted to go there anyway. I ask her all the time how come she doesn't keep kosher, and she always argues back. And her house. It's such a mess."

She does visit him occasionally. She was coming later that afternoon, to leave her cat with Moishe while she and her husband and kids went off on a short vacation. Moishe "the cleanly" was very excited about the prospect of a weekend companion. Before I left he showed me the tidy corner of his living room where he'd placed a pillow from his bed for the cat to sleep on, and asked if a smart fellow like me had any ideas about how I could make the cat's home any cozier.

Many old Jews like Moishe do prefer the threatening streets of the Lower East Side to the half-*goyishe* suburbs where their assimilated children live. They know where to find kosher butchers, stores that observe the proper Sabbath, Orthodox *shuls* that preserve the traditions they learned as children. Modern Americanized neighborhoods leave them depressed and disoriented.

Even now, in the Lower East Side's decline, there are fifty-two functioning synagogues, many of which were founded a half-century ago by landsmen from small villages in Russia or Poland who wanted to preserve their special local traditions. Each morning and night, frail old men forge their daily link to their childhood faith, *daavening*, gossiping, in the tiny, musty loft and basement *shuls*. The synagogues aren't only houses of prayer, they're centers of study and homes for the lonely, whose chatter forms a noisy counterpoint to each evening's services. Now, though, the congregants of *shuls* that once thrived often find it difficult to gather a *minyan* (the ten men necessary to recite the mourners' kaddish, the prayer for the dead) because some last surviving members are too ill—or too afraid of crime—to walk the few blocks to the nearest *shul*.

One night I went to a small basement *shul* near the old Daily Forward building on East Broadway with a man in his early sixties, a cab driver who had only become religious as he realized that death was approaching. I was always uncomfortable going to those synagogues. I kept worrying that some elderly Orthodox man would realize I didn't know the rituals and wheel at me and denounce me as an impostor. So I'd rock back and forth a little, faking a *daaven,* a prayer; I'd try to remember to turn the prayer book's pages backward, following the Hebrew text; I'd utter a few moaning sounds, hoping that whoever heard me would regard my barely audible groans as the appropriate psalm.

It was the week of Tishah B'Av, the anniversary of the destruction of the first and second temples in Jerusalem, a day of mourning for all Orthodox Jews. The *bimah*—the pulpit—was shrouded with black curtains, and only a few candles lit the murky room. The congregants chanted dirges from the Book of Lamentations. There was a fervor to the ceremony that left me unexpectedly moved, though I could only understand the tiniest portion of what was going on. The *shul,* the ceremony, belonged to the aged; I was the only person there under sixty.

After the service the cab driver made a point of waiting for two other congregants, bearded men in their eighties, wearing the caftans and wide hats of the very Orthodox. They walked very slowly, hobbling on canes. The cab driver was careful to remain a few paces behind them. It seemed to be a nightly routine, an attempt at protection. As we passed a group of Hispanic teenagers talking in rapid Spanish, I could see the cab driver grow more watchful. "Sometimes they harass the old ones. They knock off their hats or call them ugly names. It's not only them. I remember the days when the Irish and the Italians did the same thing to us. But it didn't happen so often in our own neighborhood then. At least in those days we knew that these few blocks belonged to us."

As much as they can, the Jews without money try to provide each other the kind of mutual comfort that had been so much a part of their parents' lives in Eastern Europe.

The owner of a tiny basement grocery store on Rivington Street —the survivor of a concentration camp in Russia—slips a few extra rolls each day to a senile old widow, a woman who scours the block's wastebaskets for food, who never bathes or changes her dress, who lives in pitch darkness because she can't afford to pay her tenement electric bills. I stood in the store one morning, watching the old people shop. How carefully they examined each piece of cheese, each loaf of bread; the decision of how to spend fifty cents on food was the most crucial one of the day. I noticed how the store owner's wife posed delicate questions to each customer who came in, extracting the news of their psyches. She was not asking those questions in order to pry. Her duty, she believes, is to tell Lisa Schwab, director of the Gouverneur Mobile Crisis Unit, if anyone seems on the brink of a breakdown.

After *shul* one night I watched a stooped, half-blind old man while he bought some tomatoes at a small fruit stand. He paid a dollar; he received $1.25 worth of goods. The transaction was laden with decades of accumulated, unspoken shame and pride and trust. The store owner chided me angrily when I mentioned his generosity. Later that evening I ate a dairy supper at the Garden Cafeteria, where dinner is a once-a-year luxury for someone like Moishe Kimmel. I sat with a retired tailor, born in Poland, just returned from Israel where he'd visited a cousin he hadn't seen since his parents left their village, forty years ago. The tailor lived alone and his greatest pleasure was watching comedies on TV: he was especially eager to see that night's *Carol Burnett Show*, which began at eight. But he made a point of waiting until 8:15 so he could buy a fresh copy of the *Daily Forward* from an old Jew who peddled the paper at the Garden, who needed every bit of business he could get to pay his forty-five-dollar-a-month rent.

On *Shabbos* morning the *shuls* are filled with men wearing their prayer shawls, chanting, singing Hebrew songs like "Erov Ha Shoshanim," which echo up and down the block. In some, small groups cluster around spare wooden tables, savoring long discussions of complex passages of the Talmud, disputes that have endured for centuries. Strolling home, they pause to wish each other a good *Shabbos*, or to exchange news, talking in Yiddish and in English. In the projects, you can glimpse very old people, too frail to go to *shul*, visiting each other at mealtime, spending an afternoon together, a time when the rich tide of memory washes away the present's loneliness and fear.

But the fabric of mutual support can dissolve when the outside world becomes a menacing presence.

One day I was having lunch at the Good Companion Club in the Vladecks, where about three hundred Jews and Puerto Ricans receive nourishing meals for sixty cents a day. Max Tobias, now the sexton of a synagogue nearby, was telling me about his first years in the country, when he was one of the few Yiddish-speaking members of the International Workers of the World. He remembered the anarchist, Emma Goldman, standing outside the Forward building on the day the American government deported her to Russia. He remembered the thrilling night, fifty years ago, when a huge crowd of immigrants gathered in Seward Park, in front of the same building, to await the news that they'd finally elected themselves a congressman, the Socialist Meyer London.

As we were talking about the bitter feud between the *Forward,* the main Yiddish language Socialist paper, and the *Freiheit,* a more left-wing paper, a woman came into the club, yelling that a lady who lived in a nearby building had just been robbed. I decided to go over and see what had happened. Since the victim, who was still sobbing, spoke only Yiddish, I had to ask a Jewish woman in the courtyard to translate for me.

When my interpreter first heard what had happened, she began to wail sympathetically. "Such a nice lady. She came over from Russia fifty years ago and never hurt anybody." But, as she listened to the details, relaying each one to me, she got angrier and angrier at the victim. The woman had apparently been robbed while she was standing in front of her building, counting the sixteen dollars she'd been carrying in her purse. The translator was livid: "Sixteen years in this project, and she doesn't even know enough to leave her pocketbook home? She thinks she's living on Park Avenue? This is a jungle. Listen," she said, still in English, turning to the woman and grabbing her arm, "when you go out from now on, you put your money in here." And she thrust her hand between the woman's breasts. "That's the only way you can be at all sure of staying safe."

It was about half an hour after the robbery. By then the victim had begun to wonder what I, a strange man, was doing, calmly taking notes. When the interpreter explained that I was a newspaper reporter, the victim began to cry even more loudly than she had when she'd been talking about the robbery. "She doesn't want her name in the newspaper," her translator said. "She's afraid maybe her daughter will see it. Maybe she'll get so aggravated she won't send checks anymore."

I was familiar with the request. At least half the old Jews I met on the Lower East Side asked for anonymity, in order to avoid some offspring's rage. So I said I'd describe the episode but disguise some of the details and omit her name.

Then the translator got nervous. "You're not going to use my name, are you? [I didn't even know it.] How can that help me? You can see that we're surrounded here." She gestured toward the courtyard, toward the neighboring apartments. "The police can't help. What if they find a mugger and book him? He still gets out on bail. You don't think he'd know who reported him? He would hunt you down.

"We ignore everything that goes on around us. Who knows what they can do to us? We don't even want them to know our names or what we think. So we just say, 'Hi, how are you?' We're as polite as can be. That's our only chance of being left in peace."

Then she had another troublesome thought. "Those *yentas* in the courtyard, those gossips. I'm not even going to tell them what happened here. They're sure to talk. And you"—she had a sudden inspiration—"if anyone asks you what you're doing here, say you're a messenger with a package from her daughter. Don't make trouble for us."

When the Vladeck Houses first opened, in the early 1940s, the Jews, who filled most of the apartments, saw the place as a wondrous change from the cramped, rat-filled tenements where they'd spent their earliest years in America. The apartments were spacious. They were clean. The buildings had elevators.

But all that had changed by the 1970s. As a money-saving device, the city had installed elevators that stopped only on every other floor. They wouldn't have mattered so much thirty years ago, when the project was composed mainly of young married people. But now, many of the elderly who still live there are suffering from heart ailments or arthritis or Parkinson's disease. Those who live on the odd floors must hobble down a flight of stairs to get home. The unprotected stairways, of course, are attractive turf for muggers. Frequently, the lights in the elevators are broken, which means that people don't go to their apartments unless they can find a trusted friend to accompany them.

One afternoon I was passing through the courtyard to get a cup of coffee at the Garden, when a swarm of old Jews mistook me for a repairman. They complained that the elevator had been broken since 9 A.M. They'd missed meals, doses of medicine, naps. Some were worried they'd been in the sun longer than their doctors thought was wise.

In an abandoned community like the Lower East Side, most people want desperately to believe that an outsider like me, with a smile and a moment to listen, is the representative of a mysterious, benign power that will help them—they weren't, in that way, any different from Jerry Johnson and his friends in Harlan County. I explained that I was a reporter—not a mechanic—but that didn't staunch the flow of complaints. I was a novelty, someone who would listen to sorrows their neighbors had heard to the point of boredom, someone who might possess some useful knowledge.

One woman, using the broken elevator as a pretext, reached into the sack under her stockings where she kept her precious belongings and showed me the heart pills she took twice a day. Then she showed me the special ones she was supposed to take if she had an attack. Did I think the doctors had given her the right prescription? An old man removed his dentures, showed me a deep chip where his molars should have been and asked if I knew whether his Medicaid would provide for a new set of teeth.

Sylvia Goldstein, seventy-three, was sitting on one of the courtyard benches, and she called me over to talk to her. Several days earlier I'd gone to her crowded three-room apartment with one of the Good Companion social workers. Her seventy-year-old brother and his wife, both victims of Parkinson's disease, lived in the front room. It had been early afternoon when we entered, but the shades were drawn. They were lying down on separate beds. The man, once a clothes fitter, had had the disease for twenty years and was completely bedridden. His wife, who had only gotten it three years before, could still move around the house. She got out of bed to talk with the social worker about some pills. Her whole body shook when she stood. Her voice was a faint sound from a distorting echo chamber. She could barely see or hear.

Sylvia had been trying to get the two of them into an old-age home. But she hadn't found any that would allow the man and woman to live together. The couple were childless. They had been married for fifty years. They refused to sign any papers that would let an unknown bureaucrat separate them. So Sylvia keeps them with her, defying a city regulation limiting the number of tenants who can live in a three-room apartment. She worried constantly that her transgression would be discovered and she'd be evicted. She's been going to the Good Companion for years, but it was only a few months ago that a friend told the social worker about the household couple. It took weeks to persuade her that the people who staffed the lunch program would be discreet, that they'd send meals and medicine to her brother and sister-in-law and still conceal their existence from the building authorities.

At noon every day, Sylvia likes to leave her apartment and walk across the courtyard to the club's basement headquarters. She's grateful for the food—she'd never be able to afford such solid, nourishing meals on her own. But the thing she cares about most is the free Bingo game the club conducts after lunch each day. For her, the game's excitement is particularly intense because of the chance that she might win the prize—an orange—a real delicacy for her.

The day I visited her I told her I'd be her partner one day and give her the orange if I won it. I made the remark as a half-joking stab at conversation. She took it as a firm commitment.

Now she was hollering at me in the courtyard to complain that she hadn't seen me since then. There was laughter in her voice, but the angry, reproachful tone that lay just beneath it startled me. I had to promise to join her the next day.

I couldn't get out of that courtyard. Everyone wanted to tell me a tale, to seek my advice.

One woman was looking forward to her outing in Lancaster County, Pennsylvania, the following week, with a group of people from the Henry Street settlement house. "I'll be the only white person," she said cheerfully, "a regular lily-of-the-valley."

She was a widow who lived on her $140 monthly Social Security check. Her rent was low and her diet sparse—a few pieces of American cheese, a hard-boiled egg, some tuna fish and rice every day. Still, the eleven dollars Henry Street was charging meant quite a chunk out of her budget. The cost seemed especially high since her strict observance of kosher laws would force her to forgo the sumptuous Pennsylvania Dutch meals the other travelers would enjoy. She planned to nibble on a cheese sandwich she'd pack herself.

The trip was worth it, though. She'd gone last year and had been awed by the beauty of the countryside. It was the first time she'd been out of New York City since she'd come here in 1907, as a six-year-old child.

But how the expense nagged at her! Until now, she'd been too proud to apply for welfare, but maybe she should ask for food stamps. "They'd be such a help. Maybe they'd degrade me, though. I know I'm a stubborn old woman. What do you think?"

I said I thought she should take whatever help she could get, but before we could continue talking an old man, whose breath smelled like stale liverwurst, started tugging at my shirt and talking to me. In heavily accented English, he was describing a fight between him and an old friend about the amount of money he'd paid for his daughter's wedding. I couldn't understand the details. I gathered I was supposed to be the referee. "Shut up, Bernie," said a woman who'd just joined the cluster of people around me. "Everyone knows your story." Then, shouting hoarsely, she told me she'd almost fainted crossing Grand Street a few days ago. Did I know whether Medicare could help her get a free cane?

I was beginning to feel a little hysterical when Rebecca Schwartz, pudgy, soft-spoken, invited me back to her ground-floor apartment for a cup of tea. I accepted with relief even though I knew she probably wanted to get me alone in order to describe some new problem I certainly couldn't solve.

She moved slowly, using a walker. As she let herself into her triple-locked door I noticed that she kissed her fingers and ran them lightly over the *mezuzah*. We'd never done that in my family. We'd never observed any of the Jewish customs so familiar on the Lower East Side. Yet now that ancient tribute to order and stability at home filled me with a searing, reflexive, almost racial grief for all those old people lost here in America.

In the *shtetl*, their age would have been taken as a mark of wisdom, or at least as an acceptable stage of human development, not as a burden too great for most of their offspring to bear. They'd have lived with their children and grandchildren, quarreling, of course, but accepting generational battles as a natural part of human existence. They wouldn't have aged in terrified isolation but would have remained part of a coherent community, with familiar institutions and ceremonies to comfort even those with the worst luck, the most debilitating mental and physical ailments. Beggars and rich men, cripples, fools, and sages all shared the joy of the Sabbath, the sorrow of Yom Kippur, the crazy, rollicking abandon of Purim. On the Sabbath, some of the old men who'd begged for my attention in the Vladeck courtyard would have known the mellow pride of hearing their grandsons recite a week's lessson from the Torah. Some of the women would have confidently supervised the preparations for the day of rest. And, day after day, their special talents, like Moishe Kimmel's gift for crafting things, would have remained skills useful to the whole community, not just private, isolated hobbies that seem a little sad and quirky. Those were the assumptions, the traditions, the people who'd been clamoring for my attention still carried in their pores. But they'd gotten lost somewhere along the immigrants' fifty-year voyage to modern America. These people were part of a generation still in the desert.

Mrs. Schwartz offered me some tea and an old piece of crumbling pound cake in a voice that sounded more wheedling than courteous. It looked completely unappetizing to me, though I realized that buying it had probably meant a painful, scary journey across Henry Street to the nearest food store. She'd probably been saving it as an after-dinner treat. It all seemed so desperate, so hopeless I suddenly wanted to flee. Still, I accepted the cake because I feared she'd take a refusal of her food as a sign that I was refusing her as a person. And I listened to her story.

She'd left the *shtetl* during a Russian pogrom in 1906. Her father, whose cousin had been involved in antigovernment activities, had decided to flee before the Tsar's police arrested him. He found work in a Lower East Side grocery store, sleeping on Broome Street—literally on the street—so he could save enough money to bring his wife and children over here. Those were awful years in Russia for Mrs. Schwartz. She only survived because a Gentile neighbor allowed her entire family to squeeze into the chimney of the small peasant house whenever the police appeared. Sometimes they'd hide there for three or four hours at a time. Mrs. Schwartz still has nightmares about those times.

She has lived on the Lower East Side ever since she moved to this country. She quit school at fourteen in order to help her father, who had opened his own grocery store by then. She'd married at twenty, but her husband, a sickly man, never found a steady job. He did get work, though, at a small neighborhood newsstand whenever business there was good. He died fifteen years later. The couple had never had any children. For the next thirty years Mrs. Schwartz had worked as a ticket taker in a Loew's theatre. She has lived in the Vladeck since it opened.

In June 1964, she had a stroke. Two nephews, both doctors, paid her medical bills. But they didn't assist her or visit her anymore. "What do they want with an old lady like me?" she asks. "I have enough money in the bank to pay for my rent and my food and buy my tombstone. What else do I need?"

It is hard for her to sleep at night. She goes to bed at seven or eight but usually wakes up at midnight. Then her aches, her fear that each fresh pain may bring a lonely death, keep her up for hours. She'd like to watch the late movie, but she never turns on the television for fear of bothering her neighbors. She doesn't read much English, but she spends a few hours each day, looking through the *Daily Forward*. It reminds her of the time when, as a teenager, she still used to read the paper's most popular feature, "A Bintel Brief," to her illiterate mother.

Now she gets the paper from a Jewish war veteran she's known for years. He buys it each morning and gives it to her each night. "He isn't all there," she says. "I think he was shell-shocked." He repeats himself constantly, she says, and sometimes those repetitions make her so irritable she fears she'll have another stroke. She never complains, though. She doesn't want to hurt the old man's feelings or make him so angry he'll quit giving her his used *For-wards*.

She uses several kinds of medication each day—heart pills, painkillers, pills for high blood pressure. But the previous April her Medicaid had run out. She had enough pills to get her through the summer. But what would happen next fall? That was what she wanted to ask me about.

Whenever she goes to the local health clinic to ask for a new application form, they tell her she'll have to go to the main office on 34th Street. "But how do they think I can get there? Do they think I can climb up and down the subway stairs? That I can afford to pay for a taxi? I telephone the office on 34th street. But they always give me one of those recordings that says so-and-so is too busy to speak to me now. They must be very busy up there. I've called six times and I've always been cut off before I can talk to anyone. I can't afford to waste all those dimes.

"Anyway, what good will it do for me to reach them? The same thing always happens to me when I talk to people from the government. I get so flustered I begin to cry. Then I can't remember any English. The only words that come to me are in Yiddish. But everyone down there only speaks English or Spanish. So what should I do? Some nights I can't sleep at all, I'm so worried about what will happen to me if the pills I have now run out and I don't get a new supply."

Summer 1974: In the Land of the Ancients

I hadn't imagined how deeply *"Jews Without Money, Revis-ited"* would affect *Voice* readers—or, indeed, how deeply and lastingly it would affect me.

The article coincided with a citywide effort to help poor Jews. In 1973, the Lindsay administration helped finance the United Jewish Council of the Lower East Side, which enabled a dozen people like Joel Price—a young Orthodox rabbi who was the closest friend I made while I was writing *"Jews Without Money, Revisited"*—to help senior citizens get housing, medicine, Social Security benefits. A few doors away from the council, in a build-ing called the Educational Alliance, a young, charismatic Bulgarian Jew named Mischa Avramoff headed an organization called project Ezra. Ezra's ideology and practice grew out of the gentle humanism of the early civil-rights movement, in which Mischa had participated; its funding came partly from the Federation of Jewish Philanthropies. Down the hall from Project Ezra a man named Fred Siegel—once a beatnik, now an Orthodox Jew— headed a multi-service center funded by the federation. Those three organizations all began to function in 1973. There was no way they could solve all the problems I'd heard about in the Vadeck courtyard. But they did make a difference. Once again, East Broadway was becoming a refuge for poor Jews.

Slowly, the Council and Project Ezra were finding the most invisible Jews without money—people who still lived in the decrepit tenement houses stretching from Rivington and Orchard streets to 12th Street and Avenue D. Those I met had made some contact with the agencies on East Broadway—that was how I got to know them. But they were even more isolated than the people I'd interviewed two years earlier in the projects. They didn't even have the vestige of a community to comfort them, as the people in the Good Companion food club or the East Broadway *shuls* or the Vladeck courtyards did. I'd go in the tenements, inspect the scratched old mailboxes for Jewish names, and discover that as many as fifteen or twenty of them lived on a block. But many of them were convinced that they were the last Jew in their neighborhood.

A few—mostly men—did spend all day outdoors, escaping the prison of their homes by visiting old friends. But many were so sick and scared that they rationed their trips outside. One woman I met hadn't left her apartment in two years. Most shopped once or twice a week, spent an afternoon or two on the stoop or in the park, chatting with old friends; most went to *shul* for the High Holidays. The rest of the time they stayed in their apartments, often without radio or TV, telephone or visitors.

Once the tenement dwellers had been productive workers—cab drivers, tailors, clerks, secretaries, storekeepers, printers. Now they are wraiths—men and women who have fallen out of history. It is impossible, when you talk to them, to navigate the twilight zone between neurosis and neglect, impossible to know what actions will help them, and what actions will destroy the delicate ecology of memory and complaint that actually keeps them alive.

One afternoon two social workers and I accompanied Mrs. Sylvia Lowenthal home from the efficiently run American Nursing Home to her immaculately clean apartment. It was a joyous hour for her.

She'd never wanted to go to a nursing home, she said. "But a few weeks after Passover I got a stroke in the nighttime. I saw I couldn't do nothing with my hand. I wanted to turn on the television, but I couldn't. So I called up the ambulance."

She stayed in Beth Israel hospital a month, regaining the use of her hand. She had no one at home to go home to. Her husband is dead. She's childless, with an ailing brother in Atlantic City, two nieces in Alabama, a nephew in Israel. So, the doctors, thinking they were doing her a favor, urged her to enter the nursing home. She hated the place. The food was unfamiliar and tasteless. The old people—helpless, senile—made her feel like she was already dead. She wanted to take care of herself. But the patients in a nursing home are strapped to a wheelchair because when they stand they sometimes topple over. For her, the chair was a jail. Every time an attendant touched her she felt as if her privacy had been violated.

Her caseworker found a housekeeper willing to come to her home three times a week. Medicaid would pay the expenses. That way she could go home.

She hadn't seen her apartment in three months. For an hour she went through her possessions with great excitement. The old postcards were there. The telephone worked. She flicked on the 1950s-model Dumont TV, which she thinks is brand new, since she bought it two years before for thirty-five dollars. She looked in the stove. It was clean. Her refrigerator was tidy, too. Cheerfully, she began to make ice.

It was warm and pleasant outside, the time of year when she and her husband used to go to the mountains. She'd been a garment worker—"a union lady all the time"—and her husband had been a baker, "a delegate from the bakers' union," she said proudly. Then, sadly, "He was sick for ten years, and the bills took away all our money.

"Now I have such a sickness, it works like a machine. Day and night, such a whooshing in my head. I live with pains. I lie down with pains. I sleep with pains.

"Still, maybe I can do a little bit housework. I walk not so bad, you know. I'll see if I can do something. If I do nothing, at least I'll try."

She glanced at the scroll the bakers' union had given her husband. Then she began to sort through some old clothes. She wondered how long it would be till the ice got hard. Maybe we could stay for a glass of cold water?

The social worker helped her plan her week's menu, the food she'd buy at the Essex Street Market. She smiled a little as they talked.

She looked at me. "The old generations pass away, and I'm from the old generation. I'll finish my life any day, any hour. But, if I'm going to pass away, I don't want no nursing home. It must be here."

Hedy Rose, formerly a sewing-machine operator, is barricaded behind the doors of her tenement apartment.

She is a hunched, shapeless old lady whose lined face alternately reflects inflexible pride and confused grief. When I first met her, she seemed ready to die in her four barren rooms. She seemed resigned to spending her last years staring at the chipped walls and broken bedroom windows, to bathing herself in the tub on stilts next to the kitchen stove, and relieving herself in the toilet in the hall. "I have nobody to help me. Only God," she says.

She had already made preparations for her death. The only prominent decoration in her apartment was a sign above her frayed brown couch—carefully lettered by a friend—instructing the person who found her remains to send them to a nephew, a chemical engineer in Rosedale, Long Island.

Beneath the sign is a chart from the Blau Memorial Chapel, which proves she's already paid for her burial. The cost of each item is carefully noted: $55 for removing the remains; $55 for preservation, freezing, and embalming services; $25 for the Torah room; $115 for the coffin; $65 for the hearse; $35 for the burial garments.

Three of the five apartments on Hedy Rose's floor are empty. There is a narrow ledge outside her bedroom window. A lithe burglar could walk along it easily. The two buildings next to hers are abandoned and gutted. She thinks a street gang "gangster," as she calls its teenage members—uses the empty apartment to raid her isolated home whenever she goes outside. She says they've stolen everything, from five hundred dollars in cash to her radio, toilet paper, pins, shoe polish, and *Yarzheit* candles. Most nights she can't sleep for fear of them.

Her terrors outstrip anything that might have happened to her. She thinks the gangsters plan to poison her, that they want to kidnap her. She claims she hears them vowing to kill all Jews as they dance around the bonfire of their burning cars.

The loss of the radio was particularly upsetting. Hedy had come to this country from Russia in 1915 and went right to work in the garment industry, never learning to read or write. She has no phone. Her husband is dead and she has no children. She rarely sees her nephews. All her friends have moved away from the neighborhood. So, for months at a time she is alone in that vulnerable little apartment. The radio was her friend, her clock, her calendar, the only way she knew when to pay the doctor, the rent, the installment for her burial. She won't buy a new one for fear it will tempt her tormentors.

One day she asked me to go down to the Ninth Precinct station —ten frightening blocks from her house—and describe her problems. A few days later a detective visited her. She pointed to the apartment where she thinks the gangsters live. But she refused to file a complaint or testify in court—they might kill her in revenge. The detective was relieved: He'd decided she'd be an unreliable witness. He left her a card with his phone number. Though she has no phone, he assumed she'd call him from the pay phone on the corner (which she doesn't know how to work) or walk down to the precinct station (which she'll never do). The card left her more confused than before. Was it a form of assistance or an obligation? She gave it to me the next time I visited, hoping I could find some way to use it in her behalf.

Feldstein, her landlord, wants her to move to a new neighborhood. He hasn't bought a lock for the front door of the tenement. He refuses to give her a police lock for her apartment. Last year he raised her rent from $25 to $50. She lives on a fixed income of $226 a month. When they fight he calls her a stingy old lady.

She refuses to budge from the apartment. She's lived there for forty years. "Could I go around with my sick feet, looking for rooms?" she asks. Anyway, there is only one kind of housing she'd accept: an apartment on Grand Street, the Jerusalem of the Lower East Side.

One afternoon I saw her picking her way along the street. She looked stooped and tired, but a little more cheerful than usual.

She'd just been to Beth Israel. The medical news was bad. Her blood pressure was high, 220/120. She was fifteen pounds overweight. But after her doctors were finished she went over to the hospital's social-service agency. She said someone there had called the Housing Authority and secured a one-room apartment in the Grand Street Co-ops. It was just a matter of time until she received the blessed letter telling her to move.

The hospital had given her blood-pressure pills and careful instructions about her diet. But the instructions were worthless to her since she's illiterate.

When I read them aloud to her she complained about almost every item she was allowed to eat. Chicken, I read. What good is that without salt, which is prohibited? Liver—she didn't like it. Hamburger—too expensive. Fish—too bland. Eggs—the yellow (the yolk) is dangerous. Soup—makes gas in her stomach. She'd have to stick to a diet of string beans, matzoh, potato, and American cheese.

She wanted me to guard her apartment while she shopped the next day. When I said I could come at twelve or at four, but that I had a midafternoon appointment, she became petulant and angry. Twelve was too early. Four was too late. She'd have to ask the "next door" to do the job, even though—she whispered, "he's Spanish." At first I felt guilty. Then I realized she would only accept my friendship if it conformed to her deliberately limiting set of terms.

When I called the Beth Israel Hospital the next day the head social worker checked Hedy Rose's file and found she hadn't been given an apartment. Someone there had called the co-op management and learned there was an eight- or nine-year waiting list. The best she could hope for was a place in the new Seward Park Extension, and she hadn't followed the Housing Authority rules carefully enough to gain a priority for one of those treasured rooms. Applications are supposed to be renewed every two years. She'd applied twelve years before and never gone through the process again.

Someone at Beth Israel had offered to write her a letter saying her blood pressure made her case an emergency. Maybe that echoed in the old lady's mind as the promise she wanted so desperately to hear.

There was a small, dark bruise on her cheek the next time I visited her. She'd been in her vestibule, looking for the letter from the Housing Authority, when she'd suddenly felt dizzy and collapsed. It was her blood pressure, she said. The diet of string beans and potatoes made her weak. But she didn't want to go to the hospital. Anyway, the organizer for the United Jewish Council who'd first made contact with her had read the label on her pills and told her to take them after meals, not before them. She thought that might solve the problem.

By then, three people were dealing with Hedy Rose—me, the organizer for the council, a caseworker for the Jewish Association of Services to the Aged. We decided to scrounge around for emergency housing before we told her the bad news from Beth Israel.

There were safe, pleasant places in Coney Island and Borough Park, we discovered. She could move to either neighborhood without waiting nervously through the hot, dangerous summer. She refused. She didn't want to leave the Lower East Side. Better to stay among the "gangsters" and "anti-semitten" six months longer if it means she can settle on Grand Street. "As soon as I get there I'll kiss the floor of the new building," she said.

So she forced her huddled body down the forty-two steps to her vestibule every morning. Cannily, she watched the street until the gangsters who plan to kidnap her were out of view. Then, expectations surging, she opened her mailbox in search of a letter she could never read, which will never come.

Rebecca and Martin Isaacson, survivors of Auschwitz, live in a tenement on Rivington Street. Their block is somewhat safer than Hedy Rose's. It is filled with tradesmen, peddling their used clothes and shoes, not with street gangs and gutted buildings. Their apartment is bigger, neater, and better furnished than Hedy's. Their building is always locked.

Rebecca is Martin's second wife. She was born in Czechoslovakia and widowed before the war. Still, she'd managed to care for her daughters and run a prosperous corset factory in her small town in the Carpathians. At Auschwitz the Nazis sent her to one side of the camp, her daughters to the other. She never saw the girls again.

She'd lived in the same cramped barracks as Martin Isaacson's wife. She was present the day a concentration-camp guard decided that the first Mrs. Isaacson's malnutrition, her swollen mouth, and missing teeth made her too frail to lay railroad tracks. Rebecca watched as he led her to the woods to be shot. Then, she saw the Isaacsons' daughter begin to cry. The guard took the girl away and shot her, too.

Martin Isaacson had been a truck driver in the Carpathians before the war. He'd been separated from his wife and daughter as soon as they'd reached Auschwitz and quartered with the men who worked in the coal mines. Their day began at 5 A.M. and lasted until 6 P.M. They had to crouch for thirteen hours straight and scoop up coal with their hands. There were no safety precautions. Every day several Jews were killed in rock falls. Others died of malnutrition. Their daily diet was a bowl of greasy soup apiece and one kilogram of bread to be divided among three of them. They were bound together with leg chains. The guards never let them rest. Sometimes, during those thirteen hours underground, the guards felt their foreheads and armpits. They beat the Jews who weren't sweating.

At the end of the day the guards would give the miners soap made out of human flesh. There was enough time for them to wash, but they had to leave before they could dry themselves.

They marched back to their barracks with wet bodies and filthy clothes and slept in the outfits they'd used in the mines. Those who overslept the next morning, those who complained, those who got sick, were sent to the ovens.

After the war, Martin Isaacson returned to the Carpathians. He sought his family for months. Eventually, he learned of his wife and daughters' fate and, after a period of mourning, he met and married Rebecca. In 1949, after four years, the couple left for Israel.

Though Martin was a skilled mechanic, an excellent driver, he had trouble finding work there. The jobs he landed paid little; he tried to start his own small trucking business but failed. Rebecca had contracted arthritis—in the camps, she thinks—and spent months in a Haifa hospital. Now she is a sturdy woman, but in those years her weight dropped to eighty pounds. The couple lived with five others in a single room on Mt. Carmel. The only furniture was seven beds, seven chairs, and two tables.

Soon Martin decided to leave Israel, though Rebecca wanted to stay. Their disagreement must have been bitter, for traces of it still intrude in their marriage. Martin contends, furiously, that when he decided to come to the States in 1957 the Israeli government kept the reparations money that he—like all other concentration-camp survivors—had been receiving from the German government. What a betrayal of Jewish brotherhood that was! As he talks, Rebecca shouts back at him, trying vainly to silence him. But his rage is like a volcano.

Until 1974 he'd worked in a hardware store on Orchard Street and Rebecca worked in the garment industry. Now he's retired. That spring, when Rebecca was cleaning the house for Passover, her arthritis became so severe she'd had to quit work. The financial loss was serious. Between them they receive $264 in Social Security and unemployment each month. They pay $79 for rent.

The last time I visited them Rebecca was stretched out on a couch, her legs swathed in ace bandages, trying to relieve the pain with an electric massager. She had enough strength to show me her most precious relics—some crumbling, fading pictures of her children at school in the Carpathians, before they'd been sent to Auschwitz. The realization that her daughter would have been forty-three that year made her sob uncontrollably.

She hadn't been able to go outside in four months. Martin did all the shopping. By day, she said, the pain was barely tolerable. By night, it becomes so severe she has to soak in a hot bath for hours at a time. When she's out of the tub she sits by the window and stares at Rivington Street, remembering.

She doesn't read English. Her caseworkers collected some Yiddish books for her, to help her through the night. But her greatest wish is to go outdoors. She can only do that if she moves to a building with an elevator. She hasn't heard of any safe ones whose rent she can afford. It's hard for her to get a subsidy. Her problems, hard as they are, aren't as immediate or severe as Hedy Rose's, and it was extremely difficult to get Hedy qualified as an emergency case. So, she and Martin, survivors of Auschwitz, refugees from Israel's hardships, are captives on Rivington Street, victims of their own poverty and Rebecca's failing health.

Selma Haberman, seventy-two, has a one-room apartment on Hester Street. Her mattress is shredded and roach-infested, but the frail old lady refuses to get another one. The mattress is one of the few tangible links she possesses to her murky past.

Fred Siegel, her caseworker, developed great affection for her. For months, he brought her bread, fruit, and tuna fish whenever he visited, and fed her himself. One day he noticed that a loud, gurgling sound came from her chest whenever she talked. He brought in a doctor, who diagnosed her ailment as a congestive coronary condition.

With Fred's prodding she consented to go to Bellevue. She almost collapsed as she made her way across her cluttered room to the door. She trembled as she walked down the four flights of stairs in her tenement building.

She was put in the American Nursing Home, on the sixth floor, with all the other helpless patients. Strapped to their wheelchairs, they gather in the game room for most of the day. Some are deformed, with frozen, ghastly expressions on their faces. Others, who combat senility with manic energy, screech incomprehensible curses at each other or at the nurses. One woman intones the words "help me, help me" for hours every day. Often the television, their main form of entertainment, blares out game shows for those who are free enough from pain, from their obsession with death, from their shadowy memories, to concentrate on Bill Cullen's smiling face.

The first few times I saw Selma Haberman she was confused and withdrawn. She spoke in a jumble of English and Yiddish in such a soft, parched voice you could barely distinguish between her syllables. Didn't she owe someone money? Maybe it was Fred Siegel, whose yarmulke and beard made him look like "the rabbi" to her, a figure of authority who floated through her thoughts with as little specific substance as a figure from a Chagall painting.

She talked about the past, but she possesses shreds of recollections, not memories. She doesn't know where she lived before she moved to Hester Street. Maybe on Broome Street? Maybe with a sister in Brooklyn, whose house burned down, or was sold, or condemned? Some relatives were killed somewhere. In Poland, her birthplace? In Brooklyn? She isn't sure. All that emerges from the dry rustle of random words are a few scattered events, a few recognizable place names. And a hint of the proud years, the 1930s, when she worked as a city clerk and was rewarded—by Franklin Roosevelt, she says—with six NRA medals.

Selma Haberman asked Fred Siegel to bring her bankbook to the nursing home. When he and I looked for it, rummaging through the rubble of her apartment, we realized that, until 1952, she had been a busy, worldly woman whose life had been full of invitations to this friend's wedding, that child's circumcision, a relative's funeral. She still has dozens of cards asking her to visit a sick friend or thanking her for a tasteful wedding gift—or, after 1952, begging her to leave her rooms and visit the people who love her.

From 1942 to 1952 she'd worked as a pillow stuffer. She still has a union card. She seems to have identified with the labor movement. Among her books is a heavily underlined transcript of testimony from members of the painters' union during a strike arbitrated by Fiorello La Guardia. She was quite religious. She has several prayer books, including a *siddur* written in Yiddish and printed in Warsaw, which instructs Jewish daughters on the proper way to ask the Almighty for livelihood and good health for the family and for Zion.

Once she must have cared about her looks. There are several boxes full of store-bought jewelry in the apartment, a bag with fifteen combs and three brushes, and four pairs of glasses.

She liked to read. There was a *Reader's Digest,* dated May, 1952, with articles about William O'Dwyer and Bill Veeck. Two copies of *Quick* magazine, one with a cover photo of Debbie Reynolds, the other with a picture of Julius La Rosa and Lu Ann Simms. An old copy of *Hans Brinker.* A recipe book, *Meals on Wheels,* dated 1937. *The Secret of Soviet Strength,* a pamphlet written in 1949 by Hewlitt Johnson, the Red Dean of Canturbury. *All Night Long,* a novel of guerrilla warfare in Russia by Erskine Caldwell.

During World War II, much of her energy had been spent trying to locate family members who were in Europe when Hitler's Army attacked. In 1940 the Red Cross sent answers to inquiring letters she had written—one apologizing for its inability to find two relatives who were still in Warsaw, the other bearing a message from her brother, David, who had made his way to Amsterdam. "All in good health. Praying daily for sister Rose. Any news of family in Warsaw?"

In 1941, she got a letter from Warsaw, telling her that two sisters were very sick, pleading for some food packages. She tried to mail the packages through the HIAS House, but was instructed that the Nazis wouldn't permit them to go through. The news from Amsterdam was a little better. She received two postcards from her brother. Both bore the red swastika of the Nazi censor. Both asked about other members of the family, said that life in Holland was pleasant enough, asked Selma when she planned to marry. Those were the last letters from David.

After the war, in 1947, she heard from a former neighbor of David's, who said that he'd lived in the ghetto and worked hard as a tailor, opening his store at 6 A.M. and closing it at 8 P.M., the curfew hour the Nazis had imposed. Then, one day, shortly after the first round-up of the Jews in Holland, the Gestapo routed David out of his house and led him down the street at gunpoint. The neighbor never heard from David again.

In December, 1951, Selma Haberman received a letter from Holland, the only piece of her correspondence which is disfigured. She must have read it time and time again: It has crumbled into four pieces and a few random shreds. When we reassembled the sheet we learned that David was "deported to Auschwitz via Westebrook on 24 July, 1942. He died at Auschwitz on the 14 of August, 1942. Notice of his death appeared in the *Netherlands Gazette* on 8.6.50 and a death certificate can be obtained against payment of a legal fee."

There isn't a new book, a sustained correspondence, or a hint of a job after 1953. Just rent receipts, political leaflets, bank statements, and the accreting, grimy mess.

In one of Selma Haberman's drawers, Fred Siegel found a button-shaped portrait of a bride and groom. Judging from the couple's clothes it was taken in America during the 1930s. We brought it to her at the nursing home, along with the sturdiest pair of glasses we could find. The glasses did help her see. For the weeks she'd been without them she must have lived in a shadow world.

"That's my sister, who lived in Brooklyn," she said when she looked at the picture. "I'm so sorry for her. Why did she have to die?" Fred asked her how she died. "I can't remember. I can't make my mind remember any of that." For a full five minutes she sat silently, looking fondly at the photo.

Fred and I wheeled her into the elevator and took her to a small patio outside the nursing home. After another long pause she told us how lovely the roses in the small garden looked. Then she glanced at a man sitting with some relatives at a bench near ours and said, proudly, to no one in particular, "I have some visitors, too."

All Night Long is a 300-page novel. Selma Haberman had drawn a line alongside a passage in it, and now Fred began to read it to her, half in English, half in Yiddish. "I have some sausage. It's a sign of good fortune to meet up with someone who has some bread. If we had not met, you would have eaten bread without sausage and I would have eaten sausage without bread. That proves how wise my grandfather was even in his old age. He always said if you share with your neighbors and your neighbors share with you, then both of you will have more than you did to begin with."

When Fred asked her about that passage she said something about her grandfather in Poland and how he used to believe in that.

An attendant came by with half a cherry Popsicle. Selma Haberman took a large bite, then insisted that Fred take a second, and I take a third. As we were eating, one of the people on the bench next to ours walked over to give us some watermelon. She bit into that, too, then passed it to us. We sat there, sharing the refreshing summer foods in a silent, friendly ritual.

When we prepared to wheel Selma Haberman back upstairs we saw a lean old white-haired man, evidently a deaf-mute, sitting on one of the benches, smiling benignly. As we pushed the wheelchair toward him, he began to move his hands like a symphony conductor. Then, as we drew close to him, he smiled gallantly at Selma Haberman, bowed at her, and applauded. When she passed him he kissed her.

Inside the nursing home she introduced Fred and me as her "sons," her "nephews," to some of the attendants and patients. As we wheeled her along the sixth floor, toward the game room, where the TV was still blaring, she smiled a little and waved at everyone she saw. For a moment she almost seemed happy.

CHAPTER 11

Orthodox in New York:
A Journey Through the Year 5738

For more than a year, in 1977 and 1978, I spent much of my time in New York City's Orthodox Jewish communities, particularly on the Lower East Side. It was a wondrous voyage through time. When I got off the subway—the F train—and walked down East Broadway I was suddenly in the Jewish calendar year 5738. I was in the pious world of my European ancestors.

I had felt drawn to that world ever since I wrote *"Jews Without Money, Revisited."* I talked about my feelings with some of the younger Orthodox people I met then—men and women— who had managed to integrate their religious traditions into their American lives. But the bearded, black-garbed older sages seemed unapproachable. They reminded me of my assimilation—of my ignorance of the basic Hebrew blessings, of most holidays that marked the cycle of my ancestors' years. I feared they would either treat me as an irretrievable outcast or demand that I embrace their ways. So, for the most part, their world seemed off limits.

Once, though, several years earlier, I had spent an afternoon in the Munckaczer *talis* (prayer-shawl) factory, close to the Manhattan Bridge. David Weiderman, seventy-two, born in Hungary, was weaving the exalted garments on a clattering fifty-year-old mechanical loom. His father, who had taught him the trade, had died in Hitler's Europe. Now Weiderman, isolated from his past in that small, noisy store, tried to uphold the tradition of careful religious craftsmanship he had absorbed as a boy. His prayer shawls were made only of pure Turkish wool. He was scornful of the "cheap, mixed *talisim*" imported from Israel, made of wool diluted by rayon. "Let the others do it the way they want," he said. "It's not my business. I'll do it the way it has always been done."

How proud he was of that ancient trade. For a moment I saw him as a guardian of an irrecoverable past.

That night I described David Weiderman to my father. Fascinated, he urged me to keep exploring what I'd glimpsed that afternoon.

I was surprised by his interest. Until then I'd always seen him and my mother as committed—but not religious—Jews. Like most people of their generation, they had been deeply affected by World War II. They insisted that my brother and sisters and I remember our kinship to the six million dead. In dozens of dinner-table conversations they imbued us with the idea that our history of oppression should make us sensitive to injustice: We fought for civil rights in this country and fought to end the war in Vietnam. That was *my* Judaism: the brand that made me feel so naïve in Forest Hills.

Yet my father had changed his name from Cohen to Cowan because he hated *his* Orthodox father. In my parents' house, we celebrated Christmas, not Chanukah. My brother and I attended Choate, an Episcopalian prep school, where I learned stately Christian hymns and litanies by heart. I don't remember knowing anyone who kept kosher or observed the Sabbath when I was growing up. Those acts seemed archaic customs to me. I assumed they did to my father, too.

After I wrote *"Jews Without Money, Revisited,"* my feelings about Judaism began to change. By 1976, I was fasting on Yom Kippur. And Rachel, who is not Jewish, had become even more convinced than I that simple aspects of worship—holding Passover *seders* in our apartment, fasting, gathering in close as we lit the Sabbath candles—would enrich the fabric of our family's life.

I told my father we were fasting. To my astonishment, he said that, were he in better health, he'd join us. He'd fasted every year until he was thirty, he said. He had never told me that.

We talked of other religious traditions than Yom Kippur. A few weeks earlier I had learned of a Jewish law that says holy books must be buried, for to throw them out profanes the name and the works of the Lord. My father believed that all books were sacred. He said a friend of his had searched through the Talmud and found the wording of that injunction. Now my father wanted to hang a typed copy of it in his study.

When *would* I get around to writing that article on religious Jews, he asked.

On November 18, 1976, my parents died in a fire. This chapter began as a form of mourning—and of carrying out a wish of my father's that I didn't fully understand. It came to be even more—a way of recovering part of my own lost past.

I was lucky to find a teacher, a guide—Rabbi Joseph Singer, sixty-two, born in Poland to a family of rabbis, the tenth-generation descendant of Gershon Kitover, who was the brother-in-law of the Baal Shem Tov, the founder of the hasidic movement.

He is both a rabbi and a social worker. When I first met him in his office at the United Jewish Council, he was in his cubicle, talking on the phone to an elderly woman who refused to have her phlebitis checked at Beth Israel hospital. His dark gabardine coat hung over his chair. He was pacing back and forth, shouting, joking, cajoling in a rapid mixture of English and Yiddish. As soon as he finished with the first call he answered one from a man in Brighton Beach who hadn't received a Social Security check in six months. How could he deal with city officials, the man asked Rabbi Singer. He always felt afraid in the presence of such powerful people. Rabbi Singer tugged at his beard and toyed with his *payes* (the sidelocks tucked neatly behind his ear) as he listened to the desperate voice. He arranged to go out to Brooklyn the next day and accompany his frightened client to the Social Security agency.

From the first encounter, Rabbi Singer never called me by my American name. To him I am Saul (Sha'ul). Once or twice he railed against the Biblical Paul, the early convert who laid so much of the ideological groundwork for the persecution of the Jews that would come.

He intoned my Hebrew name in such a fond, natural voice that I never worried whether he was judging my identity. Instead, I felt he was helping me enrich it with a new, special one.

Every day, at about 6 A.M. and 4 P.M., he goes to his old *shul* on Stanton Street, across from a rubble-strewn lot, to make sure that the men who pray there will be comfortable. He boils a large pot of water for coffee and tea and puts a bagful of cookies in the refrigerator. On a winter day, when the congregants come in to warm themselves, to savor a cookie or two and a few minutes of fraternity, those things are particularly important.

Some of them love to sit for fifteen minutes around a spare wooden table with Rabbi Singer, studying a portion of the Talmud in honor of the dead. Others grow impatient. Soon, someone urges the rabbi to begin the *daavening,* the praying. He smiles back. They've been doing that for years.

Then Rabbi Singer ties a black prayer belt, a *gartel,* around his waist. The ornamental garment shows his respect for the Almighty; it ensures that the passionate juices of the lower half of his body won't interfere with the purity of his prayers.

Once the *gartel* is on he walks up to the ark, where the Torah is kept, and intones prayers as he rocks back and forth with controlled dignity. Sometimes during the services, members of the congregation talk with each other—about their health or their children or the merits of a housing project. The *shamesh,* the sexton of the *shul,* wheels toward them and shouts for silence. Rabbi Singer continues to pray at his own unhurried pace.

After the service he is teasingly gentle with the congregants. He feels a deep, unquestioning affection for them. He wants them to see the *shul* as a home.

Soon after we met, during a very cold week, the synagogue's pipes broke. Rabbi Singer asked me to go with him to fix them. We hurried to the *shul.* He huddled inside his frock coat against the freezing Manhattan winter wind as we walked down Essex Street—where Rabbi Moses Eisenbach, the scribe, was correcting letters on the flowing parchment page of a Torah; past the tiny basement shop where three women bent over their sewing ma-

chines, making yarmulkes; past the cavernous old market near Pitt
Street, where the *shochet*—the ritual slaughterer—honed his knife
to be sure the chickens squawking in their wire cage would be
killed quickly and mercifully, in accordance with Jewish law.
Those people were all his friends, just as they would have been in
the *heim*, in Galicia, where he was raised. But he couldn't stop to
talk with them now. He wanted the *shul* to be clean before anybody arrived for services.

On the way over, he reminisced about the Europe of his youth,
"where the air was holy," and "a town without a rabbi was like a
wedding without music," about the Thursday nights he and his
classmates stayed in *heder*—in religious school—praying, fasting
so that they could study harder, reading from the Torah so that
the holy words would echo through the night.

He'd loved the feeling of Friday morning, when everyone went
to the market to buy fish or milk for the Sabbath and the town
square was filled with Jews from the countryside come to get their
chickens killed by the *shochet*; when the tradesmen stopped their
work to go to the *mikva*—the ritual bath—then to pray; when the
entire town was already half-bathed in the lovely amber glow of
Shabbos.

Once we entered the *shul*, we quickly began to mop the floors
in the freezing bathroom. Then Rabbi Singer got out a stepladder
and held it while I replaced some bulbs in the vestibule.

As we worked, I wondered aloud what I was doing there. But I
couldn't think of any place I'd rather have been than in that *shul*,
performing that *mitzvah*, that good deed. Why did I—why did
someone as Americanized as I—feel that way?

Rabbi Singer answered instantly. Sometimes, he said, when you
have an ancestor who was a holy man or a scholar, his piety
creates a spark that smolders through the generations until it
burns again.

My parents had never talked much about their European past.
My mother's German-Jewish ancestry was too remote. My father
wasn't sure what Eastern European country his paternal forebears
had come from. But one of his cousins had given me the name of
a great-uncle in Chicago who knew a little family history. I called
him after I talked to Rabbi Singer. In the course of our long con-

versation he told me that Jacob Cohen—my great-great grand-father—had been a rabbi in the province of Gradno, Lithuania. He'd been a Cohen, a member of the Jewish priestly caste. I realized that wasn't so miraculous. Every Jew must have a few holy people in the family tree. Still, the news delighted Rabbi Singer. And it delighted me.

Several days later, while walking down East Broadway, I heard someone call out the name "Sha'ul." I looked around. Rabbi Singer was hurrying toward me. "Did you really hear the name Sha'ul?" He asked the question several times. Assured that I had, he beamed at me through his ginger-flecked gray beard. "You see. That name is somewhere in your subconscious."

So. I was Saul Cohen with Rabbi Singer and his friends, Paul Cowan in my own world. I began to feel as if I were leading a double life. When I was on the Lower East Side, in the year 5738, I always put on a yarmulke. For a while I told myself I was doing so as a sign of respect, an attempt to conform to long-established traditions. But that didn't explain the pleasure I took in pinning the skullcap to my head. Wearing it was like fasting on Yom Kippur: not a duty but a way of reclaiming part of my identity. Sometimes, when I got off the subway on the Upper West Side, I would pause before I took the yarmulke off. I always removed it, though, always emerged from the subway bareheaded. Uptown, in the year 1978, it felt uncomfortable and a little misleading to wear it. I wasn't an Orthodox Jew; I was still in flux, still at the beginning of a voyage whose destination was not yet clear. Rachel and I were trying to figure out how to observe the Sabbath, but in a way that blended the realities of our own highly mobile, multicultured life with our desire for peace and ceremony. All I knew was that I wanted to find a place in the tradition that Rabbi Singer and my great-great grandfather Jacob Cohen represented.

I began describing those feelings to friends. Many, to my surprise, were involved in similar searches. Others seemed confused by my new interest in religion. Some, I'm sure, thought I was seeking solace. The truth was that my parents' death only intensified a feeling I have harbored for years.

I am one of history's orphans. I love the variety, the mobility of this country—the frontier dreams that are the fabric of this book

—but I have never been able to shake my feeling of personal disorientation. Because of the holocaust, I can't go back to the Jewish sectors of those German and Lithuanian towns where my ancestors came from: They don't exist. There are no long-memoried bards or precious documents, or even old libraries and cemeteries, to help me retrieve the European ghosts that must still inhabit some important corner of my very American personality. There is no way I can find out even the barest details of Rabbi Jacob Cohen's life; no way I can find out why his son Moses came to America or why his grandson Jake, a failure at business, clung to the forms of Orthodoxy with a reflexive passion that always made my father equate religion with rage; or what it meant to the hidden psyche of my family that, after all these years, we were Cowans, not Cohens, lawyers, writers, historians, entertainment entrepreneurs who had succeeded at those worldly activities but who were utterly ignorant of the intimate details of our own heritage.

How many people have been robbed of their pasts by America's relentless, subtle pressures? There were the careless immigration officers, the landsmen—the countrymen—who had been here for a year or two and saw your sidelocks, your gabardine coat, as a sure sign that you were a greenhorn. The friendly acquaintance in the shop, or the boss himself, who told you you'd "look like a Yankee" if you just shaved off that beard. The wealthy German Jews, "Our Crowd," the uptowners, who were ashamed of the Eastern Europeans, who called them "kikes" behind their backs, who established settlement houses and sent forth stump speakers to convert them to the view that it was un-American—and, some suggested, illegal—to adhere to Jewish traditions in this land. The public-school teacher who spanked a kid for speaking Yiddish in the classroom. The pal or lover, or the college admissions officer, who might accept a Cowan, but never a Cohen; a Livingston, but not a Levi.

Those are telltale details, but add them by the hundreds, spread them among the people who are thrilled to be free of the economic and political confines of the *shtetl*, who are mortified by the slightest suggestion that they are different from the mainstream America they long to enter and, miraculously, a collective identity seems to vanish in less than a century—a wink of time in the 5,739 years of Jewish history.

Rabbi Singer. There is a legend, in the Jewish tradition, that the world can't exist unless there are thirty-six just men in it. Nobody knows who they are, or what their faith is. But I have come to believe that Rabbi Singer is the kind of man who could be one of the *lamed vovnik*—one of the just.

He is immensely proud of the legacy he has carried from Pilzno, Poland, to Stanton Street, New York, of his blood relationship to the early Hasids, whose personal warmth and ecstatic religion kindled a passionate piety that swept through the *shtetls* of Eastern Europe.

It was a world in which people "felt the way of the Almighty in their soul. They felt that every little thing was from the Almighty." And that spirit endured for centuries in Pilzno, a town of about 250 Jewish familes, about a thousand Gentiles, which was located near the Vistula River. To almost all the Jews who lived in the ramshackle wooden houses that lined the town's rutted streets Rabbi Singer's grandfather—Rabbi Gershon Singer— was a man who could use his faith to make miracles. Rabbi Singer's mother used to reminisce about his holy feats in later years—after the family had moved to another part of Galicia during World War I.

Once, a boy from Lemberg, a large town, who had married a girl from Pilzno, disappeared without a trace. That was a tragedy, according to Jewish law, for the girl couldn't remarry unless she had a *gett*, a contract of divorce. "They looked for him, right and left," Rabbi Singer says. The girl's relatives advertised in newspapers in Lemberg and Cracow to see if anyone knew his whereabouts. But, he seemed to have vanished completely.

Nearly two years went by, and the girl and her parents were desperate. "Her mother bothered my grandmother, and my grandmother bothered my grandfather," Rabbi Singer says. At first the Rabbi demurred; he though a more noted *tsaddik*—holy man—in a nearby town was better equipped to help. He didn't like to promise to help people if he wasn't completely sure he could keep his vow.

Then, one night he came home from the *bet hamedresh*—the study house—where he'd been *daavening minha* and *ma'ariv*—afternoon and evening prayers—and he saw the girl had fainted in his living room. "She wasn't making believe. She was heartbroken and she couldn't take it anymore." So he and his wife gave her some smelling salts, and they talked late into the night. At last, he told the girl to "go home, rest, sleep. It's not going to be long before your husband returns." She was calm at once, Rabbi Singer says, for everyone in Pilzno believed that if his grandfather made a promise it would come true.

"Two months later a man came to town in a covered black coach, a carriage that was much finer than the horse-and-cart in which most Pilzno Jews traveled, and he went straight to my grandfather's house. When he got out, people saw that he was a long man with a high hat. Like the fancy people used to wear. They thought he was probably a well-to-do person, a German Jew." They soon learned it was the missing husband.

'He and my grandfather had a long talk. He said that when he'd left his wife he had gone to Paris. He didn't like living in a small town like ours. He had made up his mind never to come back."

"He started a business in France and he made out very well. He met a woman, and he fell in love. He was very happy. But then, during the past two months, everything he did was unlucky. His life became full of *tsouris*," a series of relentless problems. "His business went down. One day he was in a forest near Paris. He felt like his head was turning. He fell and he broke his arm.

"He had bad dreams. He couldn't sleep nights. He couldn't eat. He became very sick and had a nervous stomach.

"He dreamed about Pilzno, and he saw that his wife was crying. When his *tsouris* began, he started to feel her *tsouris*. She was alone, she couldn't get married, she had nobody.

"He decided he had to make her feel better, so he went back to Pilzno. And my grandfather didn't let him off. He called the *sofer* —the scribe—and, within two days, the *gett* was arranged.

After that, the husband want back to Paris, and he sent back letters and pictures, which showed that he was living a fine, prosperous life. But when the *gett* went through his wife was still sorrowful.

"She wondered if she would ever marry again. She began to cry even though she was happy to have the *gett*. Then my grandfather called her by name and said, 'My daughter, you're going to be very happy. You going to meet a good person.' And that's what happened. She met a wonderful man, a fine man. He was a bookkeeper and a scholar. The children and the grandchildren had such a happy life. I knew them when I was growing up," Rabbi Singer said.

He was reluctant to tell many stories like that. "The Torah likes *mitzvahs* better than miracles," he says. One of the *mitzvahs* Rabbi Gershon Singer used to perform in Pilzno a hundred years ago symbolizes the qualities Rabbi Joseph Singer seeks to embody in New York.

Every Thursday night, the rabbi of Pilzno would walk by all the Jewish houses in town, accompanied by his *shamesh*. Their mission? To inspect the chimneys of the congregants. They looked for houses where there wasn't enough smoke. Those families couldn't afford enough kindling to heat the Sabbath meal. So Gershon Singer would fetch a chicken for the *Shabbos*.

But the *mitzvah* must never be discovered. The rabbi must remain anonymous. The people who received the food must never be embarrassed by the knowledge that he was aware of their poverty.

So, between 1 and 5 A.M., when the Jews of Pilzno were asleep, the rabbi and the *shamesh* would pile the chicken and the charcoal into a wheelbarrow and place them in front of the houses. Then they would hurry away, before their goodness could be detected.

Rabbi Singer was the youngest son in a family of six boys and two girls.

His father, David, a rabbi, a *rav*, a scholar in Jewish law, lived in Pilzno until the middle of World War I. He had a house with two rooms on one of the town's main streets. In one of the rooms a large section of the floor was set aside for any traveler who needed sleep. "All my father's *seforim*—his books—were in that room, and a table for study, and a Torah, too, in case there was bad weather on *Shabbos* and we couldn't go to *shul.*"

During the day the town's Jews formed a noisy line in the back of the room and waited to consult the *rav.* He would decide whether a tiny blister on a chicken's gizzard meant the meat was kosher or *treyfe;* whether Talmudic law instructs a pious man to respect his elders by keeping a mean-spirited mother-in-law in the house or to preserve his marriage by banishing her.

Once, when the *rav* was coming home from *shul,* he saw a child crying. Why was the boy so sad, he asked. Because an older man, a fisherman, had slapped him. The *rav* decided to see whether a wrong had been committed. When he got back home, he told the *shamesh* to summon the fisherman. Then he bade the child and the adult to tell their versions of the episode. After concluding that the boy was telling the truth, the *rav* fined the man ten guilden—money that was very important to the child, since he came from a poor family. "That story went all around Galicia," Rabbi Singer says. "Everyone was impressed that my father gave so much attention to a little boy."

Throughout Eastern Europe the turn of the century was a difficult time for rabbis, for the laws and customs that had governed the *shtetls* for centuries were losing their force. Many young people were beginning to lose their faith altogether. They embraced new creeds—Communism, or a socialist brand of Zionism. They would sneak copies of Marx or Herzl into *heder* and study the heretical literature behind the holy books while they intoned the familiar Talmudic chants.

So, when Rabbi Singer was growing up, the *shtetl* was the scene of a cold war between believers and nonbelievers. "Our parents were afraid the children would mix. Of course, religious people had always argued among themselves. There were always great disputes over whether this kind of meat was kosher, that kind of meat was *treyfe.* But those people were against religion basically, against its foundation. I cannot say we hated them. But we were afraid of them. And we looked down on them because they were openly against the Almighty. There was a hydrogen curtain between us."

Besides, technology—in the form of cars and trains and steam-

ships—was transforming the once-isolated *shtetl*. America beckoned. But it also threatened. Each time a prospective immigrant
left home, his family and friends accompanied him to the railroad
station, often wailing with grief. They'd never see him again. He'd
be robbed of his piety by the lures of the new world:

"We knew that in the United States people were free—too
free. When they came back to Europe they had different opinions, different ideas. They left the religion. They left the life they
had always known."

There wasn't much that sages like Rabbi Singer's father could
do about that. Still, to solve problems that arose in the *shtetl*,
they had to span the ancient world and the modern one: to scour
Talmudic commentaries, written in ancient Babylonia or medieval
Europe, in an effort to understand how to use an invention like
electricity. Rabbi Singer's father wrote a major work on a problem
he encountered several times during World War I. Modern gov-
ernments had sent young men from Pilzno to fight a war few of
them understood, in places—like Russia and Italy—that few of
them could even imagine. Often, the soldiers never reappeared in
town. And the indifferent, inefficient army bureaucracy failed to
tell the families whether their sons or husbands were alive or
dead. Were the women who were left behind widows, free to
remarry?

It was an extremely difficult problem in Jewish law. Rabbi
David Singer, after months of study, decided that every man who
was going to war should apply for conditional *getts*—conditional
divorces—once they were drafted. If they came home, the *getts*
were canceled. If they didn't return, the divorces took effect.

The rabbi's commentaries were read in Yeshivas throughout
Europe, according to Rabbi Singer. "But his writings are all lost
now. Some were destroyed after World War I. Hitler took care of
the rest." Recently, Rabbi Singer learned that a student of his father's, now a rabbi in Israel, had preserved one of his pro-
nouncements. It is still circulating among scholars. "That was a
miracle." Someday he hopes to go to the Holy Land to recover
that scrap of his precious legacy.

It is one of the few things that remains of his youth. Toward
the end of World War I his family, like many people, fled from

the turbulence that surrounded them in Galicia; his father reset-
tled in Kashow, an eight-hour train ride away. David Singer's
health deteriorated. "He didn't eat the right foods. He didn't get
enough sleep," his son says. In 1925, he died of lung problems.

In 1934, life in Pilzno seemed normal enough for one of Rabbi
Singer's older brothers to return, to resume his family's role as
spiritual leader of the town. As the age of twenty, Rabbi Singer
accompanied him to serve an apprenticeship—to prepare himself
for a life very much like that of his father and grandfather. He
had never even contemplated another profession. His entire family consisted of "rabbis, not businessmen," he says proudly.

But, "as soon as Hitler took over Austria, we were afraid." One
day he and his brother went to Tarnow, a large city near Pilzno.
It was noontime, and they were walking down the main street,
which was filled with Jews. Some Gentiles started harassing them
—jostling them, taunting them, knocking off their hats.

"That used to happen on the side streets, or at night. But in
broad daylight, in a place that was full of Jews? That was something new. We knew that a terrible war was coming. The earth
was not sure under us.

"Until then, the great rabbis in Europe didn't let you go to the
United States. But in that time, before Hitler came, they said,
'Go, go.'"

Soon he and one brother left for America. "We were the
runners." But three brothers, all of them rabbis, and two sisters
remained behind. "I don't know exactly where they were killed.
Maybe at Auschwitz."

"I dream of those times always—about someone I knew, someone who got lost. I see him and I say, 'You're alive? You're not
alive. This is a dream.'

"How can I forget what happened? It was my memories, my
childhood. I cannot forget."

Before he left Poland he had planned to settle in a small American town—the equivalent of a *shtetl*—and "be an all-around
rabbi. I don't like to rush, and I thought that in a village I could
be a Jew in a European way. I'd be a rabbi. I'd be a scribe. If they
needed a *shochet*, I could be a *shochet*, too."

But when he got here, in 1939, he realized that it was impossible for him to settle in a small town, since most Jews who lived in those surroundings had grown so assimilated they didn't even know what a *shochet* was. He had to stay in New York City and New Jersey, in the few Orthodox communities that existed during those years.

Earlier, when Americanized Jews had returned to visit Europe, the fact that they were clean-shaven was taken as an indication they'd strayed from the faith. It wasn't exactly a religious necessity. "A lot of fine, wonderful people in Europe cut off their beards," Rabbi Singer recalls. Nevertheless, "if someone had grown up with a beard and *payes* and cut them off in America, that could be harmful to him. He cut not only his beard. He cut other things, too. He cut his religion.

"I was twenty-four years old when I came to the United States. I didn't want to cut my beard. I didn't want to change. I had a big beard—much bigger than it is now—and it was fiery red. When I got on a subway, the whole train looked at me. And everybody, even religious people, thought I was an old man because of it.

"Once, right after I came to America, I made a speech in a big synagogue in Patterson, New Jersey. Afterward, one of the *gabbaim*, the officials, came up to me and said, 'Rabbi, the people say you are an old man. But I can see in your face that you are young. Those Americans don't know. Your beard makes you look old to them.'

"I was so happy that one person knew I wasn't an old man. So I said, 'How old do you think I am?'

"'Rabbi,' he said. 'Let me say exactly. You are forty or forty-two.' Probably the other people in the synagogue thought I was sixty."

Young women were perplexed by the beard, too. "In those days, the girls were afraid of it. Maybe because it was old-fashioned, it wasn't stylish. I wanted to be old-fashioned. I'm still old-fashioned. But the girls took it differently. And the Torah says don't do things that make you look strange in the eyes of other people, as long as they are not against the religion. So I took the beard off. As a matter of fact, my cousin, he should rest in peace, an old rabbi, told me I should cut it off. I had no choice. 'But,' he said, 'make a condition, before you take it off, that you'll grow it back again.' After a while my wife said okay, I could grow it back again. And I did, too, a few years after I got married," he said with a chuckle.

In 1940, when he became the rabbi of a synagogue on the Lower East Side, he began to hear stories that showed him just how difficult it had been for the early immigrants to remain religious. "Jack, the *gabbai*, had been here thirty, forty years. He was in the garment business. He had Jewish bosses, but he had so much trouble keeping the *Shabbos*, I cannot tell you. He would say to the bosses 'Oh, you're working *Shabbos*.' And they would say, 'Get out of here. I'm a good Jew and I work *Shabbos*.' Jack was a good cutter. Finally he got a job where they said he could be religious. But on Friday afternoons they only let him leave at 4 P.M., a few minutes before *Shabbos*. Summer, it was okay. The days were big and he could get home in time for supper. But in the winter he had a terrible *tsouris*. The day was short. He *daavened minha* in the shop and walked home. When there was snow on the ground he'd get to his apartment very late. His wife would be waiting to light the candles."

Experiences like Jack's were so different from what Rabbi Singer had left behind, from the Fridays he loved when the entire *shtetl* bustled to greet the *Shabbos*. And his own life was so different from anything that he, or his forebears, had imagined. "In Europe, a rabbi was a power. Here, your president is a power. A rabbi is on a much lower level.

"Besides, a lot of them didn't care as much about religion as they did about making money."

Those things disappointed him deeply. "In 1943 and 1944, there came a boom in diamonds, and a lot of rabbis went to work in the diamond district. I did, too. I didn't give up my *shul*, but I made my living in the diamonds, as a cutter.

"Why did the rabbis go in there? Because diamonds is a Jewish line. You have no trouble with *Shabbos*. Most of the work is on contract, so you can come in whenever you want to. It is hard to be religious and punch a clock. If you want to go to the *mikva*, or if you *daaven* slow, you don't always have time for holiness since you have to get to work by eight or nine in the morning. But in the diamonds, if I went to the *mikva* and finished *daavening* at ten o'clock, I could come in at ten o'clock. And when I wanted I could always work late, since there were enough men to form a *minyan.*"

After World War II, the boom in diamonds ended. Rabbi Singer abandoned his dream of settling in a small town—an American Pilzno. He decided he could carry on his ancestors' traditions on the Lower East Side of New York.

In Pilzno there had always been a noisy group of people waiting for advice in his father's back room. Now, his cubicle at the United Jewish Council is as crowded and noisy as his father's house must have been.

Scores of pink messages—some in Yiddish, some in English— are strewn all over Rabbi Singer's desk. This man wants a safer apartment. That woman wants a new mattress. The congregation at a nearly *shul* is involved in a bitter question over the proper form of *daavening.* A cardboard box is piled high with similar requests. "You think he's a holy man?" a coworker said one day. "He's really running a bookie joint." Rabbi Singer heard the joke and smiled.

But "every little piece of paper is a trouble," he says. And a *mitzvah* that echoes back through the generations.

Itzak Hirsch, strong and raging at seventy-five, is a Jew without money. Hirsch has no family or friends—no human contact to connect him with his past. His universe consists of the splintered tables and chairs, the mounds of tattered clothes, old newspapers, magazines and girlie photos, the chipped paintings and broken phonograph records, that fill his apartment.

The management of the project where he lives has charged that Hirsch's home is a health hazard and has threatened to dispossess him. Desperate, he called on Rabbi Singer for help. But he was disoriented by his isolation in that fetid room. Wrath had become the sole filament of his human relationships. His emotions, his memories, the meager remains of his personal history, were contained in the litter he had to get rid of. Rabbi Singer, his salvation, is also his enemy.

He was appeased one day when Rabbi Singer told him that

his goods would go to charity—that he would rescue others, not himself. Nevertheless, he raged at the rabbi and five young co-workers when he saw them sorting through the possessions in his rooms, putting those he wanted to keep on one side, stuffing the ones he wanted to get rid of in garbage bags. But he let the grimy work go on.

Soon, though, he began to shout Yiddish invectives. He was watching his life vanish: each bag of trash contained the ruins of some half-forgotten dream. He stood near the dirt-streaked window, in front of an old, scavenged steamer trunk, looking like a sentry. He pointed two fingers at Rabbi Singer, as if to shoot him.

"All right, Hirsch, we'll go," Rabbi Singer said. "And tonight you'll sleep in all the garbage in the East River. How many times have I come here to help you, Hirsch? Five? Six? You're tearing my heart out. Listen, my voice is just a whisper. I don't even know if they'll hear me in my *shul* tonight."

With a laugh that was almost a caress, the descendant of the Baal Shem Tov kissed his own fingers, then stroked Itzhak Hirsch's taut, quivering hand. Hirsch's fingers remained cocked. His invective turned to obscenity. Several days earlier he had cuffed Rabbi Singer on the shoulder. Now he threatened to hit him again.

Rabbi Singer, in a gesture of intimacy that none of the younger people in the room could ever duplicate, cupped his hands over Hirsch's ears, then over his own, and glanced at the old man.

Moments later, still shouting, Hirsch stepped away from the trunk, giving us tacit permission to open it.

Occasionally, during the next hour, he even pointed out some of the garbage bags he wanted us to remove. Hirsch never was dispossessed.

One spring morning Rabbi Singer wanted Rabbi Moses Eisenbach, the scribe, to help him perform a *mitzvah*.

A few days earlier he had found some battered *tefillin* (the phylacteries Orthodox Jews put on their arms and head when they say morning prayers) in an abandoned *shul* on Henry Street. He wanted Rabbi Eisenbach to repair the scrolls inside the *tefillin* so that he could give them to some immigrants from the Soviet

Union—Jews just learning about their faith—in time for Passover.

When we entered the shop, Rabbi Eisenbach, an old man with a long gray beard, was bent over a Torah, a handwritten, flowing scroll made of sheets of parchment sewn together by thread spun from the sinews of a kosher animal. He was repairing damaged letters—with a razor blade, a turkey-feather quill, and a special black ink blended of gall nuts, copper-sulphate crystals, gum arabic, and water, whose formula had been in his family for decades.

He was performing the holiest of religious deeds: inscribing the words of the Almighty for the human race. The Torah says that *soferim*, scribes, must labor for the love of the Lord, not for wealth. Hence, in Europe, they were paid subsistence wages. Their fee was for their presence, not their output. It allowed them to labor patiently, lovingly, over each Torah, each *mezuzah*, each pair of *tefillin*.

In appearance Rabbi Eisenbach, a whisper of a man, seems to fulfill the Torah's injunction.

We waited in silence while he worked, for the task involves enormous physical and spiritual concentration. According to Talmudic law, if a *sofer* makes a mistake in writing the name of the Lord, or has a malicious or carnal thought while working, he must remove the entire parchment sheet, put it aside, insert a fresh sheet, and begin anew. And each morning the *sofer* cleanses his spirit in the mystically holy, purifying waters of the *mikva*, and goes to *shul* to *daaven shaharit*. When beginning his labor he intones the ancient Hebrew blessing that says he is making the scroll in the holiness of the Lord's name. Then, once again, he prays until his mind is free of any impure thought.

At last he finished his work and made his way to his office, a tiny desk in the back of the store. Rabbi Singer squeezed by the Torah scrolls and handed him the slightly charred *tefillin*—leather thongs and small boxes which contain four injunctions to remember the Lord, one of which, from Exodus, states:

And so it shall be as a sign upon your hand and a symbol upon your forehead that with a mighty hand the Lord freed us from Egypt.

The two men completed the transaction in Yiddish and then,

because I was there, switched to English. Rabbi Eisenbach, very reserved, talked a little about himself. He'd learned his craft in Jerusalem fifty years ago, and his time in the Yeshiva still seems like the sweetest in his life. He came to the United States in 1946, when tensions between the Arabs and the Jews began to wear on his nerves, when he found "it was hard to run a business with all those troubles." Now much of the time, he wishes he had remained in the Holy Land. He feels lonely in America, convinced that the environment here is so contaminated that it is difficult for a *sofer* to work in the proper way.

An entire body of religious law dictates that scribes must shape their letters perfectly, that their letters must not run together, that they must be written in straight lines. In Rabbi Singer's Europe, Orthodox Jews heeded that law strictly. They would travel for hundreds of miles to trade with a *sofer* who was also a *tsaddik*, who would fuse holiness and craftsmanship.

But it is different here, where many people who consider themselves religious disregard the laws Rabbi Eisenbach learned in his Jerusalem Yeshiva. They don't know—or care—about the way letters inside a *tefillin* or a *mezuzah* must be formed.

Long ago Rabbi Eisenbach decided, quite simply, that he would never risk taking on an apprentice who'd been born in this country. It wasn't only a matter of calligraphy. You can have the knack for making *alephs* and *bets*, and still not love the Lord enough to be sure that all your days are holy, that all the works of your hands are perfect.

And, according to Rabbi Eisenbach's reading of the Torah, a *sofer*'s responsibility is awesome. If he makes a flawed *tefillin* or *mezuzah* or Torah, it is likely that no one will know except himself and his Maker. Certainly, the unaware customer is not to blame. Nevertheless, he may suffer. The *mezuzah*, for example, is a small case attached to the upper third of a doorpost in a religious home and contains a small rolled piece of parchment that expresses love of the Lord and of the Torah as a way of life. Religious Jews believe a *mezuzah* affords a family spiritual protection. But if the words of the parchment are lettered imperfectly, the household might not be protected. The family could thus suffer for the scribe's mistake. So his error could become his curse, his lifelong burden, a sin that will haunt him in the afterlife.

Rabbi Eisenbach once did decide to train an American. But the younger man was hesitant to make a correction without asking the scribe's approval, and eventually he decided to leave the pressured *sofer*'s life and go into the diamond business.

I asked Rabbi Eisenbach if he ever worried that something might happen to his own highly trained hands. "What can I do?" he asked ruefully. "Insure them? Put them in a bank?" Then he went back to work.

Rabbi Singer and I stood in the store, watching him. He took such care over every letter. I could hear the traffic outside on Essex Street, but in his shop the stillness was broken only by the faint scratching of his turkey quill, the faint chipping of his razor.

There was a red light when we got to Grand Street. Rabbi Singer took my arm to prevent me from lunging ahead. He told me that the traffic light itself was a *mitzvah*, a reminder that it was a blessing to protect yourself. And, when you paused and said a *brachah*, a prayer, for such small things, you reminded yourself to be thankful for the enormous, wondrous gift of life.

It was nearly Passover, and Rabbi Singer was reminiscing.

In Pilzno and Kashow, before the holiday, ten or fifteen families would gather in the rare house that had an oven and, according to hasidic custom, sing Hallel, the Psalms of David, while the men baked the *matzot*. As the holiday drew near, everyone in the *shtetl* would search their homes for *hametz*—leavening—the removal of which serves as a reminder of the Jews' hurried flight from Egypt. They would remove every trace of it.

Such traditions have been preserved in Williamsburg, Borough Park, and Crown Heights, where thousands of hasidic Jews had settled after World War II. The traditions are observed by religious Jews all over America. They are observed on the Lower East Side, too, though many people have forgotten the exact details of the faith that pervaded their parents' lives.

Rabbi Singer feels a special responsibility to those people—especially to the "elderlies," who would have commanded so much respect in Europe and who were so often abandoned here.

For the past five years he had used a modern, spacious synagogue near East Broadway to hold free Passover *seders* for about two hundred of them. The United Jewish Council pays for those *seders* and helps arrange them.

Still, Rabbi Singer trusts no one but himself to supervise the exhausting search for the *hametz*. During the days before Passover, he takes off his black jacket, rolls up the sleeves of his white shirt, and mops the floor, scours every pan, squats in front of the synagogue's oven with an acetylene torch to be sure that he's burned away all traces of the bread crumbs.

"I know most of the people who are coming to the *seder* don't care about those things. But I do. I care for me and I care for them." There was more than a hint of loss in that wry remark.

Shortly before Passover, Rabbi Singer left the hurly-burly of his neighborhood to perform a special, personal mission in the placid, Orthodox milleu of Williamsburg. A Hasid he knew—a *rebbe* from Galicia—had promised to give him two of the especially holy round brownish *shemurah matzot*. Like the Jews in Pilzno, the *rebbe* had planted and harvested the wheat that was in them. He had ground it on a stone mill he kept in his basement, secure in the knowledge that no water or heat would cause fermentation, chanting prayers as he labored.

Children were playing tag outside the *rebbe*'s house, their sidelocks flying in the breeze. But, inside, the mood was solemn. The *rebbe*'s wife and daughter, whose aprons enveloped their long, chaste dresses, were scrubbing the houses as they would have in Europe a century before. They told us the *rebbe* was upstairs in his study.

He must have heard our voices, for he summoned us to the room where the holy book he was reading lay open on a long, wooden table. Moving slowly, he greeted Rabbi Singer, climbed on a chair, and reached to the top of a cupboard where some white boxes containing the special *matzot* were stored.

The two old friends began to talk in Yiddish. Soon the *rebbe*, looking somewhat puzzled, was staring at my clean-shaven face, my tweed cap, and my tan windbreaker.

"He wants to know how you came to me," Rabbi Singer said. "I told him our grandparents were connected."

Earlier that day he had described a place in Williamsburg where hundreds of hasidic Jews would be baking *shemurah matzot* and chanting psalms. My religious imagination was still half-conditioned by all the services I had attended in Choate's Episcopalian chapel, and, particularly, by the solemn hymns we had sung as Easter approached. So I visualized the hasidim in a staid, solemn frieze—enacting a Good Friday in Yiddish.

Instead, the place was huge and bustling, alive with throngs of men and women in traditional hasidic garb, kneading dough at separate tables. It was all done very rapidly, since Jewish law insists that all *matzot* must be baked and all the utensils washed within eighteen minutes, before fermentation begins.

Groups of Yeshiva students kept arriving. There was soon no room for them at the tables. Some stood in corners while others elbowed their way through the crowd to find a spot where they could begin their baking. Meanwhile, those who had been there awhile raced from the oven to the main room, carrying boxes full of the finished *matzot* high above their heads.

Some people standing near us chanted Hallel as they worked. Rabbi Singer's ancestors had praised the Almighty by chanting Hallel when they baked *matzot* in Galicia. More than two thousand years ago the *Kohenim*—the priests in the Temple in Jerusalem—had chanted Hallel on the afternoon before Passover, to commemorate the Exodus, the miracle that brought the Jews to that hallowed place:

Open to me the gates of righteousness, that I may enter through them and give thanks to the Lord.

"Did you take it all in, Sha'ul?" Rabbi Singer asked me later. "You've had a little taste of Europe now."

He took my arm. As we walked to the subway, people kept glancing at us. What an odd-looking pair we must have made.

Once we were on the train he held the white box close to him so that the *shemurah matzot*—so sacred in themselves, so full of precious memories—wouldn't crack on the short, jarring subway ride back to the Lower East Side.

Rabbi Singer was heading toward *shul* when Frieda Provda appeared in the window of the Masaryk Cake Box, near Grand

Street. She rapped on the pane, summoning him urgently. Anna, a widow in a nearby housing project had died of bone cancer the night before and her only relative, a brother, lived in Los Angeles.

The Masaryk Cake Box had been Anna's second home during her last years. Most days, at noon, she'd leave her radio, her closest companion, and go down there to gossip with friends or take care of the customers' children. Now Frieda Provda and her friend, Betty Fried, feeling the responsibilities of surrogate kinship, had to arrange the funeral, which, according to Jewish law, would occur the next day.

Frieda Provda was dressed for the 1970s: she didn't wear a wig or a long modest skirt as the women of Williamsburg do. She was an Americanized businesswoman—"Be kind to the next person, that's my Judaism." But she'd chosen to work in a bakery where *Shabbos* was observed, and she had no doubt about her religious loyalties. "I'm not Conservative or Reform," she told Rabbi Singer proudly. "I think she should be buried as one of us."

So she had chosen an Orthodox funeral home and asked the director to comply with age-old traditions: to be sure that there were women from a *hevrah kadishah*, a burial society, to make a *taharah*—to purify the corpse by cleaning it—and to watch it through the night. He didn't exactly refuse. But, she said, there was an unsettling hint of reluctance in his voice.

Passover was a busy season at the bakery. But Frieda Provda was worried. What if the funeral director decided to save a hundred dollars—or two hundred dollars—by omitting the *taharah?* What if he was too busy to bother calling a *hevrah kedishah?* The widow's brother was coming to New York that day. What if the funeral director convinced him to assuage his grief by purchasing an expensive coffin, not the simple pine box in which Jews are supposed to be buried. That would be a sacrilege!

What luck that she had glimpsed Rabbi Singer's gabardine coat as he rushed by. He would help her ward off the greedy bureaucrats of death.

This was a *mitzvah* he was glad to perform. He'd hated the Jewish funeral business ever since he came to America—hated the morticians who cared more about today's profits than about the afterlife. For, traditionally, death has always been the most egali-

tarian part of Jewish life. Before a funeral, rich and poor alike are
dressed in simple white shrouds—shrouds without pockets—to
show that one's soul, not one's possessions, are important to the
Almighty. All are buried in a simple pine casing, or on a bed
made of natural substances, so that the body and its casing can
decompose naturally and return to the earth.

Rabbi Singer raged while he waited for Frieda Provda to get
the funeral director on the phone:

"Who would have thought that Jews would make a chapel,
that they'd take a fancy-smancy custom—a non-kosher custom, a
goyishe custom—that they wouldn't make a *taharah* but put a
fancy-smancy suit on a body—just to make money?

"In Europe, a funeral was a holy thing. It belonged to the community. The community was the boss of what happened. And if
somebody passed away, everybody helped out, everybody knocked
a nail in the coffin. Everybody pushed to do that. It was an honor
and a *mitzvah*, not a business. Who thought about business then?

"Well," he said, answering his own question, "sometimes a rich
man passed away, and he'd be very stingy. Then the *kehilla*"—the
Jewish town council—"taxed his family. But that wasn't a business. The community used the money to pay the rabbi, the
shamesh, to fix the *shul*, to fix the *mikva*, to help the poor on
Shabbos. When the community took money from such a person it
was 100 per cent right to do so. But otherwise? A business? *Bah!*
Here the chapel is a business. There it was a sign of deep respect,
of deep feeling, to go to a funeral, to help a family."

At last, the funeral director was ready to talk. Rabbi Singer
edged past the case of almond macaroons, of marble cake made of
matzoh meal—the sweets Frieda Provda was displaying for Passover—and transformed himself into a religious diplomat as he
began to issue gentle, steely orders over a pay phone.

Of course the funeral director would call the *hevrah kedishah*.
Of course, there would be a simple pine box and a shroud. And
he'd see that a few flecks of dirt—preferably dirt from Israel—
were placed on the corpse, in conformity with the biblical injunction "ashes to ashes, dust to dust." The funeral was scheduled
for nine the next morning? Fine. Rabbi Singer or his cousin, who

had a synagogue in Washington Heights would be there . . . just to help out.

When he hung up, he was smiling with relief. But Rabbi Singer, still angry, reminisced about his past battles. "Once I had a funeral uptown. It was in a fancy place. They wanted to sell the family a casket for $1,500 or $1,800. I told them, don't take it, don't be *meshugenna*. Buy one for $150. The owners of the chapel were so angry they began to chase me. They wanted to hit me.

"Do you blame them? Do you know how much I cost them? Most chapels hate me like poison. If they could kill me, they would kill me. I spoil their business."

That dusk, we left Rabbi Singer's *shul*. As always, a police car was waiting outside, to take the rabbi home. He's on extremely good terms with the officers. Sometimes they attend services—a policewoman sat in the basement one night when we *daavaned*; an Irish cop joined the congregation as it booed the evil Haman during Purim services. Rabbi Singer invited several policemen to his daughter's wedding.

That night, though, he felt like walking; three of his congregants rode with the cops. As we cut across Pitt Street, we passed a *bodega* where three Hispanic kids were drinking Cokes. They'd seen Rabbi Singer before. In a joking voice, one of them looked at him and hollered out, "*La barba de Fidel*"—the beard of Fidel. When I translated, Rabbi Singer smiled back.

Suddenly, a bareheaded man emerged from a hardware store and ran toward Rabbi Singer, hollering in agitated Yiddish. When he caught up to us he grabbed the rabbi's tie and held it tightly. Then he and Rabbi Singer both signed a handwritten piece of paper.

He was selling his family's *hametz*—all the alcohol and medicine and cosmetics that contained leavening—with the understanding that the rabbi would, in turn, sell the *hametz* to a Gentile, who wasn't bound by the laws of the season. The transaction was a legal construct, a link to the Exodus. It involved an exchange of paper, not a transfer of property. He would seal the items with *hametz* in a closet until Passover ended, then buy them back from the rabbi and use them again. When he signed his name to a piece of paper and touched the rabbi's garment, he was heeding a Talmudic injunction, a guarantee that the contract was sealed.

Afterward, he walked back to the hardware store. Rabbi Singer glanced at him, brushing some dust off his garbardine coat. Then he touched the beard that would have been so typical in Pilzno or on the streets of Williamsburg, which had caused him such trouble when he first came to America. His coat and beard seemed to contain almost magical properties for many Jews on the streets of the Lower East Side.

"When they see me, they remember who they are," he said. "If they didn't see me they might forget."

It was a Thursday night between Passover and Shevuous, and Rabbi Singer had invited me to his home for dinner. In a few hours he would show me a modern-day reenactment of the Thursday nights in Poland, when his grandfather delivered chickens to Pilzno's poor.

His wife was waiting for him when we got to his apartment, with its lovely religious objects, its pictures of the family's European ancestors. It's not always easy to be a *tsaddik*'s wife, to wait for him while he's out performing *mitzvahs*. In their traditional marriage, she concentrates a great deal of energy on home life— talking with, and helping, her neighbors, making plans with her children, taking care of the grandchildren. Rabbi Singer is loathe to describe to her the problems he sees every day, loathe to inflict his clients' grief on her. So her conversation is rich with the details of her community, of weddings, births, bar mitzvahs; of her friends' triumphs and their losses. She's an engaging woman who loves to discuss the news she's heard on the radio, the articles she's read in the newspapers. And, sometimes, to supplement Rabbi Singer's reminiscences with stories from her own childhood in Hungary.

She had fixed a delicious meal of chicken liver, matzoh-ball soup, roast veal, kidney beans, and potato pancakes. We washed our hands, according to ritual, and then said the *motzi*, the traditional blessing over the bread. For a while, Mrs. Singer talked about a relative who was just getting her doctorate at Yeshiva

University. Then Rabbi Singer began to prepare me for our trip by describing Rabbi Gershon Singer's attitude toward charity: "He didn't want to be a show-off. Of course, sometimes it's all right to be a show-off because if you give others give, too. But the highest point of charity is anonymity. The taker shouldn't know who gave the gift and the giver shouldn't know who took it."

After dinner he took me to a tree-lined residential street in Brooklyn. Inside, about fifty hasidic men were filling grocery boxes with chicken, fish, wine, bread, and vegetables, and loading them into cars on the street outside. Soon they would distribute the cartons to needy Jews. They would drive away before the recipients could see them.

In one corner of the garage a stocky young diamond cutter had replaced his black suit with a blood-flecked butcher's apron and was cutting up carp. Three more Hasidim, still dressed in gabardine, wrapped fish in plastic bags and placed the bags in boxes. Then a young man whose father had died three weeks earlier came in. They'd been waiting for him to arrive before they *daavaned ma'ariv*; they would provide a *minyan* for him to recite a mourner's kaddish.

All work stopped. Everyone picked up their *siddurs*—their prayer books, and, facing the Eastern wall of the garage—symbolically, facing Jerusalem—they rocked back and forth; Toward the end of the service they said kaddish. A few minutes later the labor resumed.

The organizer, middle-aged, European-born, a civil servant, stood by the shelves full of packages. Writing in Yiddish, he inscribed each box with the addresses of the people who would get them. But not with their names. To spare the recipients any embarrassment, even the drivers who delivered the food would remain ignorant of their identities. My presence made him very uncomfortable. Some younger people argued that publicity might help with fund-raising, but he made me promise not to mention the organization's name—or even the area of Brooklyn it worked in—because the principle of anonymity meant more to him than the prospect of contributions.

Outside, Jacob, twenty-five, an air-conditioner salesman, almost skeletally thin, with a teenager's wispy beard and sidelocks, sat in his sleek 1977 Mercury, testing the cb radio he'd use that night when he and his friends drove to Williamsburg, Borough Park, Flatbush, the Upper West Side, and Harlem, making their surreptitious deliveries in time for the *Shabbos.*

With Rabbi Singer and me jammed into the front seat, the food jammed in the back, he tooled his Mercury down Brooklyn's streets. He would yell out greetings whenever he saw a friend. He speeded up, then slowed down, to throw a scare into a man he had known from Yeshiva. Then he congratulated the pedestrian on the birth of his new niece.

He flicked the switch of his cb, and began to talk to a friend with his space-age patois. "Breaker, breaker," he began in faintly accented English, "the handle here is Gumshoe." Then he switched to Yiddish, but his conversation was punctuated with phrases like "10-4, guy," and "negatory."

Jacob was on a tight schedule, for the recipients knew just when the packages were due, and what number to call if they were late. While Rabbi Singer and I watched he hoisted a box out of the back seat, whisked it into the lobby of the building, and rang the apartment number that was written on the package. Then he hurried down the street—a black hat and a wispy beard in the murky light—and gunned the car down the block, toward the neighborhood's main street where he'd meet some friends outside a kosher pizza parlor.

Rabbi Singer had to leave. Every Thursday night he and his son David read the Bible and some commentaries together—just as Rabbi Singer's father and grandfather had done, over candlelight, in Pilzno. This week, as the holiday of Shevuous approached, he would sit at a table in David's comfortable Borough Park apartment, rocking his two-week-old granddaughter who was strapped in a bassinet beside the *seforim*, the holy books. He'd read to his son from a commentary that discussed those mysterious days in the desert when Moses descended from Mt. Sinai and transmitted the Lord's commandments to the people who were still bewildered, still weary, from their flight out of Egypt.

As we stood near the pizza parlor, waiting for a bus, Rabbi Singer bent forward to show how his grandfather had looked when he pushed the wheelbarrow full of food through Pilzno's

dark, winding 3 A.M. streets to make *his* clandestine *Shabbos* eve
deliveries. Then the bus came, and he hurried off to study Torah
into the night.

A few days later I went back to Brooklyn to visit a friend of
Rabbi Singer's, Mrs. Dora Shapiro (as I'll call her), the wife of a
mohel, a circumciser. She lives on a quiet street in Flatbush,
among members of the hasidic sect she grew up with in Poland.
Everything else she knew as a child has perished: Dubie, her tiny
shtetl; her friends; the rest of her family of nine.

Like thousands of survivors she is a kind of living *Yarzheit* (memorial) candle. She doesn't burden you with her grief. At times
she was even merry as we sat at her plain dining-room table. I was
dressed carelessly in a slightly tattered blue and white yarmulke
and my casual American clothes. Mrs. Shapiro looks neat and tidy
in her long, modest dress and reddish bridal wig. We developed
our own special blend of Yiddish and English. Whenever she
translated a word, she'd look at me with a smile that spanned the
chasm of language and say, "There, you see how each one helps
the other."

She lives to protect the memory, and the strict religious culture,
of her dead. She was just sixteen in 1939, when Hitler's emissaries
came to Dubie and ordered the thirty-five Jewish families who
lived there to destroy the town's old wooden *shul*: "Even my father had to do it, and he was the rabbi. We worked from six in
the morning until six at night, when everyone went home. It took
many days, but we couldn't fight back. The Nazis guarded us with
guns."

When the job was done all the Jews were transported out of
town. Mrs. Shapiro escaped to the ghetto in Cracow, where she
worked as a nurse. The Nazis arrested her father. First they
promised him his freedom, then they took him to a cemetery
and buried him alive. Mrs. Shapiro didn't learn of his fate until
she met a cousin in Cracow a year later.

In 1942, the Nazis evacuated the Cracow ghetto. Mrs. Shapiro
was sent to Leipzig, a concentration camp that was administered
out of Buchenwald. There she witnessed a scene that would haunt
and inspire her for all the days of her life.

Chaim Zelig was one of the few Jews who remained openly religious at Leipzig. He always wore a yarmulke, in defiance of the Nazis. Although there was never a *minyan*, he would put on *tefillin* and pray every day.

One morning a guard, searching the barracks for the faithful, caught him worshiping. The next dawn all the ten thousand Jews at Leipzig were told to gather in a large plaza to watch as Chaim Zelig was punished. Nazi guards stood behind them, bayonets ready. A firing squad waited for Chaim Zelig on the hillock above the hushed crowd.

Despite the Nazi precautions he'd hidden his yarmulke under his shirt. He put it on his head as soon as he began to walk.

Mrs. Shapiro, who was one of the ten thousand below, remembers the thrill she felt when she saw that skullcap, that sign of bravery. She could just make out Chaim Zelig's lips moving in quiet prayer. As he climbed the gentle slope the Nazi guards jostled him so relentlessly that the yarmulke fell off his head. When he stooped over to get it, they pushed him on the ground and lashed him with their rifles.

His two sons were in the crowd, watching.

Before Chaim Zelig reached the top of the hill he managed to put the yarmulke back on his head. He resumed his prayer. Then someone from the firing squad handed him a shovel and ordered him to dig his own grave.

Then he was killed.

It was eight o'clock in the morning.

The Jews had to go to work directly after that. Mrs. Shapiro's job was sewing uniforms for Nazi soldiers.

In 1945, Leipzig was liberated by the Russians. Very little news had filtered into the camp. She had no knowledge of the full extent of the holocaust. So, like thousands of Jews, her instinct was to return to the *shtetl*. That, after all, was the traditional pattern. You were chased out of town during a pogrom, you were allowed to return in calmer times. But, as she crossed the Polish border and began her voyage to Cracow, she began to learn what the Nazis had done.

Then, when she got to Lodz, "Other Jews began to tell me that the Poles still hated us. They made a pogrom in Chelm after the war. There was still a Nazi underground. A friend of mine was in Cracow, in *shul, daavening* on *Shabbos,* when the Poles attacked. They yelled things like, 'Hitler should have killed you all,' and 'We don't want you back here.' They threw rocks at the Jews. It was even worse in the *shtetl.* There they killed the Jews at night."

In Lodz, she realized that her father's fate was a typical one. "I went back to Poland to find my family, but I had no family left," she recalled, coughing. "There was practically no one from my part of Poland left."

Mrs. Shapiro had to leave the room to compose herself. When she came back, moments later, she brought some seltzer for us both. I said the blessing Rabbi Singer had taught me before beginning to drink. She was still coughing, still upset, but she smiled approvingly. Then she continued to reminisce.

In Lodz, she said, she and her friends decided, as a matter of principle as well as faith, "that all of us should get married and have as many children as possible. We should try to bring back the six million, to be sure the Jewish nation wasn't reduced." Like many survivors, they decided to use the Jewish tradition of naming children after those who had died as a way of commemorating the victims of the holocaust.

Mrs. Shapiro has seven children and twenty grandchildren. One of her sons, a Yeshiva student, bears Chaim Zelig's name. He and his brothers and sisters know that one of Chaim Zelig's sons— who'd stood in the Leipzig courtyard that long-ago morning— nearly went mad with tormented grief after his father was killed; that finally, after twenty years, he'd settled in Jerusalem, married an Orthodox woman, and began to live a productive life. They know the entire tale by heart.

Mrs. Shapiro met her husband in Germany, in one of the camps established by the American government for wandering, disoriented survivors. He'd been a *mohel* before the war, a revered figure in his *shtetl.* He'd had a wife and two children when the Nazis came to town. On the day the Jews were to be shipped away, he carried one child toward the transport truck, his wife carried the other. A German soldier asked if he were the father. His wife answered before he could talk. "No," she said, "he's a man I just met." Then she snatched the youngster from his arms. A family woman, she was sent to Auschwitz. An able-bodied bachelor, as far as the Germans knew, he was sent to a labor camp and survived.

In the postwar years, the Americans gave him a chauffeur and a car so that he could travel from one D.P. camp to the next, circumcising the survivors' babies.

He was older than Mrs. Shapiro. When their marriage was arranged she was in awe of him. It was only after they'd had three children and moved to America that she could bring herself to drop the respectful third-person singular that her mother had used with her father in Dubie ("would the mister like") and address him with the simple, intimate "you."

To many Hasidim in those years, Israel, with its brash, Socialist pioneers, seemed like a nightmare of secularism, a horrible perversion of the Messianic dream. So the Shapiros decided to come to America, despite the warnings against this country that had resounded through *shtetl shuls* and study houses ever since the Eastern European immigration began.

Hasidic survivors like the Shapiros decided to make assets out of the very details of dress, language, and custom that earlier generations of immigrant Jews had found so onerous. There were tens of thousands of Hasidim and they constituted the first wave of militantly Orthodox Jews ever to come to this land. They owed a debt of blood and spirit to martyrs like Chaim Zelig. They decided to build themselves a wall of spiritual segregation and, by doing so, preserve a pure Torah life for themselves and their young.

The size of their communities guaranteed that the huge Yeshivas they erected in Williamsburg, Borough Park, and Crown Heights would flourish and seal their children off from the assimilationist dangers of public school. In some neighborhoods, they went even further than that and established an informal ban on television sets, movies, secular literature—anything that would bring the allurements of America into their homes. Sometimes, they bought the entire apartment buildings and reserved them for the Orthodox Jews.

There were so many of them that they could create a self-

sufficient urban economy; in the diamond trades and huge elec-
tronics and camera stores that are run by Hasidim; in the glatt
kosher restaurants and butcher shops that you now find in every
Jewish neighborhood in New York.

Mrs. Shapiro is proud of that strategy of isolation. When I told
her that the drab clothes Hasidim wear still look strange and uncomfortable to me, she laughed with unexpected satisfaction and
said, "That's the way we want it to be. Our garb is like a mask
over us. It doesn't let us go many places. If people see that you're
Orthodox, they don't come up to you with dirty intentions. Our
clothes help prevent us from feeling temptation."

Once, a decade after the Shapiros had settled in New York,
Mrs. Shapiro bought her oldest son a bicycle. A few weeks later
she wandered past a sale of used clothes and picked up a striped
short-sleeved polo shirt for the boy. That Sunday her husband saw
his son peddling down Eastern Parkway, his polo shirt furnishing
a striking contrast to his black pants and sidelocks.

Mr. Shapiro was angry enough at the bicycle, for it would allow
the boy to leave the block, leave the neighborhood, and roam uncontrollably, through sections of New York the Shapiros could
barely imagine. But the polo shirt seemed even more dangerous. If
the boy acquired a wardrobe of similar clothes, he might be exposed to the worldly contacts his parents found so perilous. Shortly
afterward, they sent him to Yeshiva in Israel. Two years later he
returned to America. Now, still a Hasid, he has a job in the diamond district.

Mrs. Shapiro says she's constantly thankful that her lapses of
judgment were countered by the unflagging piety of the man
she'd married, whom she still reveres.

That attitude, with its roots in the safe, orderly world of Dubie,
fills her with a kind of pity for the assimilated, Americanized
women, who, for their part, define her role at home and in synagogue as unbearably slavish.

She feels freed, not constrained, by the segregated seating pattern in the synagogue. In fact, when she sits in the balcony of her
shul, "I always push myself as far back as I can so that my husband, on the ground floor, can't see me. I couldn't cry if I thought
he was looking at me. I'd be ashamed. And when you daaven you

want to open up your heart to the Almighty, you have so much to say. But if I sit with men, or even see them, I worry that I'll look like a fool. I cover myself and act like I'm in a shell. If I'm alone with other women, I feel very free, very open to cry."

Doesn't it bother her, though, that the piety she respects so much in her husband makes him begin each day by uttering a prayer in which he thanks the Almighty he's not a woman?

She says she's "not resentful"; she, in turn, thanks the Almighty that she is a woman. She accepts the premise that, in his universe, her role is to stay at home while her husband's is to function in the world. "But he has all 613 *mitzvahs* to do, and a woman has only three main *mitzvahs*. There's the cooking and the preparation for *Shabbos*. But the main *mitzvah* is that she should bring up the children in the Yiddish way." That she should transmit the religion and traditions to them. "What else, in life, is more important than that?"

The children: a tribute to the dead. Nothing fills her with more anger—and more sorrow—than the idea of birth control. "These modern Jewish families! They don't want to be bothered with babies. They don't want to worry about diaper rashes and earaches, like my daughter did last week. Her child had a very high fever. She's all right now, thank the Lord, but think of the sleepless nights.

"These American men and women want all the good things in life instead of the problems. But I feel sorry for them. They're shortsighted and stupid. When they're old they'll feel useless, as if their lives had no meaning. They don't know how lonely they'll feel."

It wasn't a sermon. It was a warning, and a description of the sense of loss that never leaves her.

As we talked she fingered a ripped, faded photograph of her father, the only one that had ever been taken. The photograph stirred her memories of the *Shabbos* afternoons in Dubie, where he *zeyde*, her grandfather, would gather all the children around him and give them candies and cookies and tell tales of *his* boyhood, and of the hasidic *tsaddikim*, the holy men and wise men, who kept his own faith so strong. Those rich, indestructible mem-

ories have more to do with her Jewishness than anything she had
ever read in a book.

It was the week before Shevuous when we talked and she
reminisced, lovingly, about the beautiful spring afternoons in
Dubie when she and her brothers would gather weeping willows
and wild flowers and fill their synagogue and their home with
those simple treasures. The men would stay up all night, studying
the Bible, in commemoration of Moses' ascent up Mt. Sinai, the
act that marked "the marriage between the Torah and the Jews."
In the morning, she remembers, "we'd give them plates full of
cheesecake and kreplach and fish. My husband and I try to do
that here, but we worry about Weight-Watchers. Anyway, Dubie
was a little town where everyone was alike. It can't be like that
here."

Then, sadly, she adds that "when you meet someone from the
heim, from home, that is all you talk about. You talk about what
it was like.

"But as much as I try to tell my children, it is difficult. They
don't have much in common with us. The main thing is that the
children should know what they had and what they lost. In
Dubie, we could turn to my grandfather for that. But here the
children have no *zeyde.* I miss that more than anything. When
the Nazis killed my father they killed my family's past."

Once a Hasid, a *tsaddik,* was asked why Jews don't proselytize.
He answered, simply, that a candle glows without making an effort to give light. Religion should do that, too, he said.

Rabbi Singer doesn't proselytize. Still, by his example, he helps
to close the gulf that Mrs. Shapiro, in her ceaseless grief, thinks is
unbridgeable. It will be years before I understand the religious lessons—or the degree of religiousness—I've absorbed from my
travels through 5737 and 5738, or how to incorporate them into
my life: how to integrate Paul Cowan and Saul Cohen. But I
know now that Rabbi Singer has helped me to recover some of
what I lost. He has brought me closer to my past—and, in doing
that, helped me glimpse a kinder, more peaceful future.

CHAPTER 12

Harrisburg, Pennsylvania: Ballad for Americans

Introduction: The Specter of Main Street

I am a Jew by birth and by choice, and I'm increasingly eager to reclaim my heritage. But by background and training I'm a member of the tribe I criticize so often—the urban journalistic and political elite. I want to end this book with the experience that made me most sharply aware of this tribe's limitations, and which restored some of my faith in the heartland America we criticize so often.

It began in the winter of 1972, when I spent three months in Harrisburg, Pennsylvania, watching the Justice Department try to prove that Father Philip Berrigan, Sister Elizabeth McAlister, Eqbal Ahmad (a Pakistani-born left-wing scholar and activist), and four more priests and nuns were guilty of conspiring to kidnap Henry Kissinger, bomb federal heating systems, and raid local draft boards.

Harrisburg, in the Middle District of Pennsylvania. When I first heard the trial would be held there, I had visions of jurors lifted from the pages of Sinclair Lewis's *Main Street*. How could those conservative folk give the anti-war activists a fair trial? Some of the small towns along the Susquehanna River had harbored anti-

Catholic feelings for centuries. Some jurors would probably come from those places. How would they feel about the priests and nuns? I was worried that the trial of the Harrisburg Seven would be a 1970s rerun of the Rosenberg and the Hiss cases—and that a guilty verdict might devastate my generation of left-wing activists.

Those were difficult years for political dissenters. Richard Nixon and Spiro Agnew had convinced most of us that there was a "silent majority" of Americans who supported everything the government did in Vietnam, who wanted to suppress our protests. Nothing the anti-war movement did—not even our massive, peaceful demonstrations—seemed to convince many people in places like the Middle District of Pennsylvania that we were motivated by decent intentions, not nihilism. Often I felt as if my political views made me a stranger in my own land. Like many of my friends I was convinced that, if the government won conspiracy cases like the trial of the Harrisburg Seven, I might some day wind up underground or in jail.

The defense was worried about the Harrisburg area. It had hired a team of sociologists headquartered at Columbia University and directed by a professor named Jay Schulman to survey the region, in an effort to learn whether there were any reliable ways to locate people who would remain open-minded as they listened to the evidence. The sociologists offered two important bits of advice. The first was that most college-educated people who acquire intellectual restlessness along with their diplomas hurry away from home as quickly as possible while their more conventional classmates stay behind. The second was that, in an area where most females are programmed to be housewives, women, particularly younger women, are bored and restless—more open to intellectual adventure than their mates. So the defense should avoid college-educated people and try to make young women a numerical majority.

The jurors voted, ten to two, for acquittal. At first I attributed the verdict to the moral rectitude of the defendants; to the skills of their famous lawyers, Ramsey Clark, Paul O'Dwyer, Terry Lenzner, and Leonard Boudin; and to the sociologists' expertise. In other words, I believed that the specter of *Main Street* had been neutralized by the special skills of the urban elite.

Then, six months after the trial, I tape-recorded long interviews with seven of the twelve jurors—Robert (Fuzzy) Foresman, forty-seven, a fire-fighting instructor from Lewiston; Mrs. Jo-Anne (Tracy) Stanovich, thirty-one, a machinist's wife from Harrisburg; June Jackson, forty-eight, an interior decorator's wife from York; Pat Shafer, thirty-five, from Ettors, the wife of a construction engineer who had helped build military bases in Thailand; Harold Sheets, sixty-one, a tax accountant from Harrisburg; Anne Burnett, twenty-four, a case-worker in the Dauphin County Welfare Department; and Vera Thompson, thirty-one, a black woman who was married to a liquor-store owner in Carlisle. Those interviews gave me a new perspective on the area, the case, and myself.

Despite the sociologists' recommendations, the jurors had shared many of their neighbors' cultural feelings. Many of them found the defendants too radical—and too self-righteous—for their tastes. Some secretly wished they could have displayed their patriotism by supporting their government and voting for a conviction. During their sequestration and deliberations, some had known they would be misunderstood by their friends back home, just as they would have misunderstood people who voted for acquittal if they had been newspaper readers and not jurors.

But they didn't think the government had proved its case. And they couldn't find it in their consciences to send people to jail on such scanty evidence.

Talking to them, I realized that, for many Americans democracy is a religion. Certain tasks—like jury duty—inspire them to transcend their tribal prejudices and regard themselves as guardians of a precious faith. The civil-rights movement did that for some people; so can national crises, like the Depression; so can passionate, committed politicians, like Robert Kennedy or Franklin Delano Roosevelt. Sometimes it is possible to unify Americans in situations that call for generosity or fairness instead of dividing them into battles over physical or psychological turf. The Harrisburg jury offered a glimpse of that possibility.

My conversations with the jurors also taught me a lot about my own assumptions. They left me feeling that my attitudes toward that group of Americans (like the attitudes of most lawyers, reporters, and defendants—members of the urban elite who were connected to the case) were *just* as narrow and parochial as *their* attitudes toward us.

Part I: *The Indictment: A Fantasy on Trial*

In the early 1970s, the Catholic left played a uniquely important role in the peace movement. Its two most prominent members, Fathers Daniel and Philip Berrigan, seemed to combine the moral authority of the priesthood with the revolutionary commitment of a Che Guevara.

In those days, Daniel Berrigan, an unindicted co-conspirator in the Harrisburg case, was even more influential than his brother. An intellectual and a poet, he had participated in the widely publicized draft-board raid at Catonsville, Maryland. Then he had written a stirring play, based on the trial of the Catonsville Nine, in which he had explored his own fears and self-doubts and celebrated the courage of the resisters. Instead of going to jail for that crime, he had gone underground, emboldening thousands of liberals and radicals who were captivated by the priest's image as a "fugitive from injustice." He stayed there for months, and his elusiveness had enraged the FBI. It probably caused J. Edgar Hoover to seek revenge by announcing that Philip *and* Daniel Berrigan were behind an elaborate, disruptive plot long before any indictment was complete. The publicity Hoover's announcement generated forced the Justice Department to bring the case to trial earlier than it had planned, before it had fashioned a strong web of evidence.

Nevertheless, the government's charge wasn't completely fabricated. The draft-board raids had happened. In the early 1970s, Catholic radicals had broken into more than fifty Selective Service offices throughout America, destroying the files of thousands of young men who might otherwise have gone to Vietnam. Unlike the Catonsville Nine, most of them had acted surreptitiously. Few were ever caught.

But the draft-board raids were the only actions charged in the indictment that were reflected in reality. As was its practice in the early Seventies, the Justice Department sought to take some radicals' fantasies and prove that they constituted a conspiracy.

When the indictment was announced, Philip Berrigan, a more daring activist than his brother, had been in the Lewisburg penitentiary, near Harrisburg, for nearly two years. The draft-board raids had originally been his idea. But now, as the war escalated, they seemed a little stale and tepid. He wanted desperately to find bolder, more dramatic tactics of nonviolent resistance—and to communicate them to his friends outside prison. He needed a way of smuggling letters in and out of jail. So he enlisted the aid of Boyd Douglas, a convicted con man and forger who had convinced the prison authorities to let him attend classes at nearby Bucknell College.

Phil Berrigan liked to believe he could convert everyone he met to his political beliefs. So Douglas had no trouble convincing him that he had become a partisan of the peace movement. At Bucknell, Douglas courted two co-eds, Jane Hoover and Betsy Sandel, and persuaded them to type up Berrigan's letters and mail them to New York, to Sister Elizabeth McAlister, whom the priest would later marry. Then Douglas would smuggle Sister McAlister's letters back to Father Berrigan.

But Douglas was a paid FBI informer. He turned a copy of each letter over to his local "handler," Delmar Mayfield. At first, the FBI figured it could get some clues to Daniel Berrigan's whereabouts from the correspondence. Then some of the letters began to seem interesting in themselves. Phil Berrigan hinted that he and Fathers Joseph Wenderoth and Neil McLaughlin had toyed with the idea of using some underground tunnels for an action that would disrupt government activities. The priest discussed explosive devices, like primer cords. He wrote passages that seemed to condone the use of violence—certainly paradoxical for a man who had devoted his life to pacifism.

In August 1970, just after Dan Berrigan was caught, Sister Elizabeth McAlister wrote the depressed, caged man she loved a long letter containing a few paragraphs describing a far-fetched fantasy about kidnaping Henry Kissinger nonviolently. Shortly afterward, J. Edgar Hoover alleged the existence of the conspiracy.

No one ever denied that the letters described actual conversations. But, in those desperate years, literally thousands of people who opposed the war discussed similarly extravagant, illegal tac-

tics for ending it. Sometimes, late at night, those ideas even
seemed plausible. It was easy to see how a government infiltrator
—who was unfamiliar with the left's verbal swagger—could interpret the words as plans. Often, the government's fantasies about
the movement converged with the movement's fantasies about itself. In that atmosphere, someone like Douglas could easily convince his handlers that the Berrigan brothers intended to kidnap
Henry Kissinger. His charges fit right into the Justice Department's plan to fragment the left with a series of costly, time-con-
suming trials.

The only hard evidence the government possessed was Douglas's testimony about his conversations with the defendants and
the forty-eight-letter Berrigan-McAlister correspondence. That, it
seemed clear, was the reason the Justice Department had decided
to hold the trial in Harrisburg instead of New York, Washington,
or Baltimore, where many of the overt acts listed in the indictment had occurred. The department appeared to assume that any
jury chosen from the Middle District of Pennsylvania would
convict the defendants.

That was one of the few political points on which the Nixon-
appointed administrators and the anti-war activists seemed to
agree.

Part II: The Trial: View from the Jury Box

The most startling moment in the trial came when former Attorney General Ramsey Clark, Philip Berrigan's lawyer, contended
that the prosecution hadn't proved a thing, that the defense
would rest its case without putting a single witness on the stand.

Then the jury deliberated for six-and-one-half days, a record for
a federal case. Throughout that period it was clear that the lawyers and defendants who'd worked so carefully to choose the
twelve jurors still didn't trust them. Most of their speculation
focused on which one or two were holding out for acquittal.
There was widespread fear that the few people who were still
friendly to the defense would eventually be battered into submis-
sion by the overwhelmingly pro-government majority.

So, when it turned out that nine of the jurors had favored acquittal from the very beginning, people close to the defense evolved a set of myths to explain that unexpected behavior. All the myths—like mine—highlighted the brilliance and sensitivity of the radical defendants and their liberal lawyers. None allowed for much sensitivity on the part of the jurors.

Most outsiders believed that the jurors would have been fooled by Boyd Douglas's testimony if the defense team hadn't done such a skillful job of delving into the informer's seamy past. They thought the prosecution's case was demolished when the defense lawyers cross-examined its star witness. But most of the jurors told me they hadn't needed a dramatic courtroom confrontation to size up the informer. They'd tried to keep their minds open, but they'd disliked him from the start.

To understand their feelings, one has to imagine Douglas, with his carefully combed hair and his neat suits, his slack, pudgy face, and his droning voice, sitting in the witness chair day after day, answering every question with same carefully rehearsed set of stock responses.

"I didn't like him from the moment he walked onto the witness stand with his two-hundred-dollar Johnny Carson suit on," Tracy Stanovich told me. "And the more he talked, the deeper in the hole he got. He always sounded like Goody two-shoes. But I think he did that to impress us. Soon, I began to ask myself, is this what the government's case is all about? Who needs this?"

Tracy is a big, lively red-haired woman—a Lutheran married to the son of Serbian immigrants—who has tried to fuse her husband's culture with her own. When she was younger she'd studied ceramics in art school. Recently, she had begun to use those talents as a dental technician, molding caps for teeth, a job she enjoyed enormously. She turned out to be the jury's jokester, a free spirit who said anything that came into her mind and teased the more depressed panelists free of their self-pity.

When I asked her what she thought Douglas's motives were, she referred to a letter—which the government had inadvertently turned over to the defense—in which he asked his FBI handler, Delmar Mayfield, for $50,000 for his work as an informer. "It seemed like he had a plan," she said. "He thought, 'Well, I have it all wrapped up in my head and I'm going to walk out of here a rich man.' I think he lied about everything."

June Jackson is an older, more settled, more affluent woman than Tracy Stanovich. I interviewed her in her spacious York home, and our talk lasted for three hours. Sometimes memories of the trial made her laugh. More often they brought her close to tears. Of all of the jurors I interviewed she appeared to be the one the trial affected most deeply.

In accord with her sacred duties as a juror she tried to suspend her judgments about Douglas until the deliberations began. But, "there was just something about him I didn't trust. His eyes. His whole manner. But I tried to separate my emotional feelings about him, the way I was supposed to, and just listen to him."

She was more troubled when the FBI agent, Mayfield, took the stand. "There was something about him I didn't trust either. I mean, he should have been telling the truth. Or maybe I just want to think so because he was an FBI agent. But, call it woman's intuition or a hunch. There was just something about him that nagged at me, something I didn't like."

The men I interviewed felt more sympathy for Douglas than did the women. Even those like Fuzzy Foresman, who didn't believe the informer, found qualities about him with which they could identify.

Foresman, the fire inspector, is a warm, outgoing man, a practical jokester who loves to garden and hunt and fish. He is fascinated by his work and reads constantly to keep abreast of new techniques in fire fighting. He tries to pass those techniques on to the younger men who take a week-long course at the fire fighters' academy. But he complains that many of the people in his town, Lewiston, are limited for, until recently, they have resisted the more modern methods he tries to impart. He is a Lutheran with a Catholic wife whose children are growing up in her faith. That certainly contributed to his sense of being an outsider, as he would reveal during one of the most dramatic moments of the deliberations.

He shared a purely masculine moment of laughter with Douglas when the informer admitted to the skein of lies he'd told the Bucknell co-eds, Jane Hoover and Betsy Sandel. (In his closing argument, Ramsey Clark referred to those lies pityingly, as "a window into the man's soul.") Why had he laughed? I asked. "Because it was so much in Boyd's character, and it struck a couple of comical points in my own life, when I'd done the same thing with women in my younger days. I think Douglas was a hell of a guy. He's got a sense of humor. It was a little flakey at times, but I could go along with that.

"But I just . . . I wouldn't want to be in his company very much because he doesn't have a strong moral background to do things the way I'd do them. Not that I'm perfect or anything. But I wouldn't trust him any further than I could see him."

Most of the urban liberal defendants, lawyers, and reporters who were involved with the trial saw Pennsylvania's Middle District as a menacing foreign culture where there were few clues to correct behavior. In that setting, Ramsey Clark seemed like Jimmy Stewart—a modern-day Mr. Smith. He was a Texan, an American. With his background in the Marines and his slow, Western drawl he seemed far more likely to appeal to the jurors than Leonard Boudin, whose flashy brilliance might arouse some lurking, ancient distrust of New York Jews.

Some of the jurors were impressed by him. But most seemed to feel that his attempts at eloquence were insults to their intelligence. June Jackson saw him as "a politician who was much too oratorical and ineffective. All his eloquence didn't hit me at all. No way. No, sir."

Fuzzy Foresman was the former Attorney General's most outspoken critic. To him, Clark was "a little childish in the way he handled himself." Though he was impressed with part of Clark's closing speech, he was offended by a reference to Boyd Douglas as Judas. "He sort of left it hanging as to what the defendants were. And damn well they ain't Christ. . . . He was playing too much on our sentiments, on our emotions. And we had too much material to deal with for that sort of thing."

By contrast, the jurors felt both affection and respect for Boudin. He was theatrical, too, certainly more theatrical than Clark, but he redeemed himself with his playful, self-mocking good humor and his obvious command of the facts. Because of his heart condition—he had a pacemaker—the judge had given him permission to roam the courtroom at will, and he often walked over toward the jury or the spectators and delivered an ironic, hammed look of anguish when the prosecution—or another defense lawyer—made a point that seemed specious.

Yet there was a deep passion, behind his antics, as June Jackson sensed. "At the beginning of the trial, I thought to myself, 'I wouldn't have you if you were the last man on the earth.' But when he performed in court and I looked into his eyes I thought, 'That's the man for me if I ever need help.' He was all lawyer. He seemed to know everything."

To Foresman, Boudin was a marvel. "I teach but I'm not very good at it. I enjoy people who can think on their feet like Boudin. God, he has a fabulous mind. And he and I . . . I don't know whether I'm saying this right or whether it's correct or not, but I think he and I had a kind of rapport. We had a lot of eye contact, and we had a lot of fun together."

Throughout the trial, William Lynch, the prosecuting attorney, was a lonely, isolated figure. His quick temper and his sardonic answers to reporters' questions made him the object of a great deal of verbal abuse. One day Daniel Berrigan, whose prison sentence had ended during the Harrisburg trial, came into the courtroom, noticed the upward flap of Lynch's arms whenever he rose to object, and characterized the lawyer as a "ruptured seagull." The reporters, lawyers, and spectators all laughed appreciatively at that remark.

But none of the lawyers on the defense team received as much praise from the jurors as Lynch did. Fuzzy Foresman, Vera Thompson, Pat Shafer, and Harold Sheets were all impressed with his conduct. Tracy Stanovich thought he was a "good lawyer, though he'd get a little radical"—Harrisburgese for angry—at things.

June Jackson described her admiration for Lynch in the context of her confusion about the entire trial. I had asked her why she thought the government had brought such a frail case to court. "I don't know," she said. "That's the sixty-four-dollar question. It was my first experience with the government. And, you know"— here she began to laugh, but a little uncomfortably—"they blew it. I can't believe it. I absolutely can't." Her voice quickened, her breathing became audible. "Intelligent men. I think that Lynch is . . . oh, I'm crazy about Lynch. He wasn't flamboyant, like Boudin or young, like Lenzner. Oh, there was something about him. I really felt sorry for him. I don't know how they could have let this idiotic thing come to trial when even we, little laymen who knew absolutely nothing, saw what a farce it was. I guess that's the reason Lynch deserves an awful lot of credit. Because he did so much with"—another slightly tense giggle—"with nothing."

Before the trial began, many of the defendants believed they could use the courtroom as a forum to convert the jurors and part of the public to their belief in nonviolent resistance. That was just what Philip and Daniel Berrigan had done at Catonsville. But the trial of the Harrisburg Seven was not to be a rerun of that earlier triumph: The charges were too murky and confusing; the courtroom battle had more to do with legal wits than with political or ethnical principles. In the end, none of the defendants even took the witness stand, which they'd hoped to use as a pulpit for their passion.

They cared deeply about making converts. So they focused on their nonverbal relationships to the jurors. They were confident that their bearing in the courtroom—their ability to laugh and convey sorrow and retain visible bonds of community—would convey silent proof of their innocence, and their righteousness.

It did for some jurors. The tax accountant Harold Sheets said, "When I looked at those fellows I just kind of wondered how they could have done what they were accused of doing." Ann Burnett, the brashest, most talkative of the jurors, was impressed with their "vitality." But for others their most effective defense wasn't their sanctity or their high spirits. It was their apparent ineptitude.

On the first day of the deliberations Fuzzy Foresman said, with a laugh, "If I was ever going to kidnap anybody I wouldn't have those jokers do it." Vera Thompson, the black woman from Carlisle, had a stepson who had been a marine in Vietnam and had come home filled with technical details about explosives like

primer cords, which the priests and nuns were allegedly planning
to use. "I had sat around listening to him and his friends talk
enough to know that those people had had no dealings with
explosives whatever. Why, I knew more about it than they did."
She had originally voted to convict the defendants. One reason
she changed her mind was her recognition that even if they had
wanted to carry out their scheme they never could have done it.
"To me, it was just a dream they had. It would take an act of
Congress to actually carry it out."

The defendants' rage at the war, their dream of building a community of resisters, their ideas about mounting increasingly dramatic nonviolent protest movements, all emerged in the extensive
Berrigan-McAlister correspondence. But, possibly because none of
them took the stand, those beliefs confused more jurors than they
converted. Tracy Stanovich respected Father Berrigan's intelligence and wanted very much to meet him. "But I kept thinking,
how can a man of his education get involved in stuff like draft-
board raids? I guess he truly believed in it, but I kept thinking
that with all the knowledge he's learned he should be teaching
other people instead of doing those things." Vera Thompson said
plaintively, "If I could meet him, I'd just want to ask him why he
did all that."

And the defendants' physical appearance, far from conveying
holy fervor, kindled vagrant thoughts in the jurors' minds, whose
contents the defendants could never have imagined. Tracy
Stanovich "couldn't believe Father Berrigan's ankles and his
calves. They were so thick, I've never seen anything like that. But
Fuzzy told me it was because he came from a poor Catholic family
that exercised by kicking a soccer ball around a lot."

Some of their impressions could have contributed to a guilty
verdict if the government's case hadn't depended on the testimony of a witness the jurors found as shady as Douglas. Vera
Thompson had no use for Eqbal Ahmad, the Pakistani scholar
who was the only non-Catholic in the group. She had the idea
that he had gotten involved with the Catholic left as an agent of
his government. She thought Ahmad's plan was "to bring
America down to Pakistan's level."

Fuzzy Foresman's view of Philip Berrigan was almost as bleak. "I'm sure the defense would have done themselves some harm if they had put Philip on the witness stand. He struck me as a defendant who was chomping at the bit, someone who was just a little on the arrogant side. If he had started ranting and raving about his political insinuations, I don't think that would have helped him any. The fact is, it would have irritated me."

That last comment of Foresman's suggests a strong feeling that most of the jurors shared. For them, it was not the cross-examination of Boyd Douglas, not Ramsey Clark's eloquence, not the defendants' courtroom presence, but the shocking decision to rest the case without putting on a single witness that probably saved the defendants from a conviction. Their evident incompetence wouldn't have been enough to spare them if their testimony had allowed the government to prove they were trying to carry out a mature plan.

June Jackson recalls that when Clark first announced the decision to rest she was "in shock, in complete shock. We had ourselves all revved up for another month in court. We wanted to know what they had to say for themselves." But, in retrospect, she thought the decision to rest "was the best thing they ever did. Maybe, had they taken the stand, we would not have found them not guilty. They may have just dug their own graves, so to speak."

"That was probably what the prosecution was hoping for," I said.

"Not probably. Absolutely. We could see that. How stupid did the government think we were?"

Then I asked her whether, in her gut, she felt that the defendants might have been guilty. "Of course. Of course. Of course. I think they might have had a plan, yes. And they might have tried to carry it through. Now they didn't. They were caught before they did. But I think they were capable of doing it. They were against the war and this was their way of doing something about it. But in the evidence we had we didn't have anything where they said, 'Yes. Tomorrow we're going to go off and kidnap Henry Kissinger.' That's where the fine line was. Where does an idea become a fact? I'll be doggoned if I'd want anybody to convict me on the evidence we had to go on."

Part III: Deliberations: Twelve Anguished Jurors

Nothing the jurors saw in the courtroom left as bitter an after-taste as the interpersonal conflicts that emerged during the six weeks of sequestration and, particularly, during the six days of deliberations.

Most of the tensions revolved around Lawrence Evans, a retired supermarket owner from Dillsburg who had made a good impression on the defense during the *voir dire*. Someone had told the lawyers that Evans had decided his store should support the grape boycott. (Actually, he'd been retired for years and his son, who'd succeeded him, honored the boycott.) In 1961, he had been a Democratic ward captain and an ardent supporter of John Kennedy's. During the *voir dire* he had said that priests and nuns should be even more involved than they already were in acts of political protest. Nevertheless, he proved to be irrevocably convinced that the defendants were guilty. After the verdict was announced he criticized the decision, and some of his fellow jurors, in a series of on-the-record interviews. That night he was the only panelist who mentioned the tensions that had made the deliberations such an ordeal. Later I called him and visited his house several times to get his own, amplified version of the schisms he'd once alluded to. But he consistently refused to talk to me. So I had to rely on other jurors' accounts of their experiences.

The people I interviewed hated the sequestration, but they felt that their verdict would have been different if they had retained their contact with the outside world. Harold Sheets said, "I think it was necessary as far as I'm concerned, and I'm a pretty strong person. My wife and I run an accounting business. After the trial she told me about comments from friends of ours, people I know very well. I guess 90 per cent of them thought they were guilty. Just guilty. I'm not too sure that if I'd heard them talk I would have felt the same way about the case."

In other words, to look at the facts fairly, the jurors had to be sealed off from their own communities and, in sequestration, form a subculture of their own. They couldn't be subjected to the kinds of pressures Sheets described. Such pressures had caused Mrs. Schwerner to withhold her name when I'd first interviewed her in Forest Hills; they caused the truck driver, Ringo, to stand outdoors in the freezing Dayton night, urging the truckers who were gathered in front of the fire to "get those fucking scabs" instead of admitting that he was a scab himself; they caused the teacher in Cabin Creek's Wet Branch elementary school to disguise her true opinions in the classroom because she feared that "those parents and teachers are staring over our shoulders, waiting for us to say something immoral." Indeed, the pressures to conform were the ugly underside of the communities that seemed so stable, so orderly, when I glimpsed them as an outsider. In Harrisburg, the jurors had to be placed in an environment that would neutralize them, that would enable people with different views to deliberate freely and openly, without fear of reprisal.

So the court created a sterile, strictly policed refuge for them at the Penn-Harris Motor Inn. They weren't allowed to discuss the trial with one another until deliberations began. Marshals were present all the time, auditing their conversations. Their mail was strictly censored. They had to eat every meal together and to travel to and from court in a sealed-in bus. The only visitors they received were members of their immediate families, who could just come on weekends. Those meetings took place within the marshals' sight, which meant, of course, that the jurors were deprived of sexual relations. Ann Burnett says that many of them got very horny.

Their media diets were carefully supervised. All political and international news had to be clipped from the newspapers before they received them. They weren't allowed to watch news shows or talk shows, like Johnny Carson, where they might hear topical discussions or jokes, or dramas like *Gunsmoke* or *Ironside*, where they might see a courtroom scene or a scene of violence that could have a marginal effect on their perceptions of the case. Ann Burnett tried to bring a collection of great love stories to the motel with her, but a marshal seized it because he noticed that the book contained a short extract from the opera *Carmen*, which had an arrest scene.

June Jackson was acutely aware of the mood she shared with other jurors during those weeks. "At first, everybody stayed together, all the time. Every time we went to our rooms we cried. We missed our families. And we were scared to death. We didn't know what tomorrow would be like, what would happen to us."

The thing that troubled her most was that, throughout the trial, "We'd always have to have our party manners on. I got awfully tired of getting up every morning and smiling at everyone and putting on my makeup and combing my hair so I'd look nice in the courtroom. But it wasn't just that. You felt like you had to be on your good behavior all the time, to be nice to everybody. There were days when I got up and felt miserable, for no apparent reason. But I had to act happy-go-lucky.

"There was no one you could talk to about that feeling. It was all very private. And it was worse because we weren't allowed to discuss the trial either. And we couldn't turn off our brains as soon as we left the courtroom. But, all of a sudden, I was a party girl again—watching television, washing my hair. There were many nights when I just wanted to be alone. I used to sit at my window and watch the cars go by. What else could I do? I couldn't read. I couldn't keep my mind on that.

"I remember one night, when I was sitting in Tracy Stanovich's room, using her hair-dryer. She was putting her clothes away. And I said to myself, what am I doing here? Who is this person? I shouldn't be here at all. I should be at home, cooking dinner. You know that TV show, *Twilight Zone?* That's what the whole thing felt like. Very strange."

Most of the twelve jurors and six alternates eventually found ways of accommodating themselves to the situation, and to each other. "When you're living in one little room of one hotel, you've got to get along," June Jackson says.

Ann Burnett did that. In the first few weeks of sequestration her talkative brilliance and her unabashed descriptions of her private life created some tension between her and her colleagues. ("When that broad was born, she was vaccinated with a phonograph needle," Vera Thompson told me, chuckling.) But she learned to listen as well as talk, and she fascinated Tracy Stanovich with explicit tales of her past exploits. June Jackson and Pat

Shafer crocheted and knitted for their families. Some nights, Vera Thompson, Fuzzy Foresman, and Harold Sheets would play pinochle until midnight. Other times Fuzzy would join Tracy and some alternates in a card game called "pit." Larry Evans, a sports fan, spent his evenings reading *Sport* or *Sports Illustrated*, or practiced putting on a makeshift green he'd constructed in his room. Every morning he'd get up at five, do fifty push-ups, and work out on an exerbike. An alternate, a fisherman, spent much of his spare time tying flies. On weekends the marshals would shepherd the whole group to special events, like an ice show at the Hershey Arena or to picnic spots where they'd play touch football.

Larry Evans was the only persistent source of conflict for the jurors. At first they liked him. Tracy Stanovich recalls that "he seemed like a happy-go-lucky guy. He'd buy people drinks at night. He seemed very nice." But soon they tired of his jokes and anecdotes, which he repeated, meal after meal, day after day; they became irritated by his unshakable assumption that he knew every answer, by his unwillingness to listen to anyone else. So, by the third or fourth week of sequestration, most of them had begun to avoid his company.

By that time, many of them had been shocked by his furious competitiveness and his occasional bursts of cruelty. Tracy Stanovich remembers the night the jury went bowling for the first time and Evans lost. "He just went wild. He was really mad about the whole thing. When we asked him why he said, 'Well, I always win. I always win. I'm tops. Now I've got to win, too.'"

He was particularly hard on Ann Burnett, one of the youngest women on the jury. Ann has a quick wit and a sharp tongue, but one night Evans teased her so much at the dinner table that she ran to her room, crying.

Tracy Stanovich recalls that he was also cruel to an alternate whose body had been permanently crippled by a childhood case of polio. One weekend all the jurors were dining together at a restaurant. Evans bought a bottle of champagne to share with the alternate. Somebody else came by and took the last swig of liquor. When Evans saw the bottle was empty he accused the alternate of stealing his drink. He threatened to hit him and banged the empty bottle on the table.

During sequestration nobody saw Evans's volcanic behavior as a portent of his conduct during deliberations. June Jackson, for one, didn't notice it at all. "I knew that he was a little peculiar, but aren't we all, to a certain extent?" In conversations with Sheets, Foresman, and Tracy Stanovich, Evans did make a great point of his past experience on juries—he claimed to have served on five— and of the fact that he'd always been chosen foreman. But no one saw those boasts and his periodic hearty free-spending moods as attempts to campaign for the job of foreman of the Harrisburg jury.

Then the defense made its surprising decision to rest without putting on a case, the lawyers made their summary speeches, and Judge Herman issued a long, self-contradictory charge as to how the jury was supposed to evaluate the conspiracy indictment. (The charge was so confusing that the jury had to ask the judge to reread it three times. He never gave them a copy of it. Most of them told me they never did get it straight.) After that, at last, the jurors were free to discuss the experience that had bound them together for six difficult weeks.

Their first task was to choose a foreman. Their vote was split, six votes for Fuzzy Foresman, six votes for Harold Sheets. They flipped a coin and Sheets, the tax consultant, the more prudent and judicious of the two, was the winner. Looking back, Foresman feels that "the good Lord above had a hand in choosing the foreman."

Within ninety minutes of the beginning of the deliberations, Evans delivered a long speech that all the jurors I interviewed described as a tirade. He thought the defendants should be jailed immediately. "Larry just blew up," June Jackson recalled. "I couldn't believe it." He yelled and screamed and banged on the table. He invoked God's will and his children's future. His veins stood out and he got beet red. "I was really frightened," Ann Burnett says. "I kept thinking, this man is going to have a stroke."

Ann knew at once that Evans's fervor would make rational discussion impossible. "And I started getting very upset. At first I just stood there. I was numb. I felt like I was sinking in my chair. It was the feeling you get when you know that everything is lost. I was ready to sit there and talk for weeks on end if necessary. But what was the point of that, seeing how Larry felt? I started to cry. I was so upset I was shaking, and I had to go out and go to the ladies' room because when I get very, very upset I have something like an asthma attack. I just can't breathe."

All of the jurors were shaken by Evans's outburst and Ann's flight. Shortly afterward the day's deliberation ended.

June Jackson's room at the Penn-Harris Motor Inn was next to Evan's. At about midnight that night she was awakened by some loud knocking that seemed to be coming from his room. "I thought somebody else was in there. I walked over to the wall to listen. And I realized that he was talking to himself about another jury he had been on. Some of the other jurors had apparently talked him into acquitting a defendant he thought was guilty. Then, a few days after the trial, the defendant had died of a heart attack. And Larry was saying that God was punishing the defendant even though the other jurors had talked him out of it. And, he said, they are not going to do that to me this time. He said, if we stay here for six months, I will not change my mind. He said, they are guilty. I knew it the minute I walked into the courtroom.

"And then he started to sing 'Rock of Ages.' That's when I realized he had been talking to God. And then I kept hearing doors opening and banging shut. I stood there, absolutely petrified."

If she had left her room that night, the marshals would have intercepted her before she could talk to Foresmen or Sheets, the only people she trusted enough to help her decide what to do about Evans. She didn't want to tangle with the court-appointed authorities, and anyway she had developed a sort of clannish loyalty that made her want to protect Evans. But the next day, still terribly shaken, she did talk to Foresman and Sheets. They considered writing a note to the judge about Evans's behavior. Sheets says that "We didn't, because of my stubbornness in thinking that I could bring him out of that state. I kept thinking of the job we had to do, the decision we had to make. I didn't want to disrupt it." Instead, the men tried to calm June Jackson down and to prevent a recurrence of the situation by getting one of the marshals to let June change her room. (She never even did that.)

Sheets, the rationalist, the calm psychologist, was convinced that a hung jury would be an emotional disaster for everyone concerned. So he kept trying to devise ways to reach out to Evans. One day, he asked the other jurors to remain silent while he and Larry had a face-to-face debate about their opinions of the case. Sheets spoke for twenty minutes, describing the contradictions and gaps in Boyd Douglas's and Delmar Mayfield's testimony that had convinced him the government had failed to prove a conspiracy. Evans spoke for just a minute or two, insisting that he had read the testimony, too, and that he was serving God's will by holding out for a conviction.

By then, Evans had only one ally on the panel, Katheryne Schwartz, sixty-eight, a grandmother from York. The defense had regarded her as a potential ally because she had four sons who were conscientious objectors. But she was a religious fundamentalist, not an antiwar pacifist. She agreed with Evans that the defendants' intent was tantamount to a crime.

Few of the jurors shared Sheet's optimism that Evans or Mrs. Schwartz could be converted. For them, the six days of deliberations became a blurred, grueling, timeless period of irrational arguments; of trips into the courtroom, where they'd try to make sense of the judge's impenetrable charge; of nights at the motel, which seemed more and more like a cage. "I was sick the whole time," Tracy Stanovich recalled. "I had a terrific headache. I couldn't eat anything. I couldn't sleep."

Evans became more unbearable every day. Once, according to Tracy Stanovich, he threw some pieces of paper at Pat Shafer. Throughout the sequestration and deliberation, Mrs. Shafer had been one of the strongest, most diligent members of the jury. Since she had three school-aged children she could have been excused automatically, but she decided to serve because she wanted to do her duty as a citizen. Though she provided a comforting presence for some of the younger women, she set exacting standards of performance. But there was a moment when Evans's stubbornness shattered even Pat Shafer's calm; she began to cry, and Sheets had to comfort her.

Under the strain of sequestration and deliberations Evans developed a broad range of tactics for irritating the other jurors. Sometimes, in the midst of a discussion, he would laugh disruptively, uproariously, and walk out to the men's room until he could control himself. At other moments he was sanctimonious. He kept telling Mrs. Schwartz that "God is making us do this work, Katheryne."

Tracy Stanovich remembers one morning when a juror who was pregnant asked to ride to court in a station wagon instead of a bus because she felt sick. Evans was there, too. "He hassled her the whole way over. Finally a marshal had to tell him, 'Larry, get off her back.'"

When they got to court, the juror couldn't even bring herself to ride on the same elevator as Evans. Fuzzy Foresman noticed that and heard her sobbing. "So I walked over to her and I saw that she was extremely emotional—emotional to the point where she couldn't catch her breath. And I just took hold of her and rubbed her shoulders a little bit and just talked to her gently. I said, 'This guy isn't going to hurt you or anybody.' I just kept talking to her and calmed her down real well. She behaved pretty good after that."

But Foresman found himself getting progressively angrier at Evans. At a deeper level, his clashes with the Lutheran grocer may have represented a reenactment of fights he'd had several decades earlier, when he'd married a Catholic woman from the coal town of Shamokin, where he and his friends used to journey for carefree evenings of dancing the polka and enjoying the beautiful women.

"Before we got married, very close personal friends of mine told me that the Catholic church would do all sorts of nasty things to me. We were married in a church. A mixed marriage in a church. It was the first one the priest had performed. My Lutheran friends said it was impossible. Not only did it happen, but I invited them, and they came." Nevertheless, afterward, his friends continued to warn him about the Catholics' prejudices. "It was bullshit. I've had more trouble with the damned Protestants than I did with the Catholics, with regard to religion."

So, when Evans began to say he knew the priests and nuns were guilty as soon as he entered the courtroom, one of Foresman's thoughts was: "'Larry, I've heard all this before. I've been down this road before.' And it irritated me because the jury room was no place for that."

Foresman says he kept trying to restrain himself, to submerge anger in wit. But on the sixth day his wrath erupted. Evans had been telling him how he'd pray for him, how his insistence on the defendants' innocence was endangering his grandchildren. "I got tired of his bullshit, you know. I just had to get up on my feet and get to the front of him. So I just jumped up and yelled, 'You're never going to convince me with that method, mister. You're way out in left field. Who the hell do you think you are, telling me how to think?' I blasted right into his face. But I never intended to hit him."

Tracy Stanovich, who hates conflict, recalls that she cringed at the scene. Vera Thompson, who, by now, was furious at Evans, says, "I was hoping Fuzzy would knock him on his ass." Here is how June Jackson saw it.

"We women were already just broken. We realized that we couldn't get through to Larry, no way, nohow. Then, he really took off on Fuzzy, telling him how he should think about the case. It was another tirade. His face was beet red. No human being, no matter how strong, could take that forever.

"So Fuzzy walked over, Larry got up, and we could see there was going to be a problem. They were actually ready for a fistfight. And how we protect our own! We didn't want one marshal in there to see what was going on. So someone stood over by the door to keep them out, and Hal Sheets went over to break the fight up. As soon as Fuzzy realized what he was doing, he went back to his seat.

"Oh, we all cried for Fuzzy. We felt so sorry for him because we knew what kind of person he was and saw that he was crushed. And he apologized to us. He was ashamed of himself, and said that he just couldn't believe another human being would act the way Larry did. But somebody did. And that scared me, too. I still don't understand. I hated to see somebody break another person."

The episode convinced even Sheets that there was no chance for a unanimous verdict. Indeed, Sheets blames his unyielding desire to forge a consensus for the last terrible days of deliberation. "I'm usually able to handle people, but I just couldn't handle this one. I couldn't get through to him. That's the thing about the trial that still frustrates me."

A few minutes after Foresman and Evans had squared off, Sheets notified the judge that the jury had concluded its deliberations. And, within half an hour, those twelve men and women trooped into court to deliver their verdict.

Part IV: Aftermath: "How Stupid Did Those People Think We Were?"

After the verdict was announced the jurors returned to their motels to gather their belongings. It was a sentimental moment, the end of the most harrowing experience many of them had ever undergone. Most of them joked or cried as they prepared to leave with their kids or their spouses. But Evans kept the door to his motel room locked until all the other jurors had parted. At one point Sheets knocked on Evans's door until he finally answered. But he couldn't extract even a trace of warmth from his angry, hurt antagonist.

After the trial the jurors ceased to see much of each other. June Jackson and Pat Shafer occasionally lunched together. Tracy Stanovich joined them for dinner once. Some of them exchange Christmas cards. But there are no reunions, no lingering sense of camaraderie. Nevertheless, the seven jurors I interviewed had more in common than any of them may have realized. The trial had affected them quite deeply, shaken their faith in American justice in ways that none of them can quite communicate to their family or friends.

Indeed, Pat Shafer said that if she and her husband had had to vote, "it would be a hung jury." June's husband, Barney, respects his wife's judgment, but it's hard for him to cope with the deep emotions the trial released in her. Without quite meaning to, he made her feel hysterical and overwrought whenever she tried to talk about her new uncertainties.

Some of the jurors felt unexpectedly uneasy in the wake of the trial. Tracy Stanovich and Fuzzy Foresman, the most impulsively outspoken people in the group, both wondered aloud whether fantasies they set down in letters could—like Philip Berrigan's and Sister McAlister's—be used to bring them to trial for an unprovable conspiracy. All of the jurors I interviewed had fresh doubts about a Justice Department that could waste so much money on such an ill-advised trial. And all of them wondered about a jury system that allows men like Larry Evans to make crucial decisions about justice. They didn't know what to do with those feelings. Their frustration and rage still sat in their guts like rocks.

They wished they had been able to retain the faith in the government they brought to the trial. There was a time during every interview when the jurors said they would have supported conviction if only the government had been able to furnish one or two credible witnesses to corroborate Douglas's testimony. It was as if they had voted to acquit against their will because the government they had been trained to love violated the sense of justice they revered even more.

Yet many of them felt like objects of contempt. Not only the government's, but the press's and the defense's, too. That became particularly clear in my interview with Pat Shafer. Before the trial began an excused juror had told me he overheard her making anti-Catholic remarks. I described his charge (though I concealed her name) in a *Voice* article, where I argued the defendants couldn't possibly get a fair trial in Harrisburg. The defense had made her alleged comments the basis of a motion for a change of venue.

Maybe that was the reason she was so much more guarded in talking with me than any of the other jurors had been. But she became animated when she began to discuss the press. She showed me a sheaf of clippings that attacked the jury and, in the hurt voice of a good citizen who has been wronged, she said that no other aspect of the trial had caused her so much pain.

June Jackson felt the same anger, except in her case it was directed at the government and its attitude toward America. Still, listening to her, I felt a haunting regret about the fact that she could have been talking about the lawyers or the defendants or the sociologists or the media—or me.

After the verdict she'd become aware of the fact that the Justice Department had located the case in the Middle District of Pennsylvania because they thought the place would yield a sympathetic jury. "How stupid did those people in Washington think we were? Did they think that by just picking a certain part of the United States they could get a guilty verdict? Don't they know that people are people, whether they come from northern Florida or southern California? I mean, we all have minds and feelings. I don't care where we're from. Don't they have enough faith in human nature to know that?"

AFTERWORD

In an important way I agree with June Jackson. Though people in America do have tribal differences, and don't necessarily like to live together, most want the same things. That is true whether they come from South Boston or Columbia Point, from the Mississippi Delta or Harlan County, from Forest Hills or Campbell's Creek.

Under the right circumstances, the tribes of America could enrich each other, as dreamers from Walt Whitman on have always hoped. They could embody the sense that Rabbi Singer imparted so freely: that we are all heirs to precious pasts, with coherent humane sets of values—pasts that can help us gain some perspectives and find some meaning in these confusing times.

But instead of enriching each other the tribes of America are combating each other. I realize that, over the past seven years, I've been witnessing the dissolution of the consensus that developed during the New Deal and continued, unchallenged, through World War II and the Kennedy years. That consensus was built on the bright hope of America's promise. It foundered when it became clear that the era of limitless growth had ended, that the melting pot—with its wondrous dream of upward mobility for all—was a promise that couldn't be fulfilled. Then groups became convinced that they would be involved in an endless, brutal competition for the most rudimentary benefits.

Right now, it seems to me that the United States lacks the genuinely pluralistic language and culture, the receptive, adventurous journalistic and political forums, that would help us all make sense of this new age. It lacks the intellectual traditions—and the political party—that would make the redistribution of wealth and power an idea that could be discussed in both class and tribal terms. It lacks the shared commitment to open-mindedness and good manners that would encourage frightened, embattled people like those in South Boston and Columbia Point to see past their stereotypes of each other and glimpse the hopes and confusions that link them. There was a sense of responsibility and justice that was almost second nature to the Harrisburg jurors—but, for some reason, those qualities are rarely projected on a nation-wide stage.

The problem, for a writer and a political movement, is to find ways of interpreting the tribes of America to each other, to help define political and economic changes that will benefit them, not set them against each other—to help them get to know each other so that they can attain the goals they share instead of engaging in a destructive, never-ending war.

APPENDIX

From My Workshop

There are usually special books I read, or special records I listen to, to help me shape my prose and deepen my understanding of a subject.

I also rely on people with special knowledge to help me understand the intricacies of a battle like the truckers' strike, of the holy crafts I wrote about in "A Journey Through the Year 5738," of places like Forest Hills and Kanawha County.

Before I end this book, I want to open up my workshop for readers.

CHAPTER 1:
The Vigilantes of Highway 80

During the cold winter weeks I wrote about the truckers' strike I listened, day in and day out, to Arlo Guthrie's album *Hobo's Lullabye*, to Randy Newman's *Good Old Boys*, to Jim Croce's *Life and Times*, and *Don't You Mess Around With Jim*. All those records were imbued with the rambling, bittersweet, slightly self-mocking macho style I'd encountered when I was hitchhiking with the diesel drivers. They helped me keep my prose loose enough—raw enough—to suggest some of the wild frontier spirit that had captivated and repelled me during my journey.

Jim Drinkhill, then the investigative editor of *Overdrive: The*

Voice of the American Trucker, was very generous with his time as he told me about the intricacies of Teamster politics and, more important, the differences between the Teamsters and owner-operators, who were leading the strike.

I changed all the truckers' names and cb handles when I wrote "The Vigilantes of Highway 80" since, at the time, it seemed possible that the scabs and strikers who talked to me could be exposed to violence or arrest.

CHAPTER 2:
Still the Promised Land

Some of my feelings behind this chapter are rooted in my years as a Peace Corps volunteer in Guayaquil, Ecuador, where Rachel and I lived in 1966 and 1967. Guayaquil, an extremely poor city, was attracting tens of thousands of refugees from the country, who had no prospects in their home towns. They couldn't find work. They lived in flimsy cane shacks which remained swampy—so swampy that children occasionally drowned—during the four-month-long rainy season.

Most of them had access to radios or television sets. Some spent their spare cash on movies. So they saw commercials, TV series, films that had been made in America: They saw a country that was wealthy beyond their wildest dreams. If they listened to *Voice of America,* they heard that the United States, was a free place, too. They felt the inescapable economic lure of the promised land.

Meanwhile, as a Peace Corps volunteer, with a greal deal of access to State Department officials, I saw that our government had determined to back the politics that were rooted in Ecuador's tiny oligarchy, that were unwilling to launch programs that would help poor people. That experience provided much of the bitterness behind my book *The Making of an Un-American.*

By 1972, I was beginning to hear from some of the students I'd taught in Guavaquil. They were illegal aliens, living in Hispanic communities like Jackson Heights, New York. They weren't naïve: they knew the risks they took when they'd come here. They accepted America's immigration laws without rancor. They had to live furtive lives, but they were no more bitter about it than the Mexican I called Maximo Villa. Still, the contradiction between what this country promised through its intentional and unintentional propaganda and its highly restrictive immigration laws disturbed me deeply—more deeply, I know, than it did most of the immigrants. I wanted to show the contradiction, not editorialize about it. That was one reason I wrote "Still the Promised Land."

Immigration policy is a technical matter. When I wrote "Still the Promised Land" the author Susan Jacoby, whose book *The New Americans: Immigration in the 1970s*, will be published by Doubleday in the spring of 1979, and Michael Piore, a professor of economics at MIT with a special interest in immigration, both helped me a great deal.

I have used pseudonyms for all the Mexicans and J. B. Chapman, the Border Patrol agent in this chapter.

CHAPTER 3:
The Lower Depths of American Labor

George Orwell's book about coal mining in England, *Road to Wigan Pier*, has influenced me as much as any piece of journalism I've read. That is particularly true of the passages where Orwell describes his hours in a coal mine and makes you feel that you're walking with him, seeing every detail he sees. I reread that book before I sat down to write "The Lower Depths of American Labor," in the hopes that Orwell's methods would help me learn how to convey my anger at what I saw in New Jersey's fields and orchards without resorting to intrusive, unnecessary polemics.

Since I was posing as a day laborer, I disguised the people I met and the places I worked.

CHAPTER 4:
A Flight over America's Future

When I began researching this chapter I felt some sympathy with the creekers. I didn't see any justice in the fact that textbook editors responded to criticisms that came from feminists and ethnic minorities while they remained impervious to the criticisms that came from religious people. But I knew very little about fundamentalist Christianity.

The people I quote in the chapter taught me an enormous amount. The actions and writings of people like Julius Lester and Will Campbell, political activists who maintain a deep religious faith, showed me the renewed appeal fundamentalism has for so many Americans. Los Angeles' Robert Dornan, then a TV personality and free-lance right-wing activist, now an extremely effective conservative congressman, spent three very useful hours with me one Sunday in Kanawha County, explaining his pro-God, pro-family point of view.

Kay Michaels, who then covered education for the *Charleston Gazette*, also told me a great deal about the fundamentalists and about the county where their first important modern political struggle had occurred.

All the names in this chapter are real.

CHAPTER 5:
Jesse Jackson: A Return to the Fundamentals

Two books, Alaine Locke's *The New Negro* and Dr. Benjamin May's *The Negro and the Church*, provided some of the background I needed for this piece. So did an afternoon-long talk with Julius Lester, onetime SNCC activist, poet, author, biographer of W. E. B. Dubois, professor of black studies at the University of Massachusetts. Julius Lester's wit, honesty, and clarity of thought have influenced me for more than a decade.

While researching this piece I listened to as much gospel music as I could. I spent four or five Sundays in black churches in Chicago, Washington, and New York. It became very difficult for me to understand why so few mass-circulation publications, so few TV news executives, pay much attention to the fact that religion and its related disciplines are central, crucial features of black life in America.

Jesse Jackson and Vernon Jarrett are, of course, the real names of real people. I wrote about the Shermans under a pseudonym.

CHAPTER 6:
Housing in Forest Hills: But Not Next Door . . .

In 1975, I wrote a long article on the singer Paul Simon, raised
in Forest Hills, for *Rolling Stone* magazine. I discovered that
many of my neighbors on the Upper West Side were raised in
that neighborhood. So I had long talks with Judy Rosenberg
Pritchett, Eda Krantz, and Joanne Grumet about their childhoods
there. The author Louise Bernikow, who is writing a novel about
growing up in Forest Hills, shared some of her memories with
me. Of course, Paul Simon's reminiscences were helpful. All those
conversations provided some of the background, the atmosphere,
that had been missing from the three *Voice* articles I published
four years earlier.

I played Paul Simon's albums while I wrote this chapter. Some
of his songs, like *My Home Town* and *Kodachrome*, conveyed the
same bittersweet tone that pervaded most of my interviews about
the community. Others, like *Feelin' Groovy* and *Me and Julio
Down by the Schoolyard*, evoked the 1950s, and the Forest Hills
kids, who (in Simon's words) "assumed the nation's economy was
pegged to the price of egg cream," who spent gentle hours learning how to flip baseball cards so they fell at the base of the
nearest wall.

I also played Simon's albums because, like Isaac Bashevis
Singer, he has a marvelous sense of laconic structure—an instinct
that allows him to pack enormous meaning into a few phrases. I
wanted to acquire that talent myself.

When I revisited Forest Hills in November 1977, Dr. Marcia
Knoll, principal of P.S. 220, the elementary school across the
street from the housing development, and Jim Drinani, head of
the Neighborhood House—one of the places that makes the development so attractive—spent a great deal of time helping me
assess what had happened during the past eight years. So did Paul
du Brul, who wrote *The Permanent Government* with Jack
Newfield.

All the names in this chapter are real.

CHAPTER 7:
Busing in Boston: The Fire This Time

Before I wrote this chapter I reread James Farrell's *Studs Lonigan Trilogy* and Richard Wright's *Native Son*, both for the sense of perspective they gave me and for their naturalistic prose style, which I wanted to echo in the sections on Barbara Quinlon and Tammy Lee Russell.

I also read Steven R. Fox's biography of William Monroe Trotter, *The Guardian of Boston*, for its glimpses of life within Boston's black elite at the turn of the century; and Alan Lupo's *Liberty's Chosen Home*, a book that provides much useful, specific information on the busing crisis.

When I first wrote about busing, John Kifner of *The New York Times* and Joe Klein, then of WGBH, now of *Rolling Stone*, helped me understand what I was seeing. When I returned in 1977, J. Anthony Lukas, who is currently writing a book on busing, took the time to read the *Voice* piece I'd written three years earlier, to point out places where it was dated, where it was flawed, and to share his insights with me. In 1974 and 1977, David Smith, professor of Urban Studies at the University of Massachusetts, and his wife, Phyllis Friedman, a lawyer, discussed the busing program from their very knowledgeable perspectives. James Amalfitano, raised in South Boston, and his wife, Tracy, who lives there now, reminisced about the neighborhood's past and described its present, helping me put dozens of street-corner interviews into some kind of perspective.

My mother-in-law, Margaret Brown, who has founded more than a hundred libraries in Boston's public schools, is one of the most youthful, open-minded people I know. Her energy and her vivid descriptions of her wide-ranging work have made me feel intimately connected with Boston's schools even during the years I didn't visit them.

Sonia Beach, Tammy Lee Russell, Sharon O'Keefe, Barbara Quinlon, and her friends Maureen and Debby are all disguised. Jane Margolis is not.

CHAPTER 8:

The Mississippi Delta: Let Us Now Praise A Famous Man

In September 1977, a month after Rachel and I interviewed Hartman Turnbow, his protégé, Eddie James Carthan, was inaugurated mayor of Tchula. At the ceremony, Mississippi's governor, Cliff Finch, and two other white politicians shared the platform with Charles Evers, the one-time NAACP field secretary who, in 1973, became the first black to be elected mayor of a Mississippi town. Senator James Eastland—whose name was a synonym for racism when we worked in Mississippi in the summer of 1964—sent a telegram congratulating Mayor Carthan. At a dinner that night, the mayor introduced Hartman Turnbow as his first, most important inspiration.

CHAPTER 9:

Harlan County: The Power and the Shame

Because Harlan was so unfamiliar to me I tried to steep myself in the literature of the place. But, for all its notoriety, very little has been written about its particular culture and traditions.

In 1932, a group of left-wing writers, including Theodore Dreiser, John Dos Passos, and Sherwood Anderson, visited the county, and their *Harlan Miners Speak* is an extremely useful book. Harriet Arnow's *The Dollmaker*, a powerful novel, helps you understand some of the bleakness of life in Appalachia and some of the difficulties its people face when they migrate to the cities. Harry Caudill's *Night Comes to the Cumberlands* is a wonderful epic description of the region. I read all those books, along with Bernard Devoto's wonderful *1848: The Year of Decision*, which shows an earlier generation of mountain men—Jim Bridger, Daniel Boone, and Kit Carson—and their complex relations with northerners. Those books, taken together, gave me some perspective on what I had seen.

I reread *Road to Wigan Pier* before writing this chapter. Orwell's calm, understated prose made me feel that my *Voice* articles had been somewhat overheated. So I tried to use his style as a counterweight to mine.

All the names in the Harlan County chapter are real, except for that of Ronny, the injured coal miner.

CHAPTER 10:
Jews Without Money, Revisited, 1972

I remember the afternoon, in December 1971, when I first read Chaim Potok's novel *The Chosen*. I was covering the Forest Hills crisis then, and I needed something to read on the long subway ride back and forth from Queens. The book, with its compelling, unsentimental portrait of Brooklyn's world of Orthodox Jews, cast an immediate spell over me. I read his second book, *The Promise*, the next day. Those two novels awakened longings I never even knew I had. They made me eager to write about the Lower East Side.

At first, I thought I'd write a piece of nostalgia. It was June 1972, three years before Irving Howe's *World of Our Fathers* would become the source book for the neighborhood. But Ronald Saunders's excellent *Downtown Jews*, Ande Manners's *Poor Cousins*, Abraham Cahan's *The Rise of David Levinsky*, and, of course, Michal Gold's novel *Jews Without Money* gave me a sense of the Lower East Side's past.

I learned about the Jewish poverty that existed in the present only when I began to hang around there, to talk with some of the people who lived in the Vladecks. One of the teenagers who lived in the projects suggested I talk to Rabbi Joel Price, then in his late twenties, a youth director at the Young Israel synagogue, who was very concerned about the Jews without money. Joel was the first Orthodox Jew I'd ever known. He became a very close friend —as well, of course, as a very important source of information.

Uptown, when I talked about the Jewish poverty I was discovering, I often encountered skepticism. Dan Wolf, who was then the editor of the *Voice*—and very cynical about many of the ideas and movements that appealed to me—became emotionally involved with the problem. He encouraged me to research it as long as I wanted to, and gave me as much space as I needed to write about it. Ed Kramer of the Henry Street Settlement House's Good Companion Lunch Program and Victor Weiss of the Educational Alliance helped me meet the people I wanted to write about. S. Ellie Rosen, then the head of the Association of Jewish Anti-Poverty workers, had a network of friends throughout the city with whom I could discuss the problem.

By 1974, when I wrote my second article about the neighborhood, The United Jewish Council had been founded and Joel Price, as good-natured as ever, had a job there. He and Misha Avramoff at Project Ezra and Fred Siegel and Naomi Ickovitz of the Federation Joint Services, helped me find Selma Haberman, Hedy Rose, and others like them. During those months I felt that I was, like them a caseworker. The sense of comradeship that developed has endured ever since.

I disguised all the Jews without money.

CHAPTER 11:
Orthodox in New York: A Journey Through the Year 5738

When I began to work on this chapter, Rabbi Singer—who believes deeply that anonymity is the highest form of charity—wanted to be written about under a pseudonym. Later, his son David, Misha Avramoff, and I, out of our admiration for him, pressured him to let his name be used. Despite his reservations he did so, largely as a favor to us.

Mrs. Dora Shapiro and Itzhak Hirsch are fictionalized names for two very real people.

While I was writing this chapter I read as much avowedly Jewish literature as I could find in English: Isaac Bashevis Singer, I. J. Singer, Shalom Aleichem, for example. I wanted to move away from the rhythms of the naturalistic fiction and journalism I love, away from the highly intellectualized prose of American Jewish writers like Saul Bellow and Philip Roth, into a realm of authors who accepted the Jewish world as the natural order of things. Soon I developed strong preferences. I found myself getting angry at some of the self-conscious devices that seem to me to rob some of I. B. Singer's later fiction of the wonderful vision he displays in books like *The Magician of Lublin* and *Satan in Goray*. My admiration for Chaim Potok continued to grow. For he was able to portray the Orthodox world with a sense of calmness, with a lack of self-consciousness, that made his characters stay with me for weeks.

In writing about Judaism, the *Jewish Catalogue* proved an invaluable resource of detail, and I relied on it heavily.

Rabbi Joseph Langer, executive director of the United Jewish Council of the Lower East Side, gave me a great deal of time and patience as I researched this piece. Dr. Herman Dicker, head of reader services at the Jewish Theological Seminary, Allan Mintz, Joel Mandlebaum, Jay Greenspan, and Jacqueline Gutwirth all helped me by reading the manuscript for mistakes. In some cases I received conflicting advice on transliteration and liturgical detail and had to rely on my own eye and instincts.

CHAPTER 12:
Harrisburg, Pennsylvania: Ballad for Americans

This chapter actually grew out of a research job that was commissioned by Robert Christy, professor of sociology at Columbia, and Jay Schulman, who devised the jury-selection methods the defendants used and now heads the National Jury Project. I did all the interviewing, of course, and published my piece in the V*oice*. Schulman and Christy used the same material—which was all tape-recorded—for an article in *Psychology Today*. My article was published as a chapter in *State Secrets*, a book I co-authored with Nat Hentoff and Nick Egleson.

All the names in this chapter are real ones.